T0340632

THE CONFLICT OVER THE CONFLICT

OTHER BOOKS BY KENNETH S. STERN

Holocaust Denial (1993)

Loud Hawk: The United States versus the American Indian Movement (1994)

A Force upon the Plain: The American Militia Movement and the Politics of Hate (1996)

Antisemitism Today: How It Is the Same, How It Is Different, and How to Fight It (2006)

THE CONFLICT OVER THE CONFLICT

The Israel/Palestine Campus Debate

Kenneth S. Stern

Foreword by Nadine Strossen

NEW JEWISH PRESS
an imprint of University of Toronto Press
Toronto Buffalo London

Published by New Jewish Press
an imprint of University of Toronto Press
Toronto Buffalo London
utorontopress.com

ISBN   978-1-4875-0736-7 (cloth)   ISBN   978-1-4875-3610-7 (EPUB)
                                     ISBN   978-1-4875-3609-1 (PDF)

Library and Archives Canada Cataloguing in Publication

Title: The conflict over the conflict : the Israel/Palestine campus debate /
   Kenneth S. Stern ; foreword by Nadine Strossen.
Names: Stern, Kenneth S. (Kenneth Saul), 1953–, author.
Description: Includes bibliographical references and index.
Identifiers: Canadiana (print) 20200156780 | Canadiana
   (ebook) 20200156845 | ISBN 9781487507367 (cloth) |
   ISBN 9781487536107 (EPUB) | ISBN 9781487536091 (PDF)
Subjects: LCSH: Academic freedom. | LCSH: Freedom of speech. |
   LCSH: Education, Higher – Political aspects. | LCSH: Arab-
   Israeli conflict.
Classification: LCC LC72 .S74 2020 | DDC 378.1/213 – dc23

University of Toronto Press acknowledges the financial assistance to its
publishing program of the Canada Council for the Arts and the Ontario
Arts Council, an agency of the Government of Ontario.

 Canada Council   Conseil des Arts
for the Arts   du Canada

 ONTARIO ARTS COUNCIL
CONSEIL DES ARTS DE L'ONTARIO
an Ontario government agency
un organisme du gouvernement de l'Ontario

Funded by the   Financé par le
Government   gouvernement
of Canada   du Canada

 Canada

To the late Thomas Emerson, whose seminal work, *The System of Freedom of Expression*, is even more relevant today.

To the late James O. Freedman, former president of Dartmouth College – a mensch, a friend, who taught me that the only way to combat bigotry on campus is with methods that uphold, and ideally strengthen, academic freedom.

And to the late Gary Rubin – the smartest, wisest, and kindest Jewish communal professional I had the privilege to know.

Contents

Foreword

In July of 1991, Leonard Jeffries, a tenured professor at the City College of New York and chair of its black studies department, gave a speech in Albany, New York. He claimed that there was an anti-black "conspiracy, planned and plotted and programmed out of Hollywood," and moreover that "Russian Jewry had a particular control over the movies, and their financial partners, the Mafia, put together a system of destruction for black people." Few had heard of Jeffries beforehand, but news stories soon revealed that he also espoused a form of eugenics in which black people (whom he called "sun people") were superior to white people (whom he called "ice people") because they had more melanin in their skins. Outraged that someone holding such a prominent public position should hold and convey these views, many politicians and members of the public – including some leaders of the Jewish community – called for City College to fire Jeffries.

A few months later, I participated in a panel discussion about the Jeffries case at New York Law School, where I teach. Tensions between some members of the Jewish and African American communities, already inflamed by the Jeffries case, seemed at a fever pitch due to even more recent events. Only weeks after Jeffries's Albany speech, the Crown Heights section of Brooklyn – with its large African American and Orthodox Jewish communities – erupted in riots following the tragic death of a seven-year-old African American boy, who had been run over by a station wagon in the motorcade of a prominent rabbi. Some black youths attacked and seriously injured several Jews on the street, and killed a Jewish student from Australia.

One member of that New York Law School panel was the American Jewish Committee's expert on antisemitism, Ken Stern. I expected this leader of a Jewish organization to argue that anyone who spouts hateful propaganda, such as Jeffries, should not teach at a public university, especially given the charged context, in which Jews (among others) were being targeted with not only hateful ideas but also violence, injury, and death. Indeed, Ken pulled no punches in exposing and condemning Jeffries's racist ideas, and he explained that City College lawfully could (and should) remove Jeffries from his official leadership role as department chair, because his discriminatory advocacy was directly at odds with the College's mission. However, Ken also made forceful arguments that Jeffries's tenured teaching position should remain secure, for reasons of both principle and strategy. Ken stressed that tenure is essential even – indeed, especially – to protect freedom for "the thought that we hate," to quote Justice Oliver Wendell Holmes; and he predicted that dismissing Jeffries would, perversely, increase attention to and sympathy for him and his ideas, by turning him into a free speech "martyr." This was hardly a popular position for a Jewish communal official to take, and I was deeply impressed by Ken's staunch adherence to principle, as well as his strategic savvy.

Ever since that memorable encounter almost three decades ago, I have continued to follow Ken's remarkable career with admiration and appreciation. He continues to vigorously speak out – and to take effective actions – against both hatred and censorship, even when his is the proverbial voice in the wilderness. For example, demonstrating his expertise and vigilance concerning hate-fueled violence, Ken issued a prescient report about the militia movement just nine days before the 1995 Oklahoma City bombing, which was the worst terrorist attack on US soil until 11 September 2001. Ken's groundbreaking report documented the serious danger that these groups posed, when too many were writing them off as harmless white guys playing with guns in the woods. In the report's cover memo, Ken warned that there might well be an attack on some government official or building on 19 April 1995, the anniversary of the fiery end of the Branch Davidian cult in Texas, which to the militias epitomized government evil. Too few people remember that national news programs featured pundits who reflexively blamed the Oklahoma City bombing on Muslims, until Timothy McVeigh was arrested, thus vindicating Ken's sadly well-founded warning.

Readers of historian Deborah Lipstadt's book *History on Trial: My Day in Court with David Irving* (2005) will note Ken's contributions to the momentous 2000 London trial she recounts, which resulted in her landmark victory against Holocaust denier David Irving, who had sued her for libel. Ken, along with Lipstadt herself, consistently explains why Holocaust denial propagates antisemitism, but nonetheless opposes making it illegal. He explains that effectively combating antisemitism (and other forms of hate) requires multifaceted societal action, including education and counterspeech, and that laws punishing Holocaust denial (and other hateful speech) reduce the impetus to pursue these more promising non-censorial responses. Again, this stance illustrates major pillars that undergird all of Ken's extensive advocacy and activism, as also shown in the Jeffries case: his unwavering commitment to human rights – including equality and free speech – as well as his determination to pursue strategies that are thoughtfully designed to actually have a positive impact.

Ken has consistently been both principled and effective in advancing the anti-hate, pro-human rights cause throughout all phases of his distinguished, multifaceted career: as a trial lawyer (for example, he represented American Indian Movement co-founder Dennis Banks before the United States Supreme Court), a human rights activist, a visiting professor, a foundation executive director, and now the founding director of the Bard Center for the Study of Hate.

All of which leads to the present impressive book. Ken realizes that its topic is a "third rail," and that he will be attacked by partisans on all sides of Israel/Palestine issues. But he will not be deterred – especially because the core aim of this timely book is precisely to embolden and encourage others to robustly exercise their freedoms of thought, discussion, and debate, and to respect and indeed foster everyone else's equivalent rights, without either censorship by others or self-censorship. The book recognizes that especially insidious pressures are exerted by people with whom we are generally allies – or by our (mis)perceptions of them – because we are loath to alienate them by "deviating" from "the party line," or even questioning it.

Being married to a Columbia University professor and living on the edge of the Columbia campus, I am painfully aware of how "the conflict over the conflict" has riven that campus, with many adverse repercussions for academic freedom and campus life more generally. Let me quote a portion of an in-depth 2018 article in the daily student newspaper the *Columbia Spectator*, "Decades of Discord: What Makes the Israel-Palestine Debate Uniquely Persistent, and Personal":

> For decades, the debate has permeated discussions across multiple facets of [the Columbia] campus, including student government, academic settings, and apolitical clubs – even aspects of students' personal lives. Most significantly ... community members fear social or academic repercussions if they associate with a particular stance in the debate. As a result, students ... highlighted their discomfort with even being a member of certain clubs or taking certain classes ... Even in largely unrelated contexts ... some students said they feel uncomfortable due to their own political views. For example, activist organizations often distance themselves from Columbia University Democrats due to its perceived pro-Israel stance.

I am especially happy to write this foreword not only because it introduces such an important book but also because I had the good fortune to be present at the book's inception. I even have the *chutzpah* to claim some credit for Ken's decision to write it. Let me explain.

A few years ago, Ken reached out to me to discuss his concerns about the Israel/Palestine campus situation. Being familiar with my advocacy of free speech, open inquiry, and civil discourse, including on campus, Ken realized that I shared his concerns. We discussed how campus activists and their outside supporters on all sides of the Israel/Palestine debate were turning campuses into battlegrounds, damaging free speech and academic freedom in the process. We commiserated about incidents in which each side called out the other's transgressions, but was silent about, or rationalized, its own, thus displaying the all-too-common support of "free speech for me, but not for thee" (to quote the title of journalist Nat Hentoff's 1992 book). This particular situation is troubling enough in itself, but even worse, it typifies a broader problem, which plagues debates about public policy issues in general, on campus and beyond. Ken easily persuaded me that documenting both the problems and the potential solutions in the particular context of the Israel/Palestine debate could have a far-reaching positive impact for our campus and political discourse more broadly.

Noting that no one had written any in-depth report or book about this situation, Ken tried to persuade me to do so. Flattered as I was by Ken's suggestion, I declined, explaining to him that a certain someone else was uniquely well-qualified to "write the book" on this topic: none other than Ken Stern himself! High as my expectations were for the book that I urged Ken to write, the resulting work exceeds even those high hopes. It masterfully blends riveting insider accounts of key developments, drawing on Ken's longtime leadership role on these issues, with astute expert analysis.

In addition to his human rights and legal expertise, Ken also is a long-standing, pioneering thought leader in the emerging interdisciplinary field of "hate studies," of which he was literally a "founding father." As the book recounts, Ken worked with a few other foresightful leaders to found the very first center for hate studies – the Gonzaga University Institute for Hate Studies, which was launched in 1997. In the 2004 inaugural issue of that institute's pathbreaking *Journal of Hate Studies*, which Ken also helped to spearhead, he wrote a seminal article, whose title says it all: "The Need for an Interdisciplinary Field of Hate Studies." That article provides the following definition of the then-proposed field, which now is flourishing at a growing number of centers in the US as well as other countries: "Inquiries into the human capacity to define, and then demonize or dehumanize, an 'other,' and the processes which inform and give expression to, or can curtail, control, or combat, that capacity." Ken has continued to make essential contributions to this burgeoning field, including through his current service as the founding director of the Bard Center for the Study of Hate. The resulting insights from many fields – including evolutionary, social, and moral psychology – enhance this book, deepening our understanding of both the causes of the current polarization and the most promising countermeasures.

Of all the important aspects of this book, the one that I particularly salute is the blueprint it provides for how we can surmount the "us/them" mentality, to forge a constructive path forward. Ken outlines specific steps that we can all pursue, which will not only enrich our own thinking and enliven our interactions with others, but also lay the groundwork for mutually acceptable (and, hence, mutually objectionable) resolutions of seemingly intractable societal problems. Having been working and reading in this area intensely for many years, I nonetheless learned new and invaluable lessons about both causes of and remedies for hatred in all its ugly manifestations – hatred of those with identities and/or ideas that are different from our own.

While this book is about Israel and Palestine, it could be about any conflict that hits the jugular. It addresses a crucial question: How do we engage in and facilitate rational conversations about emotional issues? Its lessons apply to all hot-button questions, ranging from immigration, to abortion, to gun control, among countless others. It should be read by everyone who cares about critical thinking and thoughtful discourse. It deserves a place on the bookshelf of every provost, and should be required reading for all incoming college students.

Nadine Strossen is a professor at New York Law School, past president of the American Civil Liberties Union (1991–2008), and a leading expert on constitutional law and civil liberties. Her acclaimed 2018 book *HATE: Why We Should Resist It with Free Speech, Not Censorship* was selected by Washington University as its 2019 "Common Read."

Prologue

From the 1970s until a lawsuit shut it down in 2001, the Aryan Nations – perhaps America's most significant neo-Nazi group at the time – had a compound in Hayden Lake, Idaho, not far from Spokane, Washington. It was a Hitler-worshipping, Holocaust-denying, racist, and violent enterprise, and some of its members were bent on using guns and bombs to promote white supremacy.

The group "The Order" was founded by Aryan Nations members. It robbed banks to support a white supremacist revolution. In 1984 it assassinated one particularly hated Jew, Denver talk-radio host Alan Berg, who had enjoyed needling white supremacists on his program.[1]

Randy Weaver, who lived in nearby Ruby Ridge, Idaho, socialized with other white supremacists at the Aryan Nations compound. In 1992 federal agents tried to arrest him on an outstanding warrant, and during an armed standoff US Marshal Bill Degan was killed, along with Weaver's wife and son.[2]

Buford Furrow was another Aryan Nations member. He walked into a Jewish Community Center in Los Angeles in 1999, firing at least seventy rounds from a semi-automatic weapon. He wounded five people, including three children. Then he shot and killed a Filipino-American postal worker.[3]

To the human rights and Jewish communities in the Inland Northwest, the Aryan Nations and the hatred it inspired in others was a direct and constant danger. A Jewish woman bought Chanukah gift-wrap and discovered a razor blade inside. When Temple Beth Shalom (Spokane's main synagogue) was remodeled, its classrooms were placed in an inner courtyard, protected with bullet-proof windows.

Some members of the congregation came to services armed. Black law students at Gonzaga University received threatening racist letters, and some left.[4] Bombs were planted at the office of Planned Parenthood and the office of the *Spokesman-Review* newspaper.[5] In Coeur d'Alene, Idaho, a pipe bomb went off in the home of parish priest Bill Wassmuth (with him in it). Luckily, he wasn't injured.[6]

Activists in the region organized and pushed back. In 2001 the compound was closed, after Aryan Nations guards shot up a car passing by their property, and the Southern Poverty Law Center, along with local attorney Norm Gissel, filed suit.[7] The area is now vacant.[8] But the leaders in the community remain concerned about the potential for racist violence to disrupt their lives. Ten years after the compound closed, a white supremacist put a radio-controlled bomb in a backpack along the route of Spokane's Martin Luther King Jr. Day march. Many children were among the marchers, and no doubt some would have been maimed or killed if the bomb had exploded. It was filled with small fishing weights covered in an anticoagulant found in rat poison.[9] Fortunately, the device was discovered and deactivated.

These days the potential for new recruits is obvious. Confederate flag stickers or license plate holders are on the occasional vehicle. White supremacist posters have been found on lampposts in downtown Spokane.[10]

The region is small enough that most of the veterans of the struggle against the Aryan Nations and its legacy know each other. Many come from the Jewish community, and from local peace and justice groups, particularly the Peace and Justice Action League of Spokane (PJALS). They know that they need to work together to be effective. But for eight years, they didn't speak to one another. In fact, they frequently refused to be part of coalitions with the other, or even in the same room.

What would cause them to be at each other's throats, despite the threats from virulent racists who frequently were armed or had plans for murder, were endangering their children, and might be living across the street?

The problem – some might say an abstract problem – was 6,700 miles away.

Israel.

What is it about the Israel/Palestine conflict that makes people nuts? In 2018 pro-Palestinian students disrupted a program on "indigeneity" at the University of California, Los Angeles (UCLA). A protestor stormed on stage and ripped down the Armenian flag, apparently not willing to have it displayed near an Israeli one. Instead of listening to the panelists, or waiting to ask hard questions, the disrupters shouted, "We don't want two states; we want '48"[11] and "One, two, three, four, open up that prison door, five, six, seven, eight, Israel is a terrorist state."[12] Also in 2018, Israel passed its "Nation-State" law, making it easier to discriminate against non-Jews while downgrading Arabic from an official language to one with special status. A Palestinian student at Stanford University reacted with threats against his classmates, promising to "physically fight" Zionists; four hours later he amended his post to say he'd "intellectually" fight them.[13]

Within the Jewish community, Israel can be both a uniting issue and a great divider. As Rachel Sandalow-Ash, a cofounder of Open Hillel, has observed, Jewish students from all types and levels of observance can come together easily at their campus Hillel (the mainstream Jewish organization on many college and university campuses) for a meal after different services. Breaking bread with people who disagree about Israel, she says, is much more difficult, if not impossible.[14] Jews who are pro-Palestinian sometimes say supporters of Israel are racists; pro-Israel Jews sometimes call Jewish pro-Palestinian activists traitors.

I observed a similar phenomenon to the one Sandalow-Ash described during my nearly twenty-five years on staff at the American Jewish Committee (AJC is one of the two large Jewish "defense agencies"). I had Orthodox, Conservative, Reconstructionist, Reform, and secular colleagues, as well as others like me who were atheist. No one felt less part of the AJC family because of how, or if, they observed the Jewish religion. I was never asked if I was going to High Holiday services.

But there was tremendous pressure on all staff (including non-Jewish staff) to attend the annual Salute to Israel Parade[15] on Fifth Avenue in Manhattan. There were multiple memos, the tone and content of which suggested it would hurt one's career not to show up, even though the parade was on Sunday, a day off.

The organized Jewish community is particularly concerned about how Israel is portrayed on campus, for two reasons. First, tomorrow's leaders are today's undergraduates, and if being pro-Israel is part of your faith, you don't want future professors, journalists, and lawmakers to view Israel poorly. Second, you worry that Jewish students who care about Israel deeply and hear vile things about it will feel as disturbed as if someone had said something hateful about Jews. While, as we will see, there have been deeply disquieting incidents, pro-Israel activists claim that the college campus is a hotbed of antisemitism,* which it is not.

Meanwhile pro-Palestinian campus activists say these Jewish groups are using legislative and other means to suppress their First Amendment right to express pro-Palestinian political views. These claims and counterclaims, about who is trying to silence whom over Israel on campus, are taking place in an environment where many would sacrifice free speech to "protect" students from ideas they might find disagreeable.

This book is not a catalogue of every bad act by either side in the campus wars over Israel and Palestine. Rather, it is a call to action. The complexity of the Israeli/Palestinian conflict should make it an ideal subject to teach critical thinking and how to have difficult discussions. Instead, it is being used as a toxin that threatens the entire academic enterprise. How did we get here? What can be done?

My thinking about Israel has changed over my lifetime. Growing up in a Jewish household in New York City during the 1950s and 1960s, I don't remember hearing anything about Israel until my parents sent me to Hebrew school in fourth grade, to prepare for my bar mitzvah. I learned that Israel was the ancient homeland of the Jews, and the holidays we studied were about events long ago in

---

* I spell "antisemitism" lower case, without a hyphen, except when I directly quote another who uses a different format. It is a minor matter, but with the hyphen comes the suggestion that the word means being against a "Semite," which it does not (see Almog, "What's in a Hyphen?").

that faraway place. I liked those Bible stories, not for their religious connotations but for the history and interesting people facing difficult situations. We learned that Jews were reclaiming their lost land, making a deserted desert bloom. Every week we were encouraged to bring a coin and buy a leaf for a tree to be planted in Israel. We put leaf-like stickers on a paper tree, showing our progress.

By this age I was already an atheist, or if not an atheist an energetic agnostic. When we read Genesis, I asked the Hebrew school teacher how one reconciled that story with Darwin's theory of evolution. I was sent to the principal's office. My parents were called. I was sent home. I was obnoxious in Hebrew school after that. I asked, if the wind blows a leaf off a tree in Israel, do I get a refund?

One day, in sixth grade, I skipped Hebrew school because a film company was shooting on my street and had set up a camera on our driveway. The film was *Cast a Giant Shadow*, and starred John Wayne, Angie Dickinson, Kirk Douglas, Frank Sinatra, Yul Brynner, and Chaim Topol. It was about Col. Mickey Marcus, an American Jewish World War II veteran who went to Israel during the 1948 Arab-Israeli War and became the first general of Israel's army. Not knowing Hebrew, he was confronted by a sentry, and unable to give the password, was shot dead. They were filming on my block because Marcus's widow, Emma, lived across the street. The movie showed Israelis as courageous and inventive, Arabs as gullible and almost cartoonish. The narrative fit what I was learning in Hebrew school.

The first time I thought about modern Israel was in June 1967. Israel was at war with the surrounding Arab countries. It was the lead item on the evening news. My parents and Jewish neighbors were fearful in a way I had never seen. They were worried that the Jews would be slaughtered. I recall sharing their fear, although I didn't fully understand that theirs had been informed by the Holocaust, which seemed to me at that age a distant history, but to them was very fresh.

That Israel won the 1967 Six-Day War so quickly and decisively made me proud.

In Hebrew school we told jokes.

A male Israeli soldier asks a female Israeli soldier for a Saturday night date.

"What, are you crazy!" she says. "There's a war on!"

"Okay, then. Next Saturday?"

It wasn't until years later that I appreciated what I viewed as a wonderful story of survival was actually the end of an era. June 1967 turned out to be the expiration date on the world's honeymoon with the Jewish state.

I didn't think about Israel much in the early 1970s, when I attended Bard College. Yes, there was the Yom Kippur War of 1973, and it started badly, but Israel won, with a lot of materiel support from the United States. There was the Arab oil embargo, resulting in long lines of cars waiting for gas because OPEC reduced the supply of oil to countries that supported Israel. Despite prices jumping and restrictions (you could only get gas on odd or even days corresponding to the last digit of your license plate), I didn't sense anger towards Israel or Jews. And I don't recall much discussion about Israel on campus. These were the last years of the Vietnam War. That was our focus.

I started law school at Willamette University in Salem, Oregon, in the fall of 1975. I wanted to become a lawyer to fight for social justice, and volunteered with the radical lawyers practicing in Portland, Oregon. I worked with them on prison cases, and then, on 14 November 1975, an event changed my life. An Oregon State Trooper stopped a motor home and a station wagon on the interstate, right before the Oregon-Idaho border. Two occupants escaped after shots were fired. Four others were arrested. These were American Indian*

---

* I generally use "American Indian" throughout. AIM members referred to themselves as "Indians" or "Indian people," but also by the nation from which they came, using the traditional name rather than the one imposed by their conquerors (thus "Lakota" instead of "Sioux"). I understand that in Canada the term "First Nations" is preferred by many, but in this book I am referring to Indian people in the US (although in one instance I use "Native" because I am describing a confederation of nations that includes people from both sides of the US-Canada border). In the US some people use "Native American," but as the Smithsonian National Museum of the American Indian points out, while "American Indian, Indian, Native American, [and] Native" are all acceptable terms, people generally prefer "whenever possible . . . to be called by their specific tribal name. In the United States, Native American has been widely used but is falling out of favor with some groups, and the terms American Indian or indigenous American are preferred by many Native people" (see https://americanindian.si.edu/nk360/didyouknow#topq2).

activists, including American Indian Movement (AIM) co-founder Dennis Banks. They were underground, hiding from the FBI. The motor home belonged to actor Marlon Brando, who had helped buy some of their guns. I spent thirteen years – first as a law student, then as a lawyer – working on this case, which brought me further into Oregon's progressive community where, before too long, I heard a different perspective on Israel.

I became active in the National Lawyers Guild (NLG). This was a left-wing group that sought out law students to join. It had been a communist front in the 1930s, but it allowed blacks to join when the American Bar Association did not, and it counted the best labor and movement criminal defense lawyers among its members. I attended an NLG national convention in Seattle, in August 1977. Israel was the main topic, specifically whether the NLG would pass a resolution that recognized the Palestine Liberation Organization (PLO) as the "sole legitimate representative of the Palestinian people." Four decades on, this seems like a non-controversial proposition, especially since Israel and the PLO would become parties to the Oslo Accords, setting out a supposed framework for peace, sixteen years after that Seattle conference. But at the time it was contentious as the PLO was classified as a terrorist organization. Palestinian terrorists in the 1970s were hijacking airplanes and had murdered Israeli athletes at the 1972 Munich Olympics.

I was torn. Older Jewish lawyers, heroes for their work in the civil rights movement, opposed the resolution. They thought it was unfair and one-sided, stacked against Israel. And they were afraid it was going to tear the NLG apart over an issue that was not a central concern, threatening its ability to fight for legal, political, social, and economic justice in the United States. I voted for the resolution on the narrow proposition that Palestinians had the right to choose their leaders. Four decades later, I'm still conflicted about that vote.

When I joined the national staff of the AJC as its antisemitism expert in 1989, I inherited the research files on "extremist" groups and found a small manila folder on the NLG. I discovered a copy of a 1977 memo "to file" written by Morton Stavis, a legendary lawyer who was a co-founder of the Center for Constitutional Rights; the memo had been shared with the Israeli consul and then made its way to the AJC.

It was a blow-by-blow analysis of the Seattle NLG meeting, detailing Morty's effort to engineer a compromise. His main concern was that the resolution put all the blame on the Israelis, and that while it recognized the Palestinians' right to self-determination and statehood, it said nothing about parallel Jewish rights in the land of Israel.

There was a slide show during the conference that compared Israel to the racist colonialist state of Rhodesia. "Not a word was mentioned about the Holocaust or the fact that half of the Jews in Israel are refugees from Arab lands," Stavis wrote. He contemplated resignation, but decided to speak out. He noted, "I found that one of the most discouraging features of the convention was that young people who call themselves radicals responded to peer pressures to such an extent that they were afraid to oppose openly what appeared to be a consensus."[16] The resolution passed.

I graduated law school in 1979 and opened a practice in the Portland area emphasizing progressive political causes. I had also become co-counsel for the lead defendant in the American Indian Movement case – Dennis Banks. I don't recall thinking much about Israel at that time, but I did see antisemitism.

Portland, Oregon, in those days, had a small far-right community, most significantly a group named the Posse Comitatus. It was a precursor to the 1990s militia movement and was racist and antisemitic. I would run into Posse members at the county courthouse's law library, where they diligently researched their supposed right as white people to drive cars without driver's licenses or license plates (neither the Oregon State Police nor the courts shared their point of view).

They also handed out antisemitic tracts on the courthouse steps, claiming (fraudulently) that Benjamin Franklin and George Washington had warned that Jews should not be allowed in America because they ruined the country from within. Other Posse material charged Jews with secretly running the media, the banks, and the government.

I mention the Posse because in 1982 I was startled to see similar ideas expressed by my progressive friends. The war in Lebanon had broken out. I thought it ill-advised (even before the massacres of Palestinian refugees by Christian Phalangists), and joined the

demonstrations against Israeli actions. One day, I looked at literature being sold at a protest against the Lebanon War. There were
books, monographs, and newspapers, all from the radical Left.
Many had claims about Israelis that seemed cut and pasted from
the Posse Comitatus's material about Jews. And at the rally I saw a
young American Indian woman, an activist from the Dennis Banks
case. She held a sign that demanded all American military assistance be cut off from Israel. I reminded her of the 1967 war, and
the American airlift that helped save Israel in 1973, and suggested
that if her demand was listened to, Israel could be destroyed and
Israelis slaughtered. She smiled and said, "Damn right."

Portland had a radical bookstore, and I began browsing its material on the conflict. I reread the influential 1974 political statement
of the Weather Underground, which saw Israel only as a colonialist
oppressor, and the fight against it as an important anti-imperialist
struggle. Every book seemed hostile to Israel, and frequently to
Israel's existence too.

Confused and almost bereft, I sought out Frank Giese, a retired
Portland State University professor who ran the bookstore. Frank
was a friend – as a law student I had volunteered to work on
his criminal case. He was one of the last Vietnam War protestors
charged.

"Frank," I asked, "what the hell's going on?"

He said, "Your generation doesn't remember the people coming
out of the camps."

Frank was right.

Years later, when I found Morty Stavis's long memo in the AJC
files, I saw he had attached prior NLG resolutions about Israel.
The first was from February 1948, after the UN had announced
the Partition Plan, but before Israel was formally declared in May.
It made no mention of Palestinians. Instead, it called for allowing
shipments of arms to Jews, a UN police force "to defend the Jewish
State," and "equip[ping] the Haganah [Israel's army]." The NLG
also sought a UN declaration labeling "the action of the Arab states
a threat to peace."

Less than three decades later, in the summer of 1977, the NLG
had turned 180 degrees, from full-throated support for the Jewish

state to total support for Palestinians, defining each stance as "progressive."

In late 1982 I began writing op-eds for Portland's local progressive paper about Israel and the visceral hatred of it from some fellow progressives. I was convincing no one. Friends quietly told me I might have a point, but the more important thing was the struggle for Palestinian rights, a struggle I was allegedly harming.

In 1981 national leaders of the NLG were trying to recruit me for more responsibility. In 1982 they asked if I could be "rehabilitated." I felt like I was being purged for suggesting that the Israeli/Palestinian conflict was complex, rather than just a self-evident matter of justice for Palestinians. I resigned from the NLG.

My op-eds, however, caught the attention of local Jewish community organizations. I volunteered to help them confront antisemitism and work for freedom for Soviet Jews, while I continued my day job, pressing progressive legal cases, such as advocating for Portland's homeless community in a federal lawsuit. I was invited to join the board of the American Section of the International Association of Jewish Lawyers and Jurists, which included some high profile Jewish lawyers such as Alan Dershowitz and Nat Lewin. Now, when Israel came up, I was on the left flank, along with Rabbi David Saperstein, head of the Reform Movement's Religious Action Center. We argued unsuccessfully that the group should criticize Israel's close relationship with Apartheid South Africa and join the call for boycotts and sanctions against the Apartheid regime. Most of the board, while troubled with Apartheid, felt that Israel's security interests, which allegedly required cooperation with the South African government, outweighed human rights concerns.

By 1989 I had moved back to New York and had started my twenty-five-year career as the American Jewish Committee's antisemitism expert. Much of my work focused on far-right groups (like the militia movement and Holocaust deniers), and on how institutions (colleges, talk radio programs, internet providers, etc.) should deal with antisemitism and other types of hatred. None of my work was seen as contentious inside AJC or the Jewish world.

In 2011 I discovered that Israel was as much a third-rail issue inside the mainstream Jewish community as it had been inside the NLG thirty years before. I was the AJC professional responsible for the college campus. That year I wrote an op-ed on behalf of AJC, co-authored with Cary Nelson, then president of the American Association of University Professors (AAUP). It spoke of the need to address antisemitism on college campuses but decried an effort by some on the Jewish right to abuse a definition of antisemitism written in 2004 for European data collectors (I had been the definition's lead drafter). These groups wanted to threaten the federal funding of colleges that allowed speech that, in their view, transgressed this text, which included some examples of expressions about Israel. This was an attempt to impose a campus speech code that was irreconcilable with free speech and academic freedom. It also harmed Jewish students, who would be seen as trying to silence anti-Israel speech rather than answer it.

The backlash to the op-ed was intense. Funders threatened AJC. Privately, colleagues agreed with my point of view (in fact, many had been part of the drafting process). But the public perception was that I was harming efforts to "protect" Jewish students, and putting AJC's funding at risk. After much pressure, AJC withdrew its support for that op-ed.

When I had started at AJC in 1989, it proudly considered itself a "think tank," and sought out different points of view on domestic and international issues, which were discussed reasonably and intelligently. That changed over time, mostly because of the issue of Israel. The joke was that at one time AJC was all "think" and no "tank." While never entirely true (it was a combination of both), I watched as it sacrificed an instinct for serious thought, discussion, and self-reflection in favor of ardent pro-Israel advocacy. The capacity to tolerate complexities and differences, especially when it came to how Israel is portrayed on the college campus, diminished over time. Appearing "strong" in defense of the Jewish people, as both a political end and a fundraising necessity, trumped nuance. Like in the Left of the 1980s, even private, internal questioning of the wisdom of public positions on Israel became more difficult. Funders, who were parents and grandparents of college students, were deeply concerned about anti-Israel activity on campus. They wanted young Jews protected from hearing disconcerting, and in some cases antisemitic, expressions.

No one at AJC asked if I could be "rehabilitated." But when I left in 2014, it was with the sense that the stridency I had seen in the Left about Israel in 1982 was also afflicting the mainstream Jewish community.

It's even worse today. From 2014 to 2018 I directed the Justus & Karin Rosenberg Foundation, which focused on antisemitism, hatred, and the academy. Not a week would go by without an article in the paper, phone call from a student, or email from a professor, about the campus wars over Israel. Lawsuits had been filed and legislation introduced. Civil rights violations were alleged. Faculty members on both sides were blacklisted. A group with an online database threatened pro-Palestinian students that it would tell future employers that they were "radicals" and shouldn't be hired. Professors refused to write recommendations for students who wanted to study in Israel. Some academic associations voted to boycott Israeli academic institutions.

I decided that an "honest broker," someone with no track record on one side or the other about the conflict, had to write a report, documenting the toxic impact of the campus wars over Israel, and what could be done about it. I contacted the three obvious organizations: the Foundation for Individual Rights in Education (FIRE), the American Civil Liberties Union (ACLU), and the AAUP. They all passed. While every group has its plan for allocating staff and resources, and need not accommodate outside ideas, my sense was that all three organizations knew that tackling this contentious issue would upset supporters on one side (or both sides) of the conflict.

I then spoke with Nadine Strossen, the former head of the ACLU and a staunch free speech advocate, hoping she might take on this project. She said I should, but when I demurred, she connected me with scholars she thought might be appropriate for, and interested in, the task. None had staked out a strong public position on the Israeli/Palestinian conflict. All thought the idea was good, but everyone declined. Interestingly, some believed that such a report must conclude that pro-Palestinian activism caused the greater threat to academic freedom, while others believed that pro-Israel activism was the larger problem. I stressed that this conclusion, of which side was worse, seemed irrelevant. Arguments could be made (and I make them in this book) about the different nature of the dangers from each side. But whether one side is "worse" than the other doesn't change the fact that both sides are harming the academy. It's no defense to a charge of going 85 miles an hour in a 25-miles-per-hour school zone, I said, that someone else may be driving 75. The conflict over the conflict seems so intense that even people without a side felt a need to choose one. Ultimately, I was afraid if I didn't take on the task, it wouldn't get done.

What you'll see in the chapters ahead is a slightly different book than the one I described to Nadine. In places this story is told through my eyes, as a participant in some of the battles. The main point of this book is that the issue of Israel and Palestine is incredibly complex. Our desire to reduce difficult concepts to simple terms, our proclivity to see ingroups and outgroups, "us" and "them," is obvious. The campus ought to be the best place to mine this conflict and our intense views about it to help students and faculty do what they are supposed to do: think.

chapter one

Thinking about Thinking

Sometimes we look at things like we are looking through a dark lens and everything seems dark. Let's try putting on different glasses.

Robert Leahy[1]

Look at the bright side, but don't look too long, or you'll be blinded.

Emily Stern

[W]hen faced with a difficult question, we often answer an easier one instead, usually without noting the substitution ... [W]e can be blind to the obvious, and we are also blind to our blindness ... [I]t is easier to recognize other people's mistakes than our own.

Daniel Kahneman[2]

A basic principle of moral psychology is that "morality binds and blinds."

Greg Lukianoff and Jonathan Haidt[3]

In 2016 my friend Roger Berkowitz, head of Bard College's Hannah Arendt Center, asked for my help. He was organizing a two-day conference around "Difficult Questions about Race, Sex, and Religion," and was having trouble finding thoughtful pro-Israel and pro-Palestinian panelists.

I suggested Kenneth Marcus of the Brandeis Center for the pro-Israel slot. Even though Marcus and I frequently disagreed, particularly as I explain in chapter 7 about the use of Title VI of the

Civil Rights Act to address certain pro-Palestinian campus speech, I considered him a smart advocate. His organization provided legal support for pro-Israel campus advocacy.

Marcus accepted the invitation. Then Dima Khalidi, head of Palestine Legal, which helps pro-Palestinian students and faculty, agreed to speak. When Marcus learned that Khalidi and he would be on the stage together, he said no. Both Berkowitz and I tried to convince him that sharing a platform would be wise; he could confront her directly. He still refused, noting my long-standing objection to appearing alongside a Holocaust denier. I pointed out the differences. Holocaust deniers are antisemites who distort history and science to defame Jews. They shouldn't be debated, not because they have another perspective, but because of what such a joint appearance necessarily communicates. Deniers win just by being seen together with historians, survivors, or experts, because they want to create the illusion that there's a reasonable disagreement between points of view – those who allege that the Holocaust happened, and those who say it did not.[4] This is substantially different than being a zealous advocate for one side or another in a heated political debate. I told Marcus that even though I disagreed with Khalidi about many things, perhaps most things, she was a respected lawyer and an advocate for a political position, about which reasonable people may disagree.

Marcus said she was an "antisemitism denier." There is no doubt that Marcus's definition of antisemitism is different from Khalidi's; indeed, for their political purposes, Marcus's seems artificially expansive and Khalidi's artificially constricted.

Knowing that Berkowitz was facing a deadline and had no good options, I suggested Marcus and Khalidi speak one after the other. While not ideal, both could articulate their positions. I hadn't thought my suggestion through. It became obvious that the discussion about Israel and Palestine on campus was structured differently from any other session – two separate speakers, as opposed to a conversation between opposing views, like on race and sex. Before Marcus spoke (with me as introducer and moderator), Berkowitz told the audience that Marcus had a principled position against appearing with Khalidi, and that's why they would speak separately. A student challenged Marcus, asking, "Who gets to decide that you don't have to listen to another person, you don't have to share space with another person ... In my experience ... it's not always an option to opt out of a difficult conversation or sharing space with someone you don't want to share space with."[5]

For Marcus, having a debate with Khalidi was not a "difficult conversation" but an impossible one. Having a civil dialogue with someone who represented activists of Students for Justice in Palestine (SJP), who generally have a hostile view of Zionism, was simply too much.

In May 2018, a student group at Stony Brook University celebrated Israel's seventieth birthday with an information table and free food. The event was supported by the campus Hillel. Some members of Students for Justice in Palestine protested. They held signs saying "Zionism is terrorism."[6] Rakia Syed, an SJP member, told the student newspaper, "Palestinians have been suffering, and ... peace cannot truly be achieved until Israel is out of the region and out of Palestine ... We want Zionism off this campus, so we want Hillel off this campus. What we want is a proper Jewish organization that allows Jews to express their faith, have sabbath – everything like that, that are not Zionists, that doesn't support Israel."[7]

The Interfaith Center at the university, disturbed by Syed's comment, issued a statement: "While we do not expect students or student organizations to agree with everything that other groups stand for or advocate or believe, we do expect that they respect the rights of those students to observe their faith, hold by their beliefs, and celebrate their identity on our campus."[8] One of the signatories was the campus's Muslim chaplain, Sanaa Nadim. SJP then accused her of "a heinous level of betrayal to the Palestinian people by working with and aiding Zionists on their endeavors ... [I]f there were Nazis, white nationalists and KKK members on campus, would their identity have to be accepted and respected? Absolutely not. Then why would we respect the view of Zionists?"[9]

Both Marcus and the Stony Brook chapter of SJP viewed their opponents as beyond the pale. Many people who care about this conflict seem addicted to strong emotions and absolutist positions,

and allergic to reasoned discussion. And these are smart people –
college students, faculty, and professionals.

The problem is not necessarily what they, or we, think about the
conflict. It starts with something more basic, something we rarely
take time to consider, something I hope you keep in mind as you
read the rest of this book: how we as human beings process information and come to conclusions, based on who we are, especially
when our identity is tethered to an issue of perceived social justice
or injustice. We like to believe we are rational beings, and to an
extent we are. But our minds are focused on, and driven by, not
only logic but also feelings, emotions, and attitudes. We are Captain Kirk, not Mr. Spock.

This chapter is a brief introduction to aspects of the emerging
field of Hate Studies,* and particularly its disciplinary components
of evolutionary psychology, social psychology, and moral psychology. It is not meant to be an exhaustive analysis of the issue, but
rather a brief and incomplete introduction and a framing, a short
overview about how we think, especially about hot-button issues.

Our ancestral past helps define how we identify and think about ingroups and outgroups.

James Waller is a social psychologist and leading expert in genocide and Holocaust studies, who now teaches at Keene State College. In a landmark essay on evolutionary psychology for the
Journal of Hate Studies, he showed how our attitudes – instincts
perhaps – are shaped by our ancestral past. "Automobiles," he
writes, "kill far more people today than do spiders or snakes.
But people are far more averse to spiders and snakes than they
are to automobiles. Why? Because for most of our ancestral history, spiders and snakes were a serious threat to our survival

---

* Hate Studies is defined as "Inquiries into the human capacity to define, and then
  dehumanize or demonize, an 'other,' and the processes which inform and give
  expression to, or can curtail, control, or combat, that capacity" (Stern, "The Need
  for an Interdisciplinary Field of Hate Studies," 11).

and reproduction, whereas automobiles did not exist ... EP [evolutionary psychology] makes clear that our universal reasoning circuits inject certain motivations into our mental life that directly influence our behavior."[10]

Our brains were not developed in an age of jet travel, Skype, and Twitter. They were formed over millennia, starting when people lived in small groups, and survived by hunting and gathering. Sometimes our primitive ancestors confronted strangers, others. Frequently these "others" were dangerous. They competed for resources. In all cultures, even today, people feel as if they belong to some group, and define other groups as separate, some even deserving of animosity, if not suspicion and hatred.[11]

Waller writes:

Human minds are compelled to define the limits of the tribe ... We construct this knowledge by categorizing others as "us" or "them." We tend to be biased toward "us" and label "them" – those with whom "we" share the fewest genes and least culture – as enemies ...

A group of the !Kung San of Kalahari call themselves by a name that literally means "the real people." In their language, the words for "bad" and "foreign" are one and the same. Similarly, the cannibal inhabitants of the delta area of Irian in Indonesian New Guinea call themselves the Asmat, which means "the people – the human beings." All outsiders are known very simply as Manowe – "the edible ones."[12]

We are hardwired to be ethnocentric, to focus on our own group, in Waller's words, as the "right one": our group is better, other groups don't measure up, and may be dangerous to our survival.[13] Ethnocentric impulses have been documented across cultures, and are evidenced at an early age.[14] We see them in our daily news feeds, and on our sports pages. But, Waller notes, "defining what the in-group is also requires defining what it is not."[15] In other words, we are both ethnocentric and xenophobic (fearing others),[16] although there is evidence that the two phenomena are also somewhat independent (a person can favor their ingroup and discriminate against an outgroup without animus towards the latter), and that the affinity to one's ingroup is the stronger force.[17]

If you are in a room full of strangers, and someone flips a coin and divides the group in two, once a group identity is formed, experiments show that you will likely believe your group's members are better than the others', even though you know the assignment to your group was totally random.[18]

We're pre-programmed to think that way. In 1954 Muzafer Sherif conducted an experiment with twelve-year-old boys. They were as similar as he could find – white, middle class, from intact homes, Protestant. He brought them to a summer camp at a place called Robbers Cave State Park, in Oklahoma. Two groups were created, with each not knowing that the other existed. Each bonded as a unit. One called itself the Eagles, the other the Rattlers. Over time, the campers discovered they were not alone. As one chronicler of the experiment summarized:

> Sherif now arranged ... [a] series of competitive activities (e.g. baseball, tug-of-war etc.) [between the groups] with a trophy being awarded on the basis of accumulated team score ...
>
> The Rattlers' reaction to the informal announcement of a series of contests was absolute confidence in their victory! They spent the day talking about the contests and making improvements on the ball field, which they took over as their own to such an extent that they spoke of putting a Keep Off sign there! They ended up putting their Rattler flag on the pitch. At this time, several Rattlers made threatening remarks about what they would do if anybody from [t]he Eagles bothered their flag ...
>
> At first, this prejudice was only verbally expressed, such as taunting or name-calling. As the competition wore on ... [t]he Eagles burned the Rattler's flag. Then ... the Rattler's [sic] ransacked The Eagle's [sic] cabin, overturned beds, and stole private property. The groups became so aggressive with each other that the researchers had to physically separate them.
>
> During the subsequent two-day cooling off period, the boys listed features of the two groups. The boys tended to characterize their own ingroup in very favorable terms, and the other out-group in very unfavorable terms.
>
> Keep in mind that the participants in this study were well-adjusted boys, not street gang members. This study clearly shows that conflict

between groups can trigger prejudice [sic] attitudes and discriminatory behavior.[19]

What could reduce the animosity between the Rattlers and the Eagles? Towards the end of the experiment they were forced to work together to fix the camp's drinking water supply – if they didn't cooperate, the problem could not be remedied. They had a "superordinate" goal, and sure enough working together led to a reduction in the negative stereotypes about the other group. Or perhaps, in some way, working together led to the formation of a larger, transcendent group identity.

While one can criticize aspects of this experiment,[20] the import of it seems as relevant today as it was in the 1950s. People form groups, and when they do they have positive prejudices about their group, and negative ones about the "other" group, especially if that group is seen in competition. We will see many examples of this phenomenon as we examine the campus battles between pro-Israeli and pro-Palestinian advocates.

There is recent scholarship that adds another layer of understanding to our impulse to form ingroups and outgroups. "Uncertainty-identity theory" suggests that "feelings of uncertainty about one's perceptions, attitudes, values or feelings can be uncomfortable and thus motivate behavior aimed at reducing uncertainty ... Self-uncertainty is powerfully motivating because people need to know who they are, how to behave and what to think, and who others are and how they might behave, think and treat us."[21]

Michael Hogg is a leading scholar of this theory. He recognizes that all of us have multiple identities (for instance, I'm a man, a husband, a father, a Jew, a Bard College alum, a beleaguered New York Knicks fan, etc.). Some identities are more important to us than others, and some of the groups with which we identify, the ones Hogg calls "low entitativity groups," have "unclear boundaries, ambiguous membership criteria, limited shared goals and poorly defined group attitudes."[22] Higher entitativity groups, ones that "have sharp boundaries, are internally homogenous, and have a clear structure with shared goals and a common fate," are "better ... at reducing uncertainty as they provide a more prominently focused social identity that delivers a clearer sense of who we are as group members, and thus how we should behave."[23]

The attraction to "high entitativity groups," Hogg argues, is "extremitized when the group is organized around an identity and set of goals that are under threat."[24] Religion fits here. It is well-suited to reduce people's feelings of uncertainty. Hogg describes it as a "group phenomenon involving group norms that specify beliefs, attitudes, values and behaviors relating to both sacred and secular aspects of life, which are integrated and imbued with meaning by an ideological framework and worldview."[25]

Religion also provides its true believers "impermeable and carefully policed boundaries and markedly ethnocentric intergroup attitudes. Internal dissent and criticism would be discouraged and punished; consensus and uniformity would be enforced ... [along with] dehumanization of out-groups and in-group dissenters ... Ideological orthodoxy prevails and is protected by suppression of criticism and marginalization of deviance."[26]

Recall Rachel Sandalow-Ash's observation that Jewish students at Hillel can comfortably navigate different levels of religious observance, but not strong differences about Israel, and AJC's insistence on staff attending the Salute to Israel Parade. There is reason to believe that for many Jews, attachment to Israel is perhaps the strongest aspect of group association, the core part of their Jewish identity, frequently grounded in religious terms, and expressed by some as strongly pro-Israel (mostly), and by others as anti-Zionism.

When we look at the heated campus conflict over the Israeli/Palestinian conflict, it is helpful to think of the strongest proponents on each side who seek to dehumanize[27] the other side, or at least chill their speech. They are acting in ways Hogg's uncertainty theory predicts – they tend to be more strident, more connected to their group, more extreme, and to exhibit the zealotry of true believers.

Add to that one more element, the tendency of people who define themselves as part of a group to depersonalize others and themselves. Hogg writes:

> [We] depersonalize them in terms of their group's prototype, viewing
> them stereotypically and creating stereotype-consistent expectations

about their attitudes and behavior. When we categorize ourselves, precisely the same process occurs; we depersonalize ourselves in term of our in-group prototype ... [W]e conform to and internalize group norms, define ourselves in group terms, and feel a sense of belonging and identification with our group.[28]

This identification is so strong that we feel pain when someone in our group fails, but take pleasure when someone in a rival group fails.[29]

Symbols, often of no intrinsic value, have outsized importance when we think about ingroups and outgroups.

One source of tension between the Eagles and the Rattlers was over symbols – each group's flag. These were newly minted pieces of cloth. Yet each group became fiercely attached to its symbol, and intended harm to their opponent's. This is not an entirely rational process. It has much more to do with identity.[30] Now imagine how intense and extreme the conflict and prejudice between the two groups of twelve-year-olds might have been if their fathers and grandfathers had attended the same camp, and the current campers had grown up knowing its flag and seeing their family's respect for it. Think about the power that symbols of identity have in our own lives, and in history. The American flag (and the anger at those who might burn it). The power of the swastika in Nazi Germany.

Now think of the dichotomy of the Israeli flag, sporting the Star of David. It is a source of historic pride to Jews worldwide, many of whom were (and in some places still are) either oppressed for displaying that symbol, or forced to wear it by regimes that intended them harm. But it's also a permanent reminder to non-Jews in Israel that their place in the state is lesser. On the American campus, pro-Israeli students sometimes literally drape themselves in the Israeli flag, while pro-Palestinian students have been known to rip it down.[31]

Symbols are important and people will fight over them to the point where they lose themselves and their ability to think, even if the symbols are demonstrably unimportant for any practical purpose. Years ago, when I was a young trial lawyer advocating for American Indian activists, I joined them in trying to retire racist sports team mascots, from professional teams on down to elementary schools. Some schools with Indian mascots were nicknamed "the Savages."

Social scientists showed that American Indian children suffered from the presence of these mascots. Imagine how black kids would feel if Americans cheered for the football team the "Washington Niggers" (which for some is akin to "Redskin"),[32] or Jewish kids if there was a baseball team called the "Cleveland Kikes," each with cartoonish caricatures and trinkets demeaning ethnicity or religion.

Charlene Teters, an American Indian graduate student at the University of Illinois Urbana-Champaign, spoke out against the school's mascot after she saw her children, who insisted on going to a basketball game, shrink into their seats and themselves as they watched this prancing, dancing fake "Chief" abusing what they held sacred, including eagle feathers. For raising the issue, Teters received death threats.[33]

A conference was organized to explain why the university should choose a new mascot, and how the reasons alums put forward for retaining "The Chief," such as that it honored American Indians, were not only disingenuous but also demonstrably false (depictions of "The Chief" were being sold on toilet paper). In the middle of my presentation, about how we'd never tolerate similar treatment of Jews, blacks, Hispanics, or any other ethnic group, I wondered out loud about why people chose to attend the University of Illinois. They came for many reasons. It has a good faculty. Having a degree from here would help a graduate find a job. Location. Tuition. I suggested a top ten list of why someone would choose to spend tens of thousands of dollars on tuition at this university. I was sure that "having a cool mascot" would not appear among the choices. Yet the resistance to changing the mascot was fierce. Why were people holding on to it so strongly, to the point where there were death threats against Charlene, and promises from alumni to stop supporting the university if it changed its mascot?

The debate really wasn't about the mascot as much as it was about us and our identities. People were being asked to give up a part of their memories of their group, which were embodied in a symbol. Evidence that they would get past such a change, as fans of the Redmen of St. John's University did when their sports teams' name was changed to the Red Storm, didn't appear to matter. Keeping this emotional symbol seemed important, even essential, perhaps even more important than whether their team would win or lose on the field. Much of the campus battle over Israel/Palestine, which also devolves into death threats and alumni promises to punish their alma mater financially, plays out as a war over symbols.

We have a proclivity to follow authority, and we are susceptible to peer pressure. We conform. Partisans in the campus debate over Israel and Palestine are not exempt from these human tendencies.

When people think about a divisive and difficult issue like the Israel/Palestine conflict, they're not thinking on a blank slate defined by disconnected and philosophical logic. They are bringing themselves as human beings, for whom identity, and the symbols of identity, are of oversized importance. They have an ancestral impulse to see, define, and diminish an "other," especially when that "other" represents some real or perceived danger to one's group.

But that's only the beginning of how we think about difficult issues like this. Social psychology teaches us about our individual proclivities to follow authority, and how we are influenced by the actions of others.

Stanley Milgram conducted perhaps the best known experiment about respect for authority.[34] As Evan Harrington summarizes in the *Journal of Hate Studies*:

Milgram invited ordinary people from the community to participate in an experiment involving a learner, whose task was to memorize various word combinations, and a teacher, who was to administer painful electric shocks when the learner gave wrong answers. The experiment was rigged so that subjects always were placed in the role of teacher and a mild-mannered middle-aged man (working for Milgram) always was placed in the role of learner. Subjects saw the learner strapped into a chair with electrical conductors taped to his arms ... In fact, no shocks were ever given to the learner. Very soon after the experiment began the learner would begin making errors, and the teacher (i.e., the true experimental subject) would be required to give electric shocks of increasing intensity by flipping switches on a highly realistic-appearing sham shockbox designed by Milgram. The learner, seated behind a partition in another room, would make verbal protests of increasing intensity as the intensity of the "shocks" grew. In fact, the learner's screams and protests were tape recordings ... If at any point the teacher refused to continue, another actor pretending to be the experimenter ... would say various phrases to the effect that the experiment required that he or she continue to administer shocks to the learner. If the teacher became concerned about the learner's health, the experimenter would say that he would take full responsibility and that the teacher should continue with the experiment.[35]

Almost two-thirds of the subjects continued to administer the "shocks." And even in a later experiment, when the subjects weren't just pressing a button but had to hold the "learner's" hand directly to the shock plate, almost a third gave the highest level of shock. "It was a very disturbing sight," Milgram said, "since the victim resists strenuously and emits cries of agony."[36]

Milgram's work has been criticized, both for its morality and its authenticity.[37] But his observations have been replicated in other studies.[38] We tend to follow authority, even when we question the wisdom or morality of that authority. Imagine how much more pronounced this tendency would be if the authority was someone who represented a core aspect of our identity. Like someone perceived to be a strong voice standing up for the Jews of Israel, or for the Palestinians. We might abstractly question the wisdom or morality of what that person says or does, but we are less likely to criticize that person than someone on the "other side."

Our thinking process is also influenced by what we see others do. We look to the group for affirmation. Sometimes we are influenced more by the group than by our own thinking. We feel peer pressure, and worry about disapproval.

In the 1950s Solomon Asch conducted a landmark experiment in group conformity and social norms. The subject was the last to be seated in a room, around a long table. Everyone else worked with Asch. Easy questions were asked, such as which of two lines of obvious different lengths was longer. The subject was the last to reply.

Harrington describes what happened:

After making a choice, each person at the table was required to say out loud which line he thought was correct. In this way the real subject was placed in a position in which he knew the answers of the rest of the group, and they would know his. The first two trials went smoothly and all confederates picked the correct comparison line. However, as the experiment progressed, all the confederates began making the same wrong comparisons. The true subject was faced with a dilemma: Should he bravely go against the group and declare the correct answer (which was obvious)? Or should he play it safe and go along with the majority? Across 12 trials 76% of subjects went along with the group and gave an obviously incorrect response at least once (approximately one-third of the subjects could be considered frequent conformers by giving many incorrect answers) ... When one confederate in the group went against the majority and gave the correct answer, the real subject (apparently emboldened by the rebellious confederate) also gave the correct answer more frequently. Asch believed these results indicated that people do not blindly follow crowds, but rather rationally weigh the amount of disapproval they expect to face ...[39]

When we think about issues that resonate with our identity (as campus partisans do about the Israel/Palestine conflict), our thinking is influenced by our innate tendencies as humans: defining an ingroup and an outgroup, having a proclivity to listen to authority, being affected by social norms and how other people think, and being susceptible to the power of symbols associated with our group.

It is difficult to think clearly about issues like Israel and Palestine when we see the conflict in binary terms as too many on campus do – good vs. evil, settler-colonialist vs. indigenous, democratic vs. authoritarian, terrorist vs. state terrorist, and so on. How often do we step out of our ingroup or tribal affiliations and imagine what it would be like if we were born to the other team? Why do so few question the wisdom, morality, or utility of the steps "our side" take in the political battle against our opponents?

I teach a class on antisemitism and, of course, I spend a few sessions on Nazism. There's usually a student or two who have a smug reaction to Nazi ideology, essentially defining it as "yucky." How could people think such things, they ask? I respectfully jump down their throats. I tell them that if they had been Germans and had been alive then, they most likely would have been Nazis too. I force them to imagine the reality – Nazism was the norm, something their friends, neighbors, and leaders believed. And it wasn't just an abstract belief, it was sold as noble – protecting the group, including children not yet born, from the dangerous Jews.

There were, of course, people who took chances against their group and the power structure, just as there were white people in the pre–Civil War South who opposed slavery. But they were the exception, who were seen as and treated as traitors. Again, our thinking is deeply impacted by the group. As part of a group, we "deindividualize" and are less likely to act against what the group is trying to achieve, even if we believe the group's behavior is immoral. Our self-awareness becomes less. The potential for hatred of and violence against others becomes greater.[40] We'll see many examples of these tendencies in the Israel/Palestine campus debates, particularly in chapters 5 through 7.

Moral impulses drive our thinking. Partisanship is addictive. We backfill our thinking to justify what we want to believe. We become self-righteous.

In 2012 Jonathan Haidt, who teaches in New York University's business school, wrote *The Righteous Mind: Why Good People Are*

Divided by Politics and Religion. It's a study on morality, but more deeply it is a treatise about how our minds work. His central thesis is developed with a metaphor: "The mind is divided, like a rider on an elephant, and the rider's job is to serve the elephant."[41] By this Haidt means that our instincts, and our sense of morals, drive us (the elephant). Our minds (rational thought) can influence the elephant to a degree, but for the most part are just along for the ride.

Haidt is a social psychologist, and his early studies were about the role of morality in decision making. He would ask people about scenarios where there was no logical reason to object to an act, such as, "A man goes to the supermarket ... and buys a chicken. But before cooking the chicken, he has sexual intercourse with it. Then he cooks it and eats it." He posits away any rational objection – the chicken is dead, no one knows, no one is hurt. But we still sense a morally objectionable act, and Haidt, with many similar scenarios investigated in different parts of the world, defines a set of morals that he believes are universal, regardless of culture (although how they play out in different cultures varies).

Haidt identified five moral impulses: care, fairness, loyalty, authority, and sanctity. He found that people who are liberal are more likely to consider care and fairness important principles, whereas conservatives value all five. Nowhere in his book does Haidt zero in on the topic most interesting to me, and relevant to this discussion – hate. But in talking around it, Haidt offers important insights. Here are some of them:

1. "[There are] two different kinds of cognition: intuition and reasoning."[42]
2. "If you ask people to believe something that violates their intuitions, they will devote their efforts to finding an escape hatch – a reason to doubt your argument or conclusion. They will almost always succeed."[43]
3. "People bind themselves into political teams that share moral narratives. Once they accept a particular narrative, they become blind to alternative moral worlds."[44]
4. "When a group of people make something sacred, the members of the cult lose the ability to think clearly about it."[45]

5. "Extreme partisanship may be literally addictive."[46]
6. "The love of loyal teammates is matched by a corresponding hatred of traitors, who are usually considered to be far worse than enemies."[47]
7. "Why do people so readily treat objects (flags, crosses), places (Mecca, a battlefield related to the birth of your nation), people (saints, heroes) and principles (liberty, fraternity, equality) as though they were of infinite value? Whatever its origins, the psychology of sacredness helps bind people into moral communities. When someone in a moral community desecrates one of the sacred pillars supporting the community, the reaction is sure to be swift, emotional, collective and punitive."[48]
8. "Anything that binds people together into a moral matrix that glorifies the in-group *while at the same time demonizing another group* [emphasis in original] can lead to moralistic killing, and many religions are well-suited for that task."[49]

If we are honest with ourselves, we know our political views are not derived from pure, abstract logic. When we take a position on an issue about which we care deeply, we generally prefer a certain outcome. We may not see the other side's case as pure evil, but we tend to discredit it as illogical or contradictory or incomplete, while failing to examine our arguments, to see if they really hold up.

We all do this, some more than others. And all of us backfill our thinking more when we are passionate about an issue that is core to our identities. Perhaps, on some level, being pro-Israeli or pro-Palestinian can be described more as a religion than a political position. What each of us believes is a combination of what we feel and what we think. And what we feel drives what we want to think, and the evidence we accept or reject.

When people care deeply about an issue, when they see a moral principle (fairness, caring, loyalty, sanctity, authority) at stake, and when they perceive the survival of their group at risk, this tendency to have intuitions drive what we think becomes supercharged. At its extreme, it is the stuff that makes suicide bombers and soldiers who commit atrocities.

At college I saw a wonderful graffito. It said, "If I didn't believe it with my own mind, I never would have seen it." Over the decades, I've witnessed this type of myopic thinking repeatedly. It may be more pronounced by those who have given their minds and bodies over to extremist ideologies or theologies, like Holocaust deniers and militia leaders. But it is a way we all look at the world – once we accept a set of beliefs that is important to us, our thinking to a significant degree becomes an exercise to sustain and justify that belief.

When we care deeply about an issue that we see as intertwined with our identity, we tend to make certain symbols and ideas sacred – they have larger than life implications, and are difficult to abandon. As Haidt suggests, there seems to be an addictive quality to our desire to fight for something we make sacred, whether it is dying for the cross, or the Rattlers fighting over their flag, or the reestablishment of a Jewish state in Israel, or the Palestinian right of return.

Daniel Kahneman, a Noble Prize–winner in economics, has an analysis that is similar to Haidt's. Instead of an elephant and a rider, Kahneman says people have a "System 1" and a "System 2." System 1 is our ingrained, quick, intuitive mind. Examples of System 1 include "orient to the source of a sudden sound, complete the phrase 'bread and ...,' answer to 2 + 2 = ?, drive a car on an empty road."[50] System 2 requires thought and concentration, such as "brace for the starter gun in a race, park in a narrow space, fill out a tax form, [what is] 17×24?"[51]

Kahneman believes that System 2 is lazy, and we often rely on System 1: "[M]any people are overconfident, prone to place too much faith in their intuitions. They apparently find cognitive effort at least mildly unpleasant and avoid it as much as possible."[52] We "think with [our body], not only with [our] brain," and this mechanism includes the "association of ideas."[53]

Kahneman describes experiments in which participants were given one side, the other side, or both sides of a hypothetical legal controversy. The subjects knew how the experiment was constructed, and those who were presented with one side could have easily discerned the argument of the other. Yet people who saw only one side were "more confident of their judgments than those who saw both sides." Kahneman concluded that it is "the consistency of the information that matters for a good story, not its completeness ... knowing little makes it easier to fit everything you know into a coherent pattern." He describes this phenomenon as WYSIATI, short for "What you see is all there is."[54]

He argues that System 1, when "searching for an answer to one question ... simultaneously generates the answers to related questions, and it may substitute a response that more easily comes to mind for the one that was requested ... [the one that is] more accessible, computed more quickly and easily."[55]

This tendency Kahneman describes means that we generally don't consider that there are pieces of information that we don't know, but should, before we render a conclusion. And these are conclusions about hypothetical cases presented in a psychology experiment, not ones of ongoing importance, related to our identity, when one might expect our desire to seek out information that conflicts with our perspectives is even less engaged. Indeed, Kahneman says, "System 2 is more of an apologist for the emotions of System 1 than a critic of those emotions – an endorser, rather than an enforcer."[56]

He doesn't directly address the question of whether strong emotions linked to an identity cause different patterns of thinking, but his analysis suggests that this is a strong possibility. He describes how thinking that relies on System 1 can be inconsistent. For example, how people generally are more positive in their outlook when they experience the "brief pleasure of a cool breeze on a hot day," or the strong evidence that a prisoner's chance for parole is increased or decreased depending on when parole judges have breaks for food.[57] Decision making based on "formulas do not suffer from such problems. Given the same input, they will always return the same answer."[58] One has to wonder, do ideologues, who see things in black and white, exhibit more of a tendency to think in formulas, seeking the same answer?

Kahneman also describes "denominator neglect." Here is one example of many: Some people were asked to describe the dangerousness of a disease that "kills 1,286 people out of every 10,000." Others were asked to describe how dangerous "a disease that kills 24.14% of the population" would be. If you do the math, the second formulation is twice as dangerous as the first. But when people are asked these questions without the opportunity to compare (a System 2 operation), and just react, they rank the first description as the more dangerous.[59]

Even psychiatrists and psychologists are not immune from this instinct to ignore the denominator. Some were told of a psychiatric patient like a "Mr. Jones" who had a 10 per cent chance of committing a violent act if released. Another group was told that of 100 patients, you could expect 10 to act violently. "The professionals who saw the frequency format were almost twice as likely to deny the discharge."[60]

If you're a pro-Israel activist, how often do you demand to see hard numbers of problems described as ubiquitous? For example, an investigation by the newspaper *The Forward* a few years back found fourteen campuses nationwide had an "Israel Apartheid Week" event.[61] While pro-Israel students might feel personally insulted by the verbiage around the event, how alarmed would parents of Jewish college students be if Jewish organizations' fund-raising letters catastrophizing IAW said the probability of any campus having an IAW event is about 0.31 per cent?[62]

Our thinking on moral terms is also influenced by a lack of comparison. People were asked about a man who was injured during a burglary at a store; in one scenario (asked of one group), it was the store where he usually shopped, and in the second (asked of another group), the regular store was closed that day because of a funeral, and he went to a different store.

The group given the scenario where the man goes into another store gave a higher figure for compensation. The damage was the same, but System 1 gave a higher value in this situation, likely adding value to the man's probable regret that he ventured into a different store that day. Yet, as Kahneman reports:

> Almost everyone who sees both scenarios together (with a single subject) endorses the principle that poignancy is not a legitimate consideration. Unfortunately, the principle becomes relevant only when the two scenarios are seen together, and this is not how life usually works. We normally experience life in between-subjects mode, in which contrasting alternatives that might change your mind are absent, and of course

WYSIATI ["What you see is all there is"]. As a consequence, the beliefs that you endorse when you reflect about morality do not necessarily govern your emotional reactions.[63]

Here's another example, related to how we frame ideas. Kahneman asked physicians about treating lung cancer with either surgery or radiation. Long term, surgery had a better survival rate, but was more dangerous in the short term. Half the physicians were told the "one month survival rate is 90%." The other half were told that "[t]here is a 10% mortality rate in the first month." Surgery was the choice of 84 per cent of those who were asked the question framed around survival. Fifty per cent of those who answered the question framed around mortality would choose radiation instead, even though the description was exactly the same; 90 per cent survival sounds good, 10 per cent mortality scary. The "emotional words" play on System 1.[64]

If you read the primary sources I cite in the endnotes of this book, from advocates on both sides of the Israeli/Palestinian conflict, you'll see how they frame their discussions. Pro-Israel groups do not say they are anti-Palestinian, but pro-Palestinian groups are generally seen as anti-Israel. Likewise, pro-Palestinian groups generally do not say they are anti-Israeli, but say Israel supporters are anti-Palestinian. Obviously, this is not as neat a divide as saying 90 per cent survival vs. 10 per cent mortality. But how we frame things plays into the emotional response of System 1 and WYSIATI.

When I speak about antisemitism at synagogues or Jewish Community Centers, people sometimes share their hurt from the shock of antisemitic acts or comments they experienced decades ago. The pain remains fresh. Strong memories related to insults against our core identities also play a part in how we evaluate current events. As Kahneman notes, "The remembering self is sometimes wrong, but it is the one that keeps score and governs what we learn from living, and it is the one that makes decisions."[65]

So when we think about how we think about the Israeli/Palestinian conflict as its partisans battle on campus, we should be aware of our human tendencies, especially two: (1) the desire for, and ease with which we create, sacred symbols to justify our "fight," and (2) our proclivity to view opinions and positions that challenge our narrative, or worse deny or denigrate our sacred principles, as either biased or hostile. In short, we think emotionally, intuitively, and in a skewed fashion.

Opposing sides in the Israel/Palestine conflict (and campus debates) reflect the "hostile media bias phenomenon," believing the other side gets fairer coverage, which may sway those who are undecided.

In 1985, Stanford University professor Robert Vallone and his colleagues documented the "hostile media bias phenomenon."[66] They identified three groups – pro-Israel, pro-Arab, and neutral – and measured reactions to the same news coverage of the 1982 Lebanon War. It was as if the "pro-Arab and pro-Israeli subjects 'saw' different news programs … [P]ro-Arab subjects reported that 42% of the references to Israel in the news programs were favorable and that only 26% were unfavorable, whereas pro-Israeli subjects reported that only 16% of the references to Israel were favorable, and that 57% were unfavorable."[67]

And it wasn't only that each side saw mainstream news coverage as biased against its position. Both sides also "believed that this overall sample of news coverage would lead undecided or ambivalent viewers to become more hostile to the side that the partisans personally favored."[68] In other words, partisans expect otherwise "neutral" observers, such as journalists, to adopt their point of view. Strident pro-Israel groups, such as the Committee for Accuracy in Middle East Reporting in America (CAMERA), regularly see the *New York Times* as hostile to Israel.[69] Strident pro-Palestinian groups and writers make the exact opposite claim.[70] Each sees a danger that non-partisans will be swayed to support the other side.[71] Few step back to consider what it would actually take to achieve peace rather than being consumed with what one should believe, say, or do to support their "team."

A genie grants someone three wishes. The person can wish for anything, even more wishes. There's one caveat: whatever he wishes for, his neighbor gets double. The man says, "Poke out one of my eyes."

In 2007, Jeremy Ginges and colleagues published "Sacred Bounds on Rational Resolution of Violent Political Conflict,"[72] based on a study of groups living in the West Bank and Gaza – Israeli settlers, Palestinian refugees, and Palestinian students.

Some Israel supporters have said that if the Palestinians saw peace as providing economic advancement, they'd be happier and more likely to give up their demands. The Ginges study suggests the opposite – that when sacred values are in play, the additional "incentive" of material improvement may "backfire." Who wants to feel they have sold something sacred for something material?

For Jewish Israelis, the right to Israel as a Jewish state is sacred; for Palestinians, the right of return is sacred. What the Ginges study showed is that the antagonists were open to compromise in only one scenario – when they saw their opponent giving up one of their sacred values. In other words, in order for there to be peace, both sides will have to lose.

Obviously, there are important differences between how Palestinians and Israelis living in the Middle East view this conflict, and how their partisan proxies think about it on campus. People in the region have a direct stake in what happens, with implications for how many people (on both sides) will die in the process. It is perhaps easier to stake out an absolutist position from the safety of the American campus. Wrong political decisions won't put you or family or your nation at risk.

The campus battle over Israel and Palestine is fueled by identity, sacred symbols, moral impulses, and an "us vs. them / good-bad" binary. It ought to be used on campus as a picture window into how people think about such charged and difficult issues.

Many people, including students and faculty at most colleges and universities, don't care about the Israel/Palestine conflict. There are over 4,000 institutions of higher learning in the United States, and Israel is an issue on only a small percentage.[73] But those who advocate zealously for one side or the other are usually not calm, geek-like critical thinkers. They can be juiced up on partisanship, and their thinking largely directed by intuition, emotion, and the distortion of facts to fit their gut feeling.

Young people engaging with political passion is a good thing. They helped support the civil rights movement and end the Vietnam War. The difference is that whatever one believes about the Israeli/Palestinian conflict, it is happening thousands of miles away.[74] Yet, it has a powerful sway over those who choose to allow the conflict to become an important part of their identity, their "ingroup."

Colleges and universities may, abstractly, be doing a good job teaching students facts and theories associated with a wide range of academic disciplines. But they usually do not help students step back and think about *how* they think. That's a shame. Because if students were more aware of our innate tendencies, using brains developed over millennia to see ingroups and outgroups, they'd help produce graduates who crave complexity, and who think more clearly. Instead, we're seeing some campuses where students and faculty seem eager to sacrifice the academy as a place dedicated to the production of knowledge, transforming it into a battlefield over the Israeli/Palestinian conflict.

chapter two

Zionism and 1948

Our nation ... sacrificed its body to defend itself, which was laid bare by the Nakba carried out by international, Zionist and imperialist powers, which didn't have the right to allow [the creation of Israel], for those who didn't have the right [the Zionists].

Yasser Arafat[1]

Zionism is nothing more – but also nothing less – than the Jewish people's sense of origin and destination in the land linked eternally with its name.

Abba Eban[2]

On 10 November 1975,[3] the United Nations General Assembly passed Resolution 3379, by a vote of seventy-two to thirty-five. It declared "Zionism is a form of racism and racial discrimination."[4] Before we examine the conflict over the conflict on campus today, we have to look at what the fight is about at its core. In many ways, it is over Zionism. The term "Zionism" was created in 1890 by Nathan Birnbaum.[5] It means the right of Jews to self-determination in a land of their own – and, as intended by Birnbaum, in the land of Israel. As anyone familiar with the Hebrew Bible (the "Old Testament" to Christians) remembers, the story of the Jews goes back thousands of years and took place in the area now known as Israel (as well as parts of what are now Jordan, Syria, Egypt, the West Bank, and Gaza).

Even when Jews were expelled from their homeland in ancient times, the Jewish religion has remained focused on the land.

Holidays, major and minor, are largely about what happened in Israel. Festival holidays mark pilgrimages to the city of Jerusalem. Synagogues worldwide are oriented so that the ark that holds the sacred Torah faces Jerusalem's Temple Mount.

The idea of a return to the land of Zion (the name of a hill in Jerusalem) has long been part of Jewish thinking, and some Jews have always lived in the land since the days described in the Bible. In the 1890s, "Zionism" – based on an idea, a yearning – became a movement. It was spurred by political realities. For 2,000 years, since the Roman conquest of ancient Israel and the dispersion of Jews that followed, Jews were marginalized in whatever country they lived.

In the early years of Christianity in Europe, Judaism was a competitor religion. But as Christianity became entrenched, and Jews neither disappeared nor accepted the "truth" about Jesus, what was to be done? Jews were ostracized, as an example of what happens to people when they reject the "true" faith. They were forced into ghettos. They were not allowed into various professions and crafts. Some were made to wear badges so they could be identified easily (while Nazis perfected this use of fashion to dehumanize, they did not invent it). At times Jews were expelled. They were murdered during the Crusades, and later during the Inquisition.

What we now call antisemitism was rampant. Antisemitism is essentially a conspiracy theory about Jews. It alleges that Jews conspire to harm non-Jews; and it "explains" what goes wrong in the world.

In 1144 in Norwich, England, Jews were accused of abducting a non-Jewish child and committing ritual murder, crucifying him. A century later, in Germany, a different type of Jewish ritual murder was alleged – draining the blood of Christians, a "blood libel." For centuries, when Christian children would go missing, a new blood libel charge would appear (frequently around Easter time, with the assertion that the blood was used to bake Passover matzah).

During the Black Death, in the mid-1300s, about half the people of Europe died. It was because of the Jews, people believed. Jews, they said, were poisoning wells.

Throughout history, antisemitism was an oppressive condition Jews have had to endure. But sometimes it became an existential threat. During the Crusades. During the Inquisition.[6] And again, to an extent, in Eastern Europe in the 1880s.

After Russia's Czar Alexander II was assassinated in 1881, Jews were blamed. Over 200 pogroms followed. A pogrom was a riot. Jews were murdered, raped, and mutilated, and their property burned or destroyed. Some pogroms were sanctioned or organized by political leaders. Others were more "spontaneous." Police rarely interceded before much Jewish blood was spilled.

Then, in 1894, the unthinkable happened. In France, where Jews were first emancipated and felt integrated into French society, a Jewish army captain named Alfred Dreyfus was arrested and convicted of treason. It would take twelve years for him to be exonerated, even though the charges were fabricated. And it was not just Dreyfus who was defamed. Jews were stunned to hear chants of "Death to the Jews!" in the streets of Paris, and to watch antisemitism being flamed by political and military leaders.

Theodor Herzl was a young Jewish journalist covering the Dreyfus trial. It is an oft-repeated story that when he saw Jews vilified by so many Frenchmen, he concluded that Jews would never be safe as a minority in any country. The reality is more complex. Herzl's claim that the trial "made me a Zionist" was, according to Herzl biographer Derek Penslar, "an act of self-invention, which appears not to have been conscious."[7] Regardless, Herzl certainly saw raw antisemitism during the Dreyfus affair, and he later pointed to it as evidence that Jews needed to be able to defend themselves, in their own land. While Birnbaum may have coined the term, Herzl founded Zionism as a movement.

In 1896, Herzl wrote *Der Judenstaat* (The Jewish State), urging that "sovereignty be granted us over a portion of the globe large enough to satisfy the rightful requirements of a nation."[8] He led the First Zionist Congress in Basel, Switzerland, in 1897, with about 200 participants. They announced the Zionist program, with the goal of re-establishing a Jewish home in Palestine, as the land of Israel, then part of the Ottoman Empire, was known.

By 1917, in the midst of World War I, and at the urging of Zionist leaders, the British government went on record supporting Herzl's vision. Lord Balfour, the foreign secretary, wrote:

> His Majesty's government view with favour the establishment in Palestine of a national home for the Jewish people, and will use their best endeavours to facilitate the achievement of this object, it being clearly understood that nothing shall be done which may prejudice the civil and religious rights of existing non-Jewish communities in Palestine, or the rights and political status enjoyed by Jews in any other country.[9]

Britain had no control over Palestine when this single sentence was written. But when World War I ended, so did Turkish control of the region. In 1920 Great Britain received the League of Nation's postwar Mandate over Palestine (which included what is today Israel, Gaza, the West Bank, and the Kingdom of Jordan). Jewish immigration to Palestine[10] accelerated. And the British, who had the obligation to maintain order, had a problem. Important and large segments of the Arab community, feeling threatened both demographically and politically, objected to the new arrivals.*

---

* A friend who read an early draft of this chapter pointed out a problem worth contemplating: starting out with the Jewish narrative. As the epigraphs to this chapter suggest, and much of this chapter underscores, there are two conflicting, perhaps irreconcilable, national narratives colliding.

If you are more sympathetic to the Israeli narrative than the Palestinian one, how would you have felt if I had begun this chapter with Arabs living on the land for centuries, what their lives were like, and then in the nineteenth century, start bringing Jews into the picture? From that perspective the story is that Arabs were there, Jews were the outsiders who kept coming and coming until they disrupted Arab life and eventually became the dominant force, claiming the Arabs' land as their own in the name of "Zionism." A pro-Israel person might feel disquieted, having Jews recast to a secondary role, coming into the story mainly to inflict harm on others.

Which side's story goes first, and the implications of that decision, is precisely the complaint of many who prioritize the pro-Palestinian narrative, that the Arab story is seen as secondary, a reaction to the Jewish story and not as they see it, the main story. There is no way here to set out these two stories side by side. But see Paul Scham's chart, which does this, in Scham, "Modern Jewish History." See also Scham, "Israeli Historical Narratives."

While the Jewish narrative of Zionism and Israel's creation is rooted in ancient Jewish history and ethnic and religious-based yearnings, the Palestinian narrative of Israel begins in the 1880s. There was always a Jewish presence in Palestine. But in the 1880s, this region of the Ottoman Empire was overwhelmingly Arab. Some Arabs welcomed the Jewish newcomers, but the vast majority did not as it became increasingly clear that these new immigrants wanted to build a Jewish state, and on top of that they were a different Jew than the indigenous ones, who were sometimes called "Jewish Arabs." These newcomers from Poland and Russia and elsewhere in Europe were Ashkenazi Jews, many of whom were Yiddish speakers (although some preferred to speak Russian or Polish).

Of course just as the Jews in Palestine, native and newly arrived, were not monolithic, neither were the Arabs. Some were Muslim and some were Christian (of different denominations). Some were Druze. Some viewed the newcomers positively, many were hostile. The Zionist narrative is, of course, about Jews and their connection with the land of Israel. Palestinians are not central to this story. In fact, they are frequently omitted from it, except perhaps as an obstacle.

The Palestinian narrative, naturally, focuses on the Arabs, the people living on the land, the indigenous population, whose rights were given away by a European power in the Balfour Declaration. By what right did Europeans give away their land to others? And for that matter, by what right did the United Nations give away their land too? Giving away others' land is what colonialists do.

The Jews claim history, but how relevant or controlling is that? The late Columbia University professor Edward Said wrote that "the entire historical duration of a Jewish state in Palestine prior to 1948 was a sixty year period two millennia ago."* In the interim, Arabs inhabited the land. They are descendants of the people who lived

---

* Said, *The Question of Palestine*, 58. Of course, others criticize Said's description as factually wrong. As Robert Griffin notes, "Compare Martin Gilbert: 'Jewish rule in Judaea and Samaria in ancient times lasted a total of 641 years'" (Gilbert, *Jewish History Atlas*, 2nd ed. [London, 1976], 9). In any case, the issue is not length of self-rule" (Griffin, "Ideology and Misrepresentation," 618n17).

there over the centuries, Israelites included. In fact, if one is going to cite the Hebrew Bible to support claims of rights to the land, what about the Canaanites, Jebusites, and others who were there before the Jews? They too are the ancestors of today's Palestinians.[11]

One of the books I bought in Portland in 1982 was entitled *Our Roots Are Still Alive: The Story of the Palestinian People*. It began as follows:

> For centuries, the peasants of the Palestinian village, al-Yahudiyya, were a people wedded to their land ... Like other Palestinians ... they had painstakingly terraced many of the hills, converting them to usable land. Irrigation ditches built by their ancestors centuries before brought water to the land which yielded citrus, olives and grain ... The people of al-Yahudiyya used the nearby land for grazing their animals. In the late 1880s, two moneylenders gained formal ownership of this land as payment for village debts. As the peasants considered use of the land a God-given right, the passing of ownership did not worry them ...
>
> In 1878 Jewish settlers from Europe bought al-Yahudiyya's grazing land from the two moneylenders. They established an agricultural colony, Petah Tiqva ... After several years the new settlers ordered the Palestinian peasants to stop using the pastures for grazing. However, the peasants continued to use the land, and tempers flared quickly on both sides. One day in March 1886, the Jewish settlers seized ten of the Palestinians' donkeys – an act which sparked an attack by fifty angry villagers from al-Yahudiyya. Turkish authorities, who ruled Palestine at the time, immediately sent soldiers to protect the settlers at Petah Tiqva ... The fighting at Petah Tiqva was the first skirmish in what has become a century-long battle between the Palestinian people and the Jewish settlers from Europe for the land of Palestine.[12]

In other words, while Jewish settlers saw Palestine as a return to their ancestral homeland, Arabs in Palestine, quite naturally, only saw European settlers.

As Palestinian academic Sari Nusseibeh[13] observed: "[O]ur respective absolute rights – the historical right of the Jews to their ancestral homeland, and the Palestinian rights to the country robbed from them – [are] fundamentally in conflict, and ... mutually exclusive. [T]he more historical justice each side demand[s], the less their real national interests g[e]t served. Justice and interests [fall] into conflict."[14] The past, and how to think about it, is a key point of contention. Take Herzl. For a very short time he pondered whether the Jewish home he envisioned might be in South America or, temporarily, in Africa. But his movement declared there was only one choice: Palestine. Pro-Israel activists acknowledge that other national homes were briefly considered when Jews feared being killed in Europe and European colonialism was in its heyday. It was to be expected, they say, that Herzl and the other Zionist leaders used the language of the time, colonialist language, as they tried to achieve their goal of a homeland for Jews.

Pro-Palestinian activists cite this history to prove that the Jewish link to Palestine wasn't as important as suggested: a portion of today's Kenya, along the Uganda railway, was considered for the national home. And they point to the words the Zionists of that time used, describing a settler-colonialist enterprise, not so different from the British settlement of Rhodesia.

And what of Herzl's attitudes towards Arabs? Pro-Palestinian academics are much more likely to cite a diary entry from Herzl than are supporters of Israel. On 12 June 1895, Herzl wrote:

> We must expropriate gently the private property on the estates assigned to us. We shall try to spirit the penniless population across the border by procuring employment for it in the transit countries, while denying it employment in our own country. The property owners will come over to our side. Both the process of expropriation and the removal of the poor must be carried out discreetly and circumspectly. The property owners may believe that they are cheating us, selling to us at more than [the land is] worth. But nothing will be sold back to them.[15]

Is Herzl's plan, so early on, full-scale displacement of the Arab population? What was the import of the fact that while he said little about Arabs, he wrote this in his diary? Is it evidence of his real intentions, or a fleeting thought of little importance that he wrote in one of his manic periods? Was it about all Arabs, or only the poor ones? Is his comment to be excused by placing it into the context of the time, or does he not get a pass, as some of his contemporaries were speaking out against imperialism? Some scholars, such as Derek Penslar of Harvard University, wrestle with these questions – important ones for students to learn from, about how we view historical texts. Too many simply seek to weaponize such material. In fact, all material.

Consider again the claim that Israelis are "settler colonialists." On 4 July 2018, the Palestinian Campaign for the Academic and Cultural Boycott of Israel (PACBI) wrote to the Iroquois Confederacy – Native nations from New York and Canada – urging them to boycott the world championship of lacrosse, a game Natives invented (and that the Iroquois introduced to early American settlers);[16] a game they continue to excel at, and that is important to their culture.[17] The request stated, in part:

> As indigenous peoples, we have both seen our traditional lands colonized, our people ethnically cleansed and massacred by colonial settlers. This year marks 70 years of Israeli dispossession of Palestinians, which began with what we call the Nakba, or catastrophe. In the years surrounding Israel's establishment on our homeland in 1948, pre and post-state Israeli forces premeditatively drove out the majority of the indigenous people of Palestine and destroyed more than 500 of our villages and towns.[18]

Contrast this language with this passage of an essay by Judea Pearl, a noted academic (and the father of Daniel Pearl, the *Wall Street Journal* reporter who was beheaded by terrorists in Pakistan in 2002). "It is not surprising," Pearl wrote, "that misrepresenting Israel as a 'white settler-colonialist society' has become a cornerstone of BDS [Boycott, Divestment, and Sanctions] ideology and propaganda." He asks those who read such claims to "ask themselves if they can recall" any of the following:

- One case of white settlers moving into a country they perceived to be the birthplace of their history.
- One case of white settlers speaking a language spoken in the land before the language spoken by its contemporary residents.

- One case of settlers whose holidays commemorated historical events in the land to which they moved – not the lands from which they came.
- One case of settlers who did not name towns like New York, New Amsterdam and New Wales (Israeli towns are not named "New Warsaw," "New Berlin," and "New Baghdad"), but after names by which those towns were known in ancient times.
- One case of settlers who narrated their homecoming journey for eighty generations in poetry, prose, lore and daily prayers.[19]

The reality is that Israel isn't like settler-colonial states in many ways, but in other ways it is. Proponents on each side seem blind to the complexities, choosing to highlight either the differences or similarities, depending on which better suits their black/white, good/bad, us/them argument, and perhaps as Michael Hogg and his colleagues posit, depending on which one makes them feel more "certain."[20] As scholar Seth Anziska says, "Real history is the ability to navigate all these views at once. The rest is communal advocacy."[21]

This book is not intended to be a primer on the Israel/Palestine conflict. There are many good articles and books that treat this difficult history and the contrary narratives (a good introduction or refresher is Neil Caplan's *The Israel-Palestine Conflict: Contested Histories*, or *Shared Histories: A Palestinian-Israeli Dialogue* by Paul Scham, Walid Salem, and Benjamin Pogrund).* For our purposes, simply imagine you're a Jewish college student who identifies with Israel. Then imagine you are a Palestinian student whose family was displaced in 1948, or a progressive student who passionately believes Palestinians are oppressed underdogs. You'd look at each historical event in the century since the Balfour Declaration differently.

---

* There is one important aspect not covered here: While the founders of Israel were predominantly Jews from Europe, most Jews from Arab lands were expelled from their home countries after the establishment of the state. The majority of today's Israelis can trace at least part of their family history to North Africa and the Middle East.

Pro-Israel students, for example, might focus on the Arab riots of the 1920s and 1930s, in which Jews were slaughtered. Pro-Palestinian students might focus on the murders of Arabs during that period. Each would claim the British, who ruled Mandatory Palestine at the time, favored the other. Each could cite evidence in support of its view. Indeed, Israel supporters point to the restrictions the British put on Jewish immigration, especially in the 1930s when Jews were fleeing Nazi Germany and the Holocaust was looming, and again when the survivors were trying to come to Palestine after the war. Pro-Palestinian students point to Britain allowing European Jews in, in numbers that reduced Arab control over their own lives. The number of Jews in Palestine increased from census to census, as did the amount of land under their control.

Both sides also frequently use the Holocaust as a debating point. Israel's supporters will of course note that the central idea of Zionism, a return to the land of Israel, long preceded the Holocaust, so Israel's legitimacy does not rest on Nazi crimes. But they will also point to the mass murder of six million Jews to underscore the importance of a Jewish homeland, where Jews can see to their own security and not have to rely on the good will of others.[22]

Supporters of Palestinians will ask why Arabs had to give up so much because some Europeans killed other Europeans. Where's the justification in that? And some will go further, attracted by the bigoted rabbit hole of Holocaust denial. If the Holocaust didn't occur and the Jews made it up, as neo-Nazis suggest, then one of the arguments why Israel is needed – as a safe haven for Jews – is diminished.

Some pro-Palestinian actors accuse Israelis of doing to the Palestinians what the Nazis did to the Jews. This is, of course, a false comparison: Palestinians are not being herded up and sent to gas chambers. Yet, it is not entirely beyond rationality to make some limited comparisons, for example, when from time to time an Israeli leader refers to Arabs in dehumanizing terms, "like animals, they aren't human,"[23] reminiscent of how Nazi leaders spoke about Jews. And while Israelis and their supporters correctly condemn the Nazi comparisons directed towards them, some will turn around and use Nazi imagery in "support" of their views, for example Israeli prime minister Benjamin Netanyahu falsely claiming that it was a Palestinian leader who gave Hitler the idea of killing Jews,[24] or Abba Eban saying the 1967 boundaries were "Auschwitz lines."[25] More recently, Deputy Foreign Minister Zeev Elkin[26] called the 1967 border "Auschwitz borders."

The dispute over Israel and Palestine on American campuses today, of course, is largely not between Israelis and Palestinians. It is a debate involving Jews (on both sides), progressives, Evangelicals, and others.

There are some Jews for whom Israel is part of their core identity, and they have a mission to defend it against those who would defame or slander it, just as (or perhaps more fervently than) if someone maligned the Jewish religion. But there are Jews whose identity is more informed by their religion's call to repair the world and to do good. They may see this mandate as inconsistent with staying silent as Israel's occupation of the West Bank and significant control over Gaza are now over half a century old.

There are non-Jews for whom the Israeli/Palestinian conflict is the new, fashionable, cause of the Left,[27] following the tradition of the Spanish Civil War of the 1930s, the civil rights struggles of the 1960s, the Vietnam War protests of the 1960s and 1970s, and the anti-Apartheid activism of the 1980s. The Israel/Palestine conflict was lurking in the background as a secondary rallying point for many progressives since the 1967 War. With the end of the Vietnam War and then of Apartheid South Africa, this conflict attracted more attention among the Left. When the Peace Process collapsed in 2000 and the Second Intifada began, it became THE key battle for the Left, fighting what it perceived as the last great bastion of colonialism.

All these groups, each driven by its world view and set of principles, are in play on campus. There are also significant groups beyond the campus influencing these debates. On one side, there are politically conservative Jewish groups, as well as Evangelicals who support Israel because they believe the ingathering of Jews is the prerequisite to the second coming of Christ and/or believe that "whoever blesses Israel will be blessed." On the other side are groups, including Jewish ones, that are committed to supporting the Palestinian cause.

All of these groups frequently act like they have a monopoly on truth, and on justice, and sometimes display self-righteousness as an art form. Each bends the history of Israel to support its case. For the most part, the events cited are agreed upon, at least that they happened. But what happened, why, and the implications of those events become distorted through the lens of current political needs and the myopia of my-side bias.

Even though many of the campus debates today are over the Occupation (and the legacy of Israel's 1967 victory), or Israel's actions in Gaza, or the BDS movement, this is at heart a battle over 1948 and Israel's birth. In later chapters, we will explore this fact more deeply, especially as we look at BDS and the calls for an academic boycott of Israel.

For Israel supporters, 1948 was a culmination of an historic yearning and a post-Holocaust necessity. Israel's declaration as a nation in May of that year, and its survival against invading Arab armies, its latter-day David beating back Goliath, was and is a source of pride. And until 1967 that was the shared narrative by most Jews and by the Left, which after the end of World War II saw the new state, with its socialist leaders and collectives (kibbutzim), as a counterforce to British imperialism. It was a feel-good story. Movies like *Cast a Giant Shadow* and *Exodus*, the writings of Leon Uris, told a compelling narrative of Holocaust survivors reclaiming their homeland, beating back threats, making the desert bloom.

And what of the Arabs in Palestine in 1948? They were seen as a fifth column. They refused to accept the UN's partition (and, if they had, they would have had a state). And most, it was alleged, ran off when the leaders of Arab countries told them to leave their homes and get out of the way, so their brethren could drive the Jews into the sea, after which they could return.

But starting in the 1980s a group of Israeli historians,[28] accessing new information from archives, began documenting a more complicated picture. Yes, some Arabs left. But others were pushed from their homes, expelled at the point of a gun. While pro-Israel activists might point to the bravery of soldiers who withstood attacks to save the Jews of the old city of Jerusalem, or the horrid murder of Jewish doctors and nurses at Mt. Scopus, or the desecration of Jewish cemeteries by Jordanian solders (who turned tombstones into latrines), there were now documented instances of Arab villages – men, women, and children – being forced out, even on occasion slaughtered. There were also instances of rape.

Each of these events, which Israelis call the War of Independence and Palestinians call the Nakba (the "catastrophe"), has to be looked at in the context of the times, recognizing also that politicians and commanders were making life and death choices in the moment. There is no excuse for war crimes and massacres, but the forced evacuation of various Palestinian towns during the course of a war were not all of a piece. Benny Morris's *1948: A History of the First Arab-Israeli War* and Ari Shavit's *My Promised Land* underscore the complexities and personalities involved.

Yet partisans on each side, in Israel/Palestine and on the American college campus, spin 1948 to their own group's purposes. When Israel's "new historians" began writing, they were frequently blasted as traitors. Palestinians and their supporters, who believe the creation of Israel was not only unjust but has to be undone, used these new revelations of massacres and forced removal as justification for their views.

If you want an image of the crux of the conflict, the different narratives, in fact the different realities of each group, consider the contrasting images of May 2018. On the seventieth anniversary of Israel's birth, the United States moved its embassy to Jerusalem, with much fanfare and celebration. Forty miles away, thousands of Palestinians approached the fence separating Gaza from Israel, with the stated intention of returning to their 1948 homes.[29] There was literally a split screen: The celebration in Jerusalem. The shooting, killing, and wounding of Palestinians in Gaza.

This is still a battle over 1948, over the success of Zionism. And as the disruptors of the UCLA program on indigeneity made clear in their shouts against two states, and for "1948," this is the crux of the campus conflict too.

chapter three

Free Speech and Academic Freedom

Without a vibrant commitment to free and open inquiry, a university ceases to be a university.

> Geoffrey Stone, paraphrasing University of Chicago
> president Robert M. Hutchins, who confronted a "storm
> of protest" when the university invited the Communist
> Party's candidate to speak on campus in 1932[1]

[A] function of free speech under our system of government is to invite dispute. It may indeed best serve its high purpose when it ... stirs people to anger. Speech ... may strike at prejudices and preconceptions and have profound unsettling effects ... That is why freedom of speech, though not absolute ... is nevertheless protected against censorship or punishment ...

> Justice William O. Douglas, *Terminiello v. Chicago*, 337 US 1 (1949)[2]

When we care about something deeply, especially an issue connected to how we define ourselves, our families, our morality, our values, our group, or our children's future, it's difficult to acknowledge we might be dead wrong. When was the last time you heard someone who passionately believes abortion is the same as taking a baby out of a crib and killing it say they might be mistaken?

Some of the same stridency exists on both sides of the Israel/Palestine debate. As we discussed in chapter 1, aspects of this binary are inescapable. You have groups that are defined in opposition and competition with each other, fighting over the same land, the national identity of one threatened by the national identity of the other.

But on the American college campus, the focus should be on learning about this conflict, why it is so complicated, how we think about it, perhaps even what can be done about it. Yet the trend is exactly the opposite: to stake a side and fight a battle, rather than to think and learn. It is as if blood allegiances are to people, or perhaps to our imagination of who those people are, thousands of miles away in Israel and Palestine, rather than to classmates and colleagues.

Some of the brightest people I know, when expressing an opinion, start by saying, "I might be wrong, but ..." The acknowledgment that one's truth, even sacred truth, might be mistaken is the essence of what a college education should be about. This doesn't mean that you hold your views less tenaciously or act on them less energetically; rather, it means that you are open to re-examining them, understanding that no person or ideology or theology is infallible. Recall that people were once killed for suggesting that Earth wasn't the center of the universe. Some who professed what seemed like odd ways of thinking were burned as witches. And people are still being murdered today for believing in the "wrong" god.

I don't know how many college students today study John Stuart Mill's "On Liberty," but it is something they should take to heart. Mill explained why liberty requires the airing of presumably "wrong" opinions:

> [T]he peculiar evil of silencing the expression of an opinion is, that it is robbing the human race; posterity as well as the existing generation; those who dissent from the opinion, still more than those who hold it. If the opinion is right, they are deprived of the opportunity of exchanging error for truth: if wrong, they lose, what is almost as great a benefit, the clearer perception and livelier impression of truth, produced by its collision with error.[3]

You might say that Mill's view is idealistic. Why should we allow harmful ideas to gain currency, when we know too well how naturally hate resonates in our souls, and is so easily stoked? That is a discussion postponed until later in this book, about what is effective against hateful speech. The question at hand is not how ideas are communicated and acknowledged in the world generally, but how they play out on the campuses of colleges and universities. The purpose of higher education is not that of trade schools. While people may get a degree in one or more of a variety of subjects, what they are being taught is how to think. Of course, it is difficult to have a philosophical, thoughtful, maybe even Socratic tussle with difficult ideas if you are feeling harassed, intimidated, or threatened. That's the contradiction of hateful ideas on campus: They need to be examined critically, but a hateful environment causes human beings stress, and influences their thought processes. Ideas are important, and they can also upset us deeply.

"I wish they had hit me."

That was the opening line in my first major report as the American Jewish Committee's specialist on antisemitism. AJC hired me in 1989. My initial task was to investigate how college campuses should handle allegations of antisemitism.

I went to Baltimore and read a large collection of press clippings about campus bigotry, archived by the National Institute against Prejudice and Violence. Three things became clear. First, the worst campus disruptions occurred when students felt an incident of bigotry had not been combated, or at least acknowledged promptly and seriously, by the college's president. Second, universities were not going to adopt new structures to combat antisemitism alone, but new mechanisms designed to address all forms of campus bigotry would help Jewish students as well. Third, the hardest cases were those about expression. Assaults, graffiti, and other physical acts were, at least in theory, easier to address. What does one do about a hateful comment, poster, or speaker?

The opening quote in the report was the lament of a Brown University student. An Asian American, he had been taunted by seven white male students. "I felt empty," he said. "I wish they had hit me ... At least I would be able to *physically* show the scars the words 'ching' and 'chang' left on my being. [Authorities and fellow students] would not care to hear how [I was] chipped away emotionally. They want blood. They want proof that it happened. Only then could [I] truly have been hurt – in their eyes."[4]

AJC attracted many committed and knowledgeable lay people, including the late Robert Hess, then president of Brooklyn College. Bob was struggling to come up with better ways to handle problems of bigotry on his campus. About the time that I was copying newspaper clippings in Baltimore, three Jewish students at Brooklyn College were seriously injured by a group of twenty white men, who hit them with "fists, feet and beer bottles,"[5] according to the police, while yelling ethnic slurs. That same fall Bob attended a meeting of college presidents, about this issue. He was frustrated. "The many distinguished experts ... talked mostly about the free speech limitations of college disciplinary codes," he wrote. "My colleagues and I heard what we couldn't do, not what we could do."[6]

Episodes of campus bigotry were seemingly increasing and deeply troubling for college presidents. Students felt afraid. Parents, alumni, and donors were alarmed. Prospective students, it was feared, might shy away. There were news reports of swastikas, cross burnings, slurs, racist literature, and hate-mongering speakers. Graffito: "You're a fucking asshole and I hope you die eating matzoh." A piece of paper with the word "Spic!" slipped under a student's door. One sent through the mail said, "Custer should have finished off your entire degenerate race."

The trend had been to enact "speech codes" to address the problem. The idea was to give the campus community, especially students, a set of expectations of what type of speech was permitted, and what would get one in trouble. Thoughtful people pondered what a code might contain. The University of Michigan's code had Talmud-like distinctions. Apparently, its authors recognized that there were different speech interests at different campus venues. Classrooms should have the most freedom because they were the formal loci of discussion and learning. Perhaps there was a lesser free speech interest in a dining hall, and even less in a dorm, which was like a home, although one might argue that a college works best when classroom discussions are so engaging that they are continued over meals and late into the night.

Students at the University of Michigan found the intersections of these different physical spaces and wrote "free speech zones" in chalk. That code was not upheld in the courts as violating free speech (nor were others like it). But the codes were also bad policy. Who would expect a drunken student at 2:00 a.m. to measure his words against a speech code that calibrated what was okay to say depending on where on campus he happened to be?

Then consider the fact that the distinction to be made is actually not about speech, but expression. Ideas can be expressed by speech of course, but also by other means: writing, signs, art, posters, placards, demonstrations. Conversely, words can be used to harass, intimidate, even terrorize. We want campuses that are open to expression – including, perhaps even especially difficult and disturbing ideas – but which protect students from real harassment and intimidation. Hate speech codes were efforts to say that ideas themselves can harass and intimidate. Ideas can and should make one uncomfortable (a comfortable college education is a wasted college education). But harassment is something different. For example, it is permitted to say that one believes all fill-in-the-blanks should die. Such speech should, obviously, be robustly condemned. But it is not permitted to send an email blast to every student of a particular ethnicity that says you have a mission to hunt and kill them.[7]

When hate speech codes of the 1980s and 1990s were being debated for campuses in the United States, First Amendment scholars weighed in. Since American jurisprudence has strong protections for the expression of opinions, including against prior restraints, these experts disagreed about the smallest of gray areas, in which few cases would play out.* By focusing on questions of speech and its supposed limitations, people ignored the other things that colleges and universities should have been doing to address the problem, among them surveying their students to see

---

* The First Amendment applies to government, not individuals, so it limits restrictions on speech at public institutions, not private ones. Yet, because a campus is supposed to be a place to examine ideas, even private colleges should be guided by First Amendment principles.

how they experience bigotry on campus, training staff (sometimes campus police and other staff treat students of color differently than their white classmates), setting up mechanisms to report bias incidents, pre-planning what to do if a hate incident were to occur (such as having a crisis team in place), reviewing curriculum, and so much more.

The articles in the Baltimore archives showed that an incident of bigotry which tears the campus apart is almost always the last in a series. It becomes the tipping point when students feel that their experiences with everyday bias and hateful events have been ignored by the campus leadership.

In the years following the release of my report, I trained over 200 college presidents on a blueprint of how to manage bigotry on campus, steps which, as outlined above (surveys, training, etc.) required resources, a steadfast commitment to academic freedom and free speech, and a lot of work on their part. Hate speech codes were also bad policy because they allowed university leadership to be lazy, to say they were doing something about the problem of bigotry on campus, without having to do any of the difficult things needed to cultivate a climate that actually rejected bigotry, through research, training, and education.

Bob Hess also emphasized what he called "the myth of the institution." When divisions threatened the campus, whether over an act or a speaker perceived by some as hateful, he would emphasize that "we're all part of the Brooklyn College family." He was pointing the students towards their shared group identity, rather than their other identities (like pro-Palestinian or pro-Israeli) that threatened to tear the fabric of the campus apart. Bob Hess instinctively understood the social psychology of groups, and how to use it to counter bigotry.

In 2004 a pro-Israel group, The David Project, made a film called *Columbia Unbecoming*. It charged Columbia University with doing nothing about professors who were allegedly not only biased against Israel and Jews but who had also "intimidated students who try to express reasonable and alternative viewpoints"[8] (the controversy is discussed later, in chapter 4). Columbia's president Lee Bollinger, while deeply concerned about the allegations, was also distressed that outside forces, including elected officials, were calling for the firing of the professors in question, in large part because of their views about Israel.

Bollinger, seeing the academy and free speech under attack, decided to give a lecture on the history and importance of academic freedom, delivered at the Association of the Bar of the City of New York. Grounding academic freedom in two related concepts – the "freedom to teach" and the "freedom to learn"* – he said:

> Historians trace the codification of academic freedom … to a series of conflicts in the late 1800s that pitted individual faculty members against university trustees and administrators.
>
> The most famous was a case involving Edward A. Ross, a Stanford [academic] who made a series of speeches in support of the Democrat William Jennings Bryan in 1896. Jane Lathrop Stanford – widow of Leland Stanford, ardent Republican, and sole trustee of the university – was so outraged by Ross' activism that she demanded his dismissal. The president of the university eventually acceded to her demands; Ross was forced to resign in 1900.[9]

As Bollinger made clear, Ross's treatment led to the foundational document of the American Association of University Professors, the 1915 "Report on Academic Freedom and Tenure," co-authored by Arthur Lovejoy, one of Ross's Stanford colleagues who resigned after Ross was forced out. The report, Bollinger said, "sought to remove university trustees as arbiters of research and teaching, and to assert instead the authority of self-governing faculty members." It stated:

> The distinctive and important function [of professors] … is to deal at first hand, after prolonged and specialized technical training, with the

---

* Academic freedom and free speech are related, but different, concepts. I have the free speech right to say the Earth is flat, but someone teaching rocket science who says that can be investigated on a campus as a matter of competence. Yet, for most issues, and certainly ones related to history, identity, nationalism, and so forth, the protection of free speech is essential for the promotion of academic freedom.

sources of knowledge; and to impart the results of their own and of their fellow-specialists' investigations and reflection, both to students and the general public, without fear or favor ... The proper fulfillment of the work of the professoriate requires that our universities shall be so free that no fair-minded person shall find any excuse for even a suspicion that the utterances of university teachers are shaped or restricted by the judgment, not of professional scholars, but of inexpert and possibly not wholly disinterested persons outside their ranks.[10]

The idea that Bollinger stressed – "that faculty members, not external actors, should determine professional standards for the academy" (meaning the faculty's jobs and research must not be jeopardized by outside political interference) – is not only "foundational" but also an idea that routinely has to be defended. During World War I, Columbia's board of trustees required their entire university to subscribe to a loyalty oath. Opposition to the war effort was prohibited. Nicholas Murray Butler, who was then Columbia's president, explained, "What had been tolerated before became intolerable now. What had been wrongheadedness was now sedition. What had been folly was now treason."[11] Some professors who opposed the war effort were fired.

Near the beginning of the McCarthy era, James B. Conant, Harvard's president, said that members of the Communist Party were "out of bounds as members of the teaching profession."[12] Approximately 600 professors lost their jobs, not because they were poor teachers but simply because of their alleged political affiliations.

In 1953 the state of New Hampshire's legislature adopted a resolution directing the attorney general of the state "to make [a] full and complete investigation with respect to violations of the subversive activities act of 1951 and to determine whether persons as defined in said act are presently located within this state."[13] Paul Sweezy was a professor at the University of New Hampshire. The attorney general compelled Sweezy to appear. The AG laid "great stress upon an article which [Sweezy] had co-authored. It deplored the use of violence by the United States and other capitalist countries in attempting to preserve a social order which the writers thought must inevitably fail."[14]

Sweezy affirmed that he was a "classical Marxist" and a "social-ist."[15] Then he was called back for a second meeting. He was asked questions about progressive groups, and the political affiliations of others, including his wife. He refused to answer. He was questioned about a lecture he gave to students in a humanities course in 1954 at the request of a colleague. "What was the subject of your lecture?" he was asked. "Did you ... espouse the theory of dialectical material-ism?"[16] Sweezy refused to answer. He was held in contempt.

The United States Supreme Court reversed, not only on First Amendment grounds but also because of the importance of academic freedom. The Court said:

> The essentiality of freedom in the community of American universities is almost self-evident. No one should underestimate the vital role in a democracy that is played by those who guide and train our youth. To impose any strait jacket upon the intellectual leaders in our colleges and universities would imperil the future of our Nation. No field of education is so thoroughly comprehended by man that new discoveries cannot yet be made. Particularly is that true in the social sciences, where few, if any, principles are accepted as absolutes. Scholarship cannot flourish in an atmosphere of suspicion and distrust. Teachers and students must always remain free to inquire, to study and to evaluate, to gain new maturity and understanding; otherwise our civilization will stagnate and die.[17]

It continued:

> Insights into the mysteries of nature are born of hypothesis and speculation ... The problems that are the respective preoccupations of anthropology, economics, law, psychology, sociology and related areas of scholarship are merely departmentalized dealing, by way of manageable division of analysis, with interpenetrating aspects of holistic perplexities. For society's good – if understanding be an essential need of society – inquiries into these problems, speculations about them, stimulation in others of reflection upon them, must be left as unfettered as possible. Political power must abstain from intrusion into this activity of freedom ... except for reasons that are exigent and obviously compelling.

... Suffice it to quote the latest expression on this subject. It is also perhaps the most poignant because its plea on behalf of continuing the free spirit of the open universities of South Africa has gone unheeded.

"In a university knowledge is its own end, not merely a means to an end. A university ceases to be true to its own nature if it becomes the tool of Church or State or any sectional interest. A university is characterized by the spirit of free inquiry, its ideal being the ideal of Socrates – 'to follow the argument where it leads.' This implies the right to examine, question, modify or reject traditional ideas and beliefs. Dogma and hypothesis are incompatible, and the concept of an immutable doctrine is repugnant to the spirit of a university. The concern of its scholars is not merely to add and revise facts in relation to an accepted framework, but to be ever examining and modifying the framework itself ... It is the business of a university to provide that atmosphere which is most conducive to speculation, experiment and creation. It is ... to determine for itself on academic grounds who may teach, what may be taught, how it shall be taught, and who may be admitted to study."[18]

Erwin Chemerinsky co-taught a class on free speech when he was dean of the law school at University of California, Irvine (he is now the dean of the University of California, Berkeley, School of Law). His students surprised him. He started the class with a case then in the news, a videotape of racist speech by fraternity members from the University of Oklahoma. If one of the students was expelled, and then sued the university, he asked, who should win? It was a unanimous vote for the university. When the students were polled again at the end of the semester, they split.

Erwin, like me, grew up during the civil rights movement and the Vietnam War protests. He wrote about how free speech was viewed at that time:

Much of the speech that was considered important to protect was raucous and even profane. Protesters burned draft cards, flags, and bras; cities prosecuted people who wore T-shirts that expressed obscene sentiments about the draft; authors, publishers, and even comedians risked jail by pushing against historic prohibitions against indecency or obscenity. We saw firsthand how officials attempted to stifle or punish protesters by claiming that they were defending community values or responding to threats to the public peace. We also saw how stronger principles of free speech assisted the drive for desegregation, the push to end the war, and the efforts of historically marginalized people to challenge convention and express their identities in new ways. In our experience, speech that was sometimes considered offensive, or that made people uncomfortable, was a good and necessary thing for progress.[19]

For many baby boomers like Erwin and me, free speech was a necessary precondition for positive social change. This wasn't only about burning draft cards or the ability to wear clothing that said "Fuck the Draft," but about challenging a power system that denied Americans equal rights. Rosa Parks's refusal to move to the back of the bus wasn't only a question of public accommodation, it was a protest, and an act of expression, an assertion of an idea. Plus, we knew from our parents, or at least I did, about the horrors of the McCarthy era, when government stripped people of their livelihood and even jailed some because of their political ideas and associations.

Today's students seem to know little of this history. Many don't regard protection of free speech, including speech with which one fundamentally disagrees, as important for the promotion of democracy and human rights. Erwin also noticed that today's students had grown up with anti-bullying programs. The anti-bullying message worked: students understand that words can hurt, and that they have an obligation not to inflict harm and also to stop others from bullying.

In the spring of 2018 I was invited to speak on a panel at the annual J Street conference. J Street is a progressive, largely Jewish organization that was established a decade earlier in 2007. It is a home for Israel supporters who are uncomfortable with the Israeli occupation of the West Bank, and the tendency of mainstream Jewish organizations in general, and the American Israel Public Affairs Committee (AIPAC) in particular, to remain on the sidelines when strong advocacy for a two-state solution is needed, even if Israeli officials don't appreciate the pressure.

I was asked to participate in a panel discussion about free speech, and in particular the issue of "no platforming." A few months before, Steve Bannon, a founding board member of the Breitbart News Network and an associate of President Trump, had been invited to speak at the University of Chicago. Progressive students saw Bannon's views as racist, and they of course had a right to protest Bannon's ideas and even his invitation. But they demanded that the university not allow him to speak, that it provide him no platform.

J Street has an active campus operation, and there was a chapter at the University of Chicago. It wanted to join with other groups demanding that Bannon not be allowed to speak on campus. That was the "progressive" stance, and the J Street students felt pressure to be part of it. The parent organization explained that while it supported the students' desire to make their displeasure with Bannon known, signing on to a "no platform" statement would be against J Street's free speech policy. Indeed, there had been many instances when the right wing of the Jewish community had shut out J Street from the communal table, simply because it found J Street's views abhorrent.

The students insisted anyway. Bannon's speech, they believed, was an attack, a type of verbal violence. It was racist, Islamophobic, and caused real pain. The students decided to ignore the parent organization's guidance. But then the Students for Justice in Palestine chapter on campus reportedly refused to allow the J Street group to sign on with the other progressive organizations. Apparently, in SJP's view, any support for Zionism was inherently not progressive, perhaps racist, and thus J Street's participation was not welcome.

A University of Chicago J Street student joined me on the conference panel, as did my old friend Joe Levin, co-founder of the Southern Poverty Law Center, and a second student, this one from Stanford.

Joe is a lawyer, as I am, and he outlined the reasons why free speech had to be protected, not only as a matter of legal principle and court decisions, but also because, in his experience, when the government attempts to restrict speech, it is progressive forces that are targeted.[20]

The Stanford student had been a leader in an effort to deny Charles Murray the ability to speak on his campus. Murray is an academic who had co-written *The Bell Curve*, a 1994 book which alleges that the reason blacks score lower on intelligence tests is associated with both genetics and environment. In 2017 students at Middlebury College in Vermont had shouted Murray down, called him a eugenicist, and refused to let him speak during a confrontation that turned violent, injuring a faculty member.

The Stanford student saw Murray's invitation as illegitimate and an attack on students of color. He believed there was no value in anything Murray might have to say and no justification for allowing him a platform.[21] He equated Murray's views with a form of violence, asserting that students have a right not to be oppressed by such hatred in their midst.

There was clearly a generational divide on this panel. These were smart students, but they seemed certain that allowing hateful speech was worse than having the authorities suppress it.

I offered a different analysis, beyond the historical reasons to support free speech as necessary for democracy and progressive politics. First, even if one believed that offensive speech should be banned, the Supreme Court's decisions have been clear. Very few expressions (threats to the president and defamation in certain circumstances, for instance) are beyond First Amendment protection. And as offensive as some expressions may be – neo-Nazis marching in a community of Holocaust survivors, or anti-gay religious zealots picketing near a soldier's funeral – the government has no business deciding which expressions it likes and which it doesn't. We tried content-based suppression during World War I and during the McCarthy era. When the government can stop or chill speech based on its content, it frequently harms speech that the government views as critical of its policies. If speech is to be suppressed, it can't be based on the viewpoint the speech expressed. One can, of course, put time, place, and manner restrictions on speech; for example, you can't protest outside someone's house with a bullhorn at 2:00 a.m. But it doesn't matter if the proposed speech is something the homeowner would like or not. The restriction is content neutral.

The Supreme Court has also made it clear that there has to be some sort of emergency, an exigent circumstance, to stop an expression. If I stand at a street corner and say, "I think all blacks should be killed," as awful as that expression is, it is legally protected. If I'm with a crowd of baseball bat-carrying skinheads and say the same thing, pointing to a group of blacks across the street, that same sentence would likely not be protected. It's not the message that is being suppressed, it's the imminent danger from the context in which those words are expressed.

There really is no such thing as "hate speech," meaning speech that would otherwise be protected under the First Amendment, but which loses that protection because it conveys a message of hate. There is hateful speech, which should be opposed, but legally it won't work to seek its censorship.[22]

By trying to censor, rather than expose and combat, speech the students perceived as hateful, they were actually helping the alt-right and white supremacists. It's no coincidence that the white nationalists in recent years have wrapped their racist and antisemitic messages around the concept of free speech.[23] Why would progressives allow these haters to steal the bedrock democratic principle of free speech, disingenuously saying this is what their fight is about? By trying to deny alleged racists platforms, progressives are helping white supremacists recast their vile message as noble protection of a right.

Most importantly, I asked why they were defaulting to suppression when there were other more effective things to do? For example, in 2007 Iranian president Mahmoud Ahmadinejad spoke at Columbia University. Many in the Jewish community insisted that Ahmadinejad not be allowed to speak, given his hateful track record, which included Holocaust denial. I supported the invitation. In planning for the event, Columbia leadership reached out to a variety of groups and individuals to think through how to approach it, and I was among those offering advice.

I'm reasonably confident President Lee Bollinger would have preferred that Ahmadinejad not come. What university president needs such a headache, one that would likely result in some funders deciding not to support the university financially, in protest? But the rules that allow faculty, students, and departments to invite speakers to campus had been followed, and a college president should not overrule such an invitation based on distaste for the speaker's message. Indeed, the idea that the campus community can invite speakers so that students can learn firsthand from primary sources is an important requirement for academic freedom.

But precisely because Ahmadinejad represented so much hate, Bollinger felt he had an obligation to use his free speech rights too. He issued a statement in advance of the event, outlining his plan to introduce Ahmadinejad with "sharp challenges" on many issues, including his Holocaust denial and his "public call[s] for the destruction of the State of Israel," and Iran's support for terrorism, its dangerous nuclear program, and its suppression of women, journalists, and scholars.[24] My one small suggestion – also mention Iran's persecution of homosexuals, which Bollinger did.

When Bollinger finished his hard-hitting talk, Ahmadinejad spoke, and then the dean of Columbia's School of International and Public Affairs (SIPA) followed up with questions that had been submitted by students and faculty in the audience. One asked why Iran "imposed draconian punishments, including execution on Iranian citizens who are homosexuals?"[25] Ahmadinejad's answer: "In Iran we don't have homosexuals like in your country."[26] The remark was met with laughter; more importantly, it was the headline of many press reports, as well as the genesis of biting parodies, including a *New Yorker* cover and a *Saturday Night Live* skit.[27] The event damaged the Iranian president's reputation.

So, I told the J Street students, they were making a tactical mistake by framing the question as whether a hater gets to speak. Instead, they should work hard to figure out how to expose him, which may require more research and coordination and planning than merely demanding he not be given a platform. If they did this, they could actually help combat hate, increasing the chance the speaker they detest would leave their campus diminished, deflated, maybe even discredited.

Second, I told them about a college that had invited a Ku Klux Klan leader to campus. The school was in an uproar, but the invitation had been made through the proper procedures. Eventually, the session with the KKK leader was allowed to continue, off campus. And why was the KKK leader invited? It was a journalism class, and the professor wanted to teach students how to interview a white supremacist. I explained that the press's poor performance was a great frustration during neo-Nazi David Duke's campaigns for office in Louisiana. Journalists would ask him a question like "Are you a racist?" He would say "No," and they'd move on to the next question. Very few journalists knew how to interview and expose a white supremacist. Wouldn't students want to increase the capacity for journalists to do a better job covering people who promote hatred?

Third, I told them about neo-Nazis planning a march in western Montana. This wasn't an on-campus problem, but it was a valuable lesson in how to fight hate that could be replicated at universities, if students were willing to do the work.

A white supremacist named Andrew Anglin had threatened the small Jewish community in Whitefish, Montana,[28] as well as the human rights activists who spoke up to defend their neighbors. Anglin then said he would lead a group of armed skinheads on a march through the town on Martin Luther King Jr. Day, 2017, which he called "James Earl Ray Day," in honor of King's assassin.

I worked with the local human rights community to create a "Project Lemonade" response. Rather than seek to deny Anglin a right to march and exercise his free speech rights (and let him assume the mantle of free speech), we turned his rights on their head, making his speech anything but free. We announced we would gather pledges from people across the country who would give money based on how long Anglin's march lasted. The longer he marched, the more money would be raised for things he would detest, such as increased security for the people he threatened, hate crime training for the police, anti-bias education in the schools, and so forth.[29] This approach gave Anglin a disincentive to appear, allowed those under direct threat to know that others had their back, and gave people from around the country a way to help. We'll likely never know fully why Anglin decided not to march, but the human rights activists in the community say this strategy may well have had the desired effect.

So, I asked, rather than try and bar Steve Bannon from speaking, why not have him raise money for Syrian refugees, lawyers for immigrants targeted by the Trump administration, and other uses that he would hate? And while they're at it, why not work with journalism students and aspiring lawyers to plant questions that might lead Bannon into the type of statements that would undercut him, as happened with Ahmadinejad?[30]

I offered the students an open door – I'd be happy to work with them to implement such a strategy on their campus, whenever a hateful speaker was invited. So far, no one has taken me up on that offer.

Students today live on campuses where "trigger warnings," "safe spaces," and a focus on "microaggressions" may be part of the culture. These concepts are not speech codes, but in many ways function to limit expression and intellectual inquiry on campus. When I trained college presidents about campus bigotry, one of my main recommendations was that they conduct surveys into the campus climate. Colleges should be concerned when students report they are told they don't belong ("you're only here because of affirmative action"), or are otherwise made to be uncomfortable and not participate fully in campus life (including its intellectual life) because of who they are.

Campus leadership must also cultivate an environment in which students don't have to self-censor. For education to work, students and faculty must feel comfortable saying what they think, in an atmosphere that allows for the testing and recalibration of ideas. It is better to try out ideas and be wrong than to spout what you think others profess to be correct. When I teach I tell students the surest way to get a bad grade is to parrot back to me what they think I think. The purpose of a college is to teach students how to think, not what to think. Yet in some places students are being told what not to say, perhaps not to think, so that no one is offended.

The two goals a campus must seek to achieve simultaneously are partly contradictory. Students have to feel free to be who they are so they can articulate what they think. But if everyone feels free to say what their views are, surely some will be offended. Some students will say things that others perceive as hateful, such as support for Palestinians, or support for Israelis.

What a campus has to do is maximize Bob Hess's "myth of the institution." Leadership has to use the tools of education, research, and training to make sure everyone feels at home as much as possible. Students need to accept that they will hear ideas that disturb them. A campus is, after all, the best and safest possible place to battle over ideas.

But the push towards "safe spaces" and "trigger warnings" and against "microaggressions" is actually undermining the intellectual life of the campus. The premise is that students should not be disturbed. Universities, in my view, should tell students that if they don't want to be made uncomfortable by ideas, they should apply somewhere else. The purpose of an education IS TO BE DISTURBED. How else does one learn how to wrestle with difficult and challenging concepts?

Yet many of the students who want their universities to ban Charles Murray and Steve Bannon and other disapproved speakers don't just want to stop outside voices from visiting, or to win a political battle that they simplistically divide into "good" vs. "evil," they also want to transform the campus into a cocoon, insuring that no allegedly hateful or disquieting idea gets through. The basic idea of "trigger warnings" and "microaggressions" and "safe spaces" have some rationality behind them. They reflect something positive: young people's concerns with racism, discrimination, and injustice, and as noted above, the responsibility of each of us to care about other human beings. But on some campuses these concepts have become larger-than-life over-zealous missions rather than cautions or something to consider.

Someone who has been raped has been traumatized. It is certainly possible that if that student reads a book or sees a movie with a rape scene, they might have a flashback or otherwise relive their ordeal. So, the idea is to give students notice that specific disturbing material will be assigned. Faculty won't know what trauma which students have experienced. The warnings are supposed to make students less uncomfortable; in theory, they can choose to skip a disquieting assignment.

Faculty should have the right to give trigger warnings if they want, but I never do, and I think the idea is a horrid one. I teach *Mein Kampf*. It's disturbing – get over it. College should prepare one to be an adult, and there are no "trigger warnings" after graduation day. Why are we encouraging students to be ostriches? Shouldn't they, rather, be learning how to navigate things that will likely unsettle them over the rest of their lives?

Likewise, the idea of safe spaces has some logic. Imagine you're one of the few black students on a campus. It is probable that you will have stress that a white student will not. You may get looks of disapproval, classmates might presume you are only there because of affirmative action, campus police might treat you differently, and if racist flyers are found on campus, you'll have good reason to feel a higher level of threat. So, the idea goes, that in order to make this student as comfortable on campus as his/her white classmates, there needs to be a "safe space," where, black students can go and simply be themselves.

Some "safe spaces" are self-generating or built around organizations, like black or Hispanic or LGBTQ students gravitating to those with similar backgrounds or experiences or interests; like Jewish students seeking out a Hillel House for a meal or services or community. When colleges undertake surveys, it's important to find out if self-segregation is a manifestation of people who have something in common and who want to be together, which is understandable, or evidence that students feel under siege.

It's one thing for colleges to make sure that students aren't harassed or physically assaulted. But the purpose of safe spaces on some campuses is to segregate students from *ideas* that might make them uncomfortable, to create a place where their minds will not have to wrestle with expressions and concepts and opinions that might disturb.

CNN commentator Van Jones, a strong civil rights proponent, opposes "safe spaces" on campus:

> I think that's a terrible idea for the following reason: I don't want you to be safe ideologically. I don't want you to be safe emotionally. I want you to be strong. That's different. I'm not going to pave

the jungle for you. Put on some boots, and learn how to deal with adversity. I'm not going to take the weights out of the gym. That's the whole point of the gym.

You can't live on a campus where people say stuff that you don't like? ... You are creating a kind of liberalism that the minute it crosses the street into the real world is not just useless but obnoxious and dangerous. I want you to be offended every single day on this campus. I want you to be deeply aggrieved and offended and upset and then to learn how to speak back.[31]

The concern about "microaggressions" – defined as "a comment or action that subtly and often unconsciously or unintentionally expresses a prejudiced attitude toward a member of a marginalized group (such as a racial minority)"[32] – makes sense too, but again in the abstract. Words can hurt. We ought to be mindful of how we use words that can cause others unnecessary pain. But that's quite different than campuses promoting lists of what to say and what to avoid saying, reminiscent of Orwellian Newspeak.

In my lifetime, I've seen what's acceptable and what isn't go through changes, mostly for the good. While we still have the Washington Redskins, my children didn't speak like my classmates and I did in elementary school, calling allegedly duller kids "retards," or a variety of people from the far and middle east "Orientals" (as in rugs). No longer do we address an adult woman differently if she is married to a man (few contemplated that there could be same-sex marriages in the 1950s and 1960s) than if she is single.

The University of New Hampshire's website has a "Bias-Free Language Guide."[33] It includes these following gems:

- [Don't say] "The new international student is having language challenges." [Instead say] "The new international student is concentrating on learning a new language."
- [Don't say] "Poor person." [Instead say] "Person who lacks advantages that others have."
- [Don't say] "Senior Citizens" or "Elders." [Instead say] "People of advanced age."

- [Don't say] "The Homeless." [Instead say] "Person-experiencing homelessness."
- [Don't say] "Rich." [Instead say] "Person of material wealth."
- [Don't say] "Normal, able-bodied, healthy or whole." [Instead say] "Non-disabled."
- [Don't say] "Foreigners." [Instead say] "International people."
- [Don't say] "Obese" or "overweight people." [Instead say] "People of size." (Although the guide notes: "'Fat,' a historically derogatory term, is increasingly being reclaimed by people of size and their allies, yet for some, it is a term that comes from pain.")

You don't want people calling each other offensive names, but you have to wonder whether an official scorecard of how to self-monitor speech also sends students a destructive message: If there are preferred words, are there preferred thoughts, preferred ideas, preferred opinions? Are we now too sensitive? You won't offend me if you call me a slightly overweight old fart (at least if you say it with a smile).

More fundamentally, colleges should empower young people to think, individually. It is likely that those who proposed the University of New Hampshire's guide to speech thought they were empowering students, but weren't they actually doing the opposite – articulating an abdication of individual agency to a form of group-think?

The Foundation for Individual Rights in Education (FIRE) has pointed to a correlation between intolerance for free speech on campus and the growing number of comedians, like Chris Rock, who refuse to perform at colleges and universities.[34] My generation grew up with comics who used jarring language to make critical comments about culture, injustice, and politics. Lenny Bruce, Dick Gregory, Richard Pryor, George Carlin, Mort Sahl. The state sometimes tried to arrest or fine them, but progressives saw their biting comedy as shining a light on hypocrisy and showing us new ways to look at the human condition. Perhaps the principle that no one should be offended has been turned into a dogma. Perhaps dogmas and humor are incompatible. But FIRE is right to worry about the capacity for free speech on campus if we can no longer take a joke.

In 2014, in the midst of discussions about campus speech and attempts to restrict what can be said, the University of Chicago issued a clear statement, recommitting itself to open debate on campus. Many other colleges and universities have endorsed the University of Chicago's view:

> Because the University is committed to free and open inquiry ... it guarantees ... the broadest possible latitude to speak, write, listen, challenge, and learn ...
>
> Of course, the ideas of different members of the University community will often ... conflict. But it is not the proper role of the University to attempt to shield individuals from ideas and opinions they find unwelcome, disagreeable, or even deeply offensive ...
>
> In a word, the University's fundamental commitment is to the principle that debate or deliberation may not be suppressed because the ideas put forth are thought by some or even by most members of the University community to be offensive, unwise, immoral, or wrong-headed. It is for the individual members of the University community, not for the University as an institution, to make those judgments for themselves, and to act on those judgments not by seeking to suppress speech, but by openly and vigorously contesting the ideas that they oppose ...
>
> Although members of the University community are free to criticize and contest the views expressed on campus, and to criticize and contest speakers who are invited to express their views on campus, they may not obstruct or otherwise interfere with the freedom of others to express views they reject or even loathe. [W]ithout a vibrant commitment to free and open inquiry, a university ceases to be a university.[35]

The University of Chicago has it right, although it is distressing that a university should have to articulate what should be self-evident about its mission. Chicago's statement wasn't needed only because some students and faculty failed to understand free speech and academic freedom. It was also needed because outside groups see issues they care about – such as the Israeli/Palestinian conflict – playing out on campus, and want to make sure their group wins and their opponents lose, not caring about the damage done to the institution itself.

As we will see, especially in chapters 6 and 7, campus partisans on each side of the Israel/Palestine debate repeatedly corrode the academy's core value of academic freedom, as they try to censor and suppress their opponents. This is largely because the campus debate over Israel and Palestine is supercharged with the building blocks of hatred – ingroup and outgroup, good and evil, justice and injustice, perceived threats, conflicting narratives, sacred symbols, moral principles of fairness and loyalty, aversion to uncertainty. The people on and off campus who advocate the most strongly on one side or the other appear to have the most strident views of their opposition, and rather than examine why the other side thinks as it does, too often default to name calling and dehumanization. Some pro-Israel groups and their supporters sometimes call pro-Palestinian activists "terrorists."[36] In a debate over whether an international academic association should have its next meeting in Tel Aviv, a Jewish member (associated with Jewish Voice for Peace) said, "You wouldn't have this meeting next to a concentration camp in Germany."[37] Such devil imagery, disquieting as it is from either side, has to be allowed, and exposed, on a campus. And while this type of language isn't new, as mentioned in the prologue about the 1970s and 1980s, many of today's campus manifestations can be traced, in part, to a conference in South Africa in 2001.

chapter four

Durban and Its Aftermath

For once, Israel's critics and cheerleaders agree on something: the Jewish state risks greater international isolation. Pro-Israel groups ... say a new assault is on the way. [An] Israeli-Palestinian activist group in Jerusalem ... says that advocating a boycott is no longer always treated as anti-Semitism. Both sides have a motive to exaggerate such claims. But "boycotts, divestments and sanctions" (known in the activist world as "BDS") do seem to be growing ... Pro-Israel lobbyists see this as part of what they call the "Durban strategy," devised by activists at a United Nations anti-racism conference there in 2001, which marked a new high point for Israel-bashing.

"Boycotting Israel: New Pariah on the Block,"
The Economist, 13 September 2007[1]

In the summer of 2000, US president Bill Clinton made a last-ditch effort to bring about peace between Israelis and Palestinians at Camp David. It would have been a good bookend to his administration's efforts, following up on the Oslo Accords and the famous handshake between enemy leaders on the White House lawn in 1993.

The effort failed. Each side, of course, blamed the other, and there is probably truth and distortion in both narratives. Regardless of how a mythical, completely independent observer would allocate the relative faults, the failure was soon followed by Ariel Sharon's provocative visit to the Temple Mount, near two Palestinian and Muslim sacred places: the Dome of the Rock and the Al-Aqsa Mosque. The Second Intifada began, with attacks on Jews on the streets of Israel.

A year later, with the Intifada raging, the United Nations World Conference against Racism, Racial Discrimination, Xenophobia, and Related Intolerance was held in Durban, South Africa, from 31 August to 8 September 2001.[2] Its mission was to find ways to counter racial hatred and bias, but instead it energetically promoted hatred of only one country – Israel. There was also clear hatred of Jews.

Leading up to the event, its Inter-ministerial Committee on Human Rights met on a Saturday. Jewish groups asked that it be moved to a different day, so they could attend. Among the responses: "Here we go again with the Jewish lobby." "Why should we accord special privileges to Jews?" "Have the rabbi give you special dispensation!" "Enough of Auschwitz." "Jews always put on their victim act."[3]

At another preparatory meeting, held in Iran (where Jewish groups could not attend), a draft document not only claimed that Israel engaged in "a new kind of Apartheid, a crime against humanity" but also bemoaned "the emergence of racist and violent movements based on racist and discriminatory ideas, in particular the Zionist movement, which is based on racial superiority." Not decided: whether the Holocaust should be spelled with an upper-case H or a lowercase h, with some countries saying the Holocaust had been made up.[4]

Israeli Deputy Foreign Minister Michael Melchior said that the draft document was worse than if the United Nations had reinstituted its 1975 resolution equating Zionism with racism. The UN repealed this equation in 1991, but during the time the resolution was on the books, Israel was demonized and Jews were discriminated against. In the UK, for example, a Jewish student group was barred because it was presumed if you were a Jew you were a Zionist, therefore a racist, and racist student groups were not permitted.

Melchior saw something more pernicious in Durban:

> What it is really saying is that everything that has to do with the birth of the State of Israel, with Israeli government policy, and in general with the Jewish people, its past, its suffering, and its future, is not legitimate ... [Y]ou can only find a compromise if you keep and stick to the conflict being a ... national conflict, as a territorial conflict.

Then you can sit around a table and divide territory. But if you [make it] an existential [conflict] then there is no possibility [of] negotiating. You don't negotiate with the devil; he can't be a half-devil. You don't negotiate with apartheid. If the whole of the being and existence of Israel is apartheid, racism, is the devil, is the anti-Christ … there can only be a justification of violence and terror and eventually to wipe out this entity from the face of the Earth.[5]

The Durban meeting had three parts – a youth summit, a gathering of non-governmental organizations (NGOs), and the main conference. Banners and literature about Jews and Israel seemed ubiquitous, as were comparisons between Israel and Nazi Germany, some claiming Israel was worse. Swastikas were imposed on a Star of David. Cartoons showed Jews with large hooked noses, with fangs dripping blood. One poster said "Hitler should have finished the job."[6] A leaflet showed Hitler, with a caption: "What if I had won? The good things: there would be NO Israel and NO Palestinians' bloodshed. The bad things: I wouldn't have allowed the making of the new Beetle."

Antisemitic tracts were easily available. Demonstrators demanded an end to Israel. Someone shouted "Kill the Jews."[7] Other less threatening but still deeply disturbing comments were heard:

- You don't belong to the human race! "Chosen people?" You are cursed people!
- I won't talk to you until you take off that thing [referring to a yarmulke].
- Why haven't Jews taken responsibility for killing Jesus?
- Arabs are Semites, too, and should be listed as victims of the Holocaust and be compensated.
- Jews are not members of the human race!
- I believe in a Jewish state … on Mars.[8]

Some Jews hid their name tags. Some men wore caps to hide their yarmulkes.[9] The Jewish Center was closed, as a precaution, as was a session on Holocaust denial. A press conference by Jewish groups was disrupted, journalists unable to ask questions over the chants of "Zionism is racism!"[10]

Both the draft statements for the NGO meeting and that of the main UN meeting of countries were infested with venomous anti-Israel language. Israel, rather than the legacy of slavery or the ongoing suffering of millions of people from racism worldwide, became the defining issue of the conference.

Secretary of State Colin Powell pulled the US delegation out of the conference, declaring:

> Today I have instructed our representatives at the World Conference Against Racism to return home. I have taken this decision with regret, because of the importance of the international fight against racism and the contribution that the conference could have made to it. But ... I am convinced that will not be possible ... [Y]ou do not combat racism by conferences that produce declarations containing hateful language, some of which is a throwback to the days of "Zionism equals racism," or supports the idea that we have made too much of the Holocaust, or suggests that Apartheid exists in Israel, or that singles out only one country in the world, Israel, for censure and abuse.[11]

Commentator Charles Krauthammer wrote: "This was a universal conference whose overriding objective was to brand one country and one people as uniquely, transcendently evil. The whole point was to rekindle the Arab campaign to delegitimize the planet's single Jewish state – and thus prepare the psychological and political ground for its extinction."[12]

Durban wasn't only an orgy of anti-Israel animus, it was intended to be the opening shot in a new international movement of anti-Israel organizing, dusting off and repurposing the tools that had isolated and eventually overthrown Apartheid South Africa. Like the anti-Apartheid movement, the anti-Israel organizing was supposed to have a significant student component. But the plans had to be put on hold. The attacks of 11 September 2001 on America occurred three days after Durban ended.

The anti-Israel campaign on some American college campuses began in earnest in February 2002. Petitions were circulated, asking universities to divest from companies that did business in Israel. They appeared at Columbia, Cornell, Duke, Harvard, MIT, Princeton, Rutgers, St. Lawrence University, Tufts, University of California, University of Massachusetts, University of Illinois, University of Maryland, University of Michigan, University of North Carolina, University of Pennsylvania, Wayne State, and Yale.[13]

Back in the 1980s, when students organized against the racism of the South African regime, there were no significant voices arguing a pro-Apartheid position. But now, soon after the anti-Israel divestment petitions were circulated, counterpetitions were organized, frequently with many more signers, among them thousands of alumni.

President Lawrence Summers of Harvard University denounced the divestment push, saying those promoting it were "advocating and taking actions that are anti-Semitic in their effect if not their intent."[14] President Lee Bollinger of Columbia University called the petition's comparison between Israel and South Africa "grotesque" and "offensive," and said Columbia would not divest.[15]

Around that time, a cinder block was thrown through a window of the Hillel building at Berkeley, and someone tagged the building with "Fuck Jews."[16] At San Francisco State University, Jews attending a peace rally were threatened. Professor Laurie Zoloth described the scene:

> [They were] surrounded by a large, angry crowd of Palestinians and their supporters ... They screamed at us to "go back to Russia" and they screamed that they would kill us all, and other terrible things. They surrounded the praying students, and the elderly women who are our elder college participants, who survived the Shoah, who helped shape the Bay Area peace movement, only to watch as a threatening crowd shoved the Hillel students against the wall of the plaza ... [They screamed] at the Jews to "Get out or we will kill you" and "Hitler did not finish the job."[17]

At Concordia University in Montreal, a riot by pro-Palestinian students prevented then-former Israeli prime minister Benjamin Netanyahu from speaking. Chairs were thrown. A window was smashed.[18] A rabbi and his professor wife were spat upon and hit.

Others were assaulted too, and some men wearing yarmulkes had them "knocked off."[19]

I consulted colleagues in Canada and Berkeley, and spoke at length with Professor Zoloth. She said that speakers on her campus had portrayed

> Jews as the source of sinfulness in the world. Jews as the killers of innocent children. Jews as perhaps having an odd divided loyalty [suggesting that] "they seem like they're here but they really are agents of foreign Zionism," and then finally the notion that the campus itself was not a location that was safe for Jews. And this was said publicly at large rallies and privately to me by senior colleagues ... who felt it would be inappropriate for us to put up anything ranging from a succah ... to having a peace demonstration ... [T]here was a widespread concern that even expressing any solidarity, or any speech that had to do expressly with Israel, was, in fact, provocation.[20]

A poster on her campus showed a dead Palestinian baby, with the caption "canned Palestinian children meat, slaughtered according to Jewish rites under American license."[21]

I then called university presidents I knew and respected, in particular former Dartmouth president James O. Freedman and Brandeis president Jehuda Reinharz. A plan was developed. Jim and Jehuda took the lead in drafting a statement, and with their help I contacted a group of college and university presidents seeking their endorsement. Ultimately, it was printed in the *New York Times*, with over 300 presidents signing on.[22]

The statement read:

> In the current period of worldwide political turmoil that threatens to damage one of our country's greatest treasures – colleges and universities – we commit ourselves to academic integrity in two ways. We will maintain academic standards in the classroom and we will sustain an intimidation-free campus. These two concepts are at the core of our profession.
>
> Our classrooms will be open to all students, and classroom discussions must be based on sound ideas. Our campus debates will be conducted without threats, taunts, or intimidation. We will take

appropriate steps to insure these standards. In doing so, we uphold the best of American democratic principles.

We are concerned that recent examples of classroom and on campus debate have crossed the line into intimidation and hatred, neither of which have any place on university campuses. In the past few months, students who are Jewish or supporters of Israel's right to exist – Zionists – have received death threats and threats of violence. Property connected to Jewish organizations has been defaced or destroyed. Posters and websites displaying libelous information or images have been widely circulated, creating an atmosphere of intimidation.

These practices and others, directed against any person, group or cause, will not be tolerated on campuses. All instances will be investigated and acted upon so that the campus will remain devoted to ideas based on rational consideration.

We call on the American public and all members of the academic community to join us.[23]

There were, of course, some difficult moments in putting this statement together. One president (a Jewish one) refused to sign because the text included the word "Zionist." One of the original sponsors pulled out because it didn't mention attacks on Muslim and Arab students too. I understood his point, but agreed with the other presidents that there was no need to provide such "balance" here. There had been statements – including from Jewish organizations – denouncing attacks on Muslims and those mistaken as Muslim after 11 September 2001. No one thought at the time that such statements needed to include reference to Jewish students, just as when statements are put out about attacks on black students or LGBTQ students, there's no requirement to mention attacks on white students or straight students. The presidents' statement clearly applied to all students, and spoke of the duty of the president of an institution of higher learning to cultivate an environment for learning and to stand against thuggery.

This strong statement demonstrated the wisdom of James O. Freedman, which he shared with me: when opposing campus bigotry, do things that enhance, rather than restrict or have to explain away, academic freedom and free speech. The presidents' statement did just that.

In 2004, the off-campus, pro-Israel group The David Project, previously mentioned, released a film called *Columbia Unbecoming*. Jewish students from Columbia University told their stories, complaining about its Middle East and Asian Languages and Cultures program (MEALAC). An Israeli student said when he had asked a professor a question, the professor refused to answer unless the student first said whether he had served in the Israeli military, and if so had he killed any Palestinians? A second student described a conversation she had with a professor after class; the professor said, because she had green eyes, she had no claim on the land of Israel, but because he had brown eyes, he did. A third student had asked if it was true that Israel gave warnings before it destroyed buildings, to which a professor replied, yelling: "If you're going to deny the atrocities being committed against Palestinians, then you can get out of my classroom!"[24]

The charges were serious, but also not entirely consistent. The film seemed a work in progress, with many versions being released,[25] and some claims altered. It also turned out that the alleged episode with the IDF veteran did not occur in a classroom. The student was not even enrolled in the professor's class; the incident supposedly happened during a lecture at a sorority.

The film, despite its problems, did highlight a concern that Columbia took seriously – it lacked an adequate procedure for students to report alleged incidents of intimidation, while also preserving faculty members' due process rights.

Meanwhile, other outside Jewish groups and politicians attacked Columbia, some calling for the firing of one of the professors in question, Joseph Massad, who was in the process of coming up for tenure. Massad was viewed by some academics as an inferior scholar, and it had been hoped that he would be denied tenure because of that. But after the dismissal calls began, other faculty, including professors around the country, announced their support for Massad. They saw him representing their academic freedom rights. Inside AJC at the time, some colleagues and I began, with equal parts humor and distress, to call these other Jewish groups and politicians "The Committee to Ensure Joseph Massad Gets Tenure." He did.

The outside groups also blasted Columbia when it announced a committee to investigate The David Project's allegations, and the committee included professors who had supported divestment from Israel, as well as Massad's former thesis adviser. If these outside groups had taken the time to reach out to the Jewish leaders on campus – Hillel, professors, and others – they would have understood the damage they were doing, and the erroneous assumptions underlying their advocacy. The issue at hand was not whether a faculty member can have a political position but whether a faculty member violated his duty to be a fair teacher. Did he discriminate against or harass students because of their heritage or political positions? As one anti-BDS professor told me, to suggest that a professor couldn't fairly judge another faculty member's conduct because the professor signed a BDS petition made no more sense than saying he, who signed the anti-BDS petition, couldn't be trusted to serve on such a committee either.

I thought the composition of the committee was a gift. If it had been made up of all Israel supporters, and had concluded the professors mentioned in the film had acted wrongly, its conclusions would be written off by faculty and others as biased. But if it concluded, as it did, that some of the assertions were factual, it would be believed.

The Hippocratic oath for doctors – "First, do no harm" – should apply to outside groups that, too often, do not care to do due diligence on a campus, presume to know "the truth," and then create messes for others to clean up. Scholars for Peace in the Middle East, the Zionist Organization of America, and others created such a mess at Columbia in 2005. Ignoring the advice of the Columbia Hillel director and others, they brought in non-academics and hardline pro-Israel activists for a program on campus. Three students who had organized in support of The David Project's film were cheered. But when they listened to the speakers, some of whom were vilifying Muslims, the students felt compelled to say they didn't agree. One of the students – Bari Weiss, who would later become a leading journalist, and as of this writing is working at the opinion pages of the *New York Times* – said: "In an environment where words like 'Israeli' and 'Zionist' are being used interchangeably with 'Nazi' and 'fascist,' it's very important we don't fall into the same sort of vicious inaccuracies." She and the other students, applauded only minutes before for their bravery on speaking out about their experiences at Columbia, were then shouted at angrily.[26]

Shortly thereafter, Simon Klarfeld, then director of the Columbia/ Barnard Hillel, invited me to run a workshop on antisemitism. Some of his students had been asking him if things they were hearing and reading on campus were antisemitic; claims about Jewish power, influence on the media or political process, and so forth.

I asked my old friend Eric Ward, a longtime anti-racist activist, to join me. The students had been specifically invited – Jews who were not necessarily active in the campus Hillel, but were campus leaders, such as those involved in the Amnesty International chapter or LGBTQ organizations. Eric and I did the program, explaining antisemitism and anti-Zionism, and helping the students understand the complexities. We had dinner with them. We continued talking.

To the best of my recollection, it was around 11:00 p.m. and a few of us were still around a table. One student said this was the first time she felt free to say what she really thought about Israel. Why? Because, she said, she had to gauge whether if she said what she believed, she would jeopardize a grade or a friendship. I asked the others if they had the same experience. They did. Only about Israel? No, this self-censoring was about other issues as well. Did their friends at other schools have to double-check their thoughts before expressing them too? Yes, they said. The students seemed refreshed that evening. They enjoyed asking difficult questions and the pleasure of inquiring, with no perceived downside of being "wrong," and thus little self-censoring.

I walked out somewhat depressed. I liked these students and learned more from them than they had from me. But they were in college. No one was going to kill them or knee-cap them for saying something wrong. Yes, they were teenagers and young adults, and we all care about our reputations and what others think. But I felt they were selling themselves short, playing it "safe," and thus not squeezing every bit of intellectual growth they could out of their college experience.

chapter five

The Academic Boycott of Israel

I would appreciate it if the announcement made clear that [I] was appointed as a scholar and unappointed as an Israeli.

Gideon Toury[1]

When I began working at AJC in the late 1980s, I met many capable people who led its chapters across the country. They had to balance the national office's directives with the unique needs of their local communities. Jonathan Levine, one of my favorites, directed the Chicago office. He would sometimes tell his staff, as he pointed out the window (overlooking Lake Michigan), that AJC's headquarters was 733 miles away. The point was that no one was looking over their shoulders every minute, and if they believed something was important to be done locally, they should do it. Although I worked in the national office, I too had a few moments when I was glad I was a great distance from New York.

During a conference on campus antisemitism held in Amsterdam, I was on a panel debating David Matas, an old friend and noted Canadian human rights lawyer. David was frustrated with what he saw as my near-absolutist defense of academic freedom. If my recollection is correct, we had been discussing the Leonard Jeffries case. Jeffries was a professor of black studies at City College of New York, and chair of the department. He gave a speech in the early 1990s in which he said that "rich Jews" had financed the slave trade. He was also known for teaching a reverse eugenics in which blacks were allegedly biologically superior to whites, because they had more melanin.

When Jeffries was stripped of his departmental chairmanship, I wrote a legal brief for AJC in the ensuing lawsuit. We argued that the college was permitted to fire him from his chairmanship. After all, the board of a college can fire its president for a racist statement. The university has the right to its own reputation as being critical of racism, and Jeffries was in a ministerial position, representing a part of the university.

But he could not be fired from his professorial position for his racist views. There was no showing that he discriminated against students based on the color of their skin or their religious affiliation. And, in any event, the benefit that Jewish students and others received from tolerating a few bigots, who usually would be shunted off to the margins of campus life by their colleagues, was well worth the cost of protecting everyone else's academic freedom.

Matas believed that if someone had these horrid views, he should not be allowed to teach and, as a good lawyer, he posed the most difficult hypothetical case. "Would you fire Hitler?" he asked.

Relatively confident that my comments were not likely to be reported to AJC headquarters, I replied, "Does he have tenure?"

Tenure, which enshrines academic freedom, is a protection against those who would disqualify scholars, especially because of political considerations. As discussed in chapter 3, at times professors have been targeted because they opposed war efforts or because they were communists. The same danger applies when there are attempts to disqualify or shunt aside scholars because of their nationality.

The idea of an academic boycott of Israel began in April 2002, in the United Kingdom. Two Jewish academics, Steven Rose of Open University and Hilary Rose of the University of Bradford, initiated a petition (signed by about 120 people initially) that complained about Israel's "violent repression against the Palestinian people in the occupied territories." They wrote:

> Odd though it may appear, many national and European cultural and research institutions, including especially those funded from the EU

and the European Science Foundation, regard Israel as a European state for the purposes of awarding grants and contracts. Would it not therefore be timely if at both national and European level a moratorium was called upon any further such support unless and until Israel abides by UN resolutions and opens serious peace negotiations with the Palestinians along the lines proposed in many peace plans, including most recently that sponsored by the Saudis and the Arab League.[2]

Two months later, one of the signers of the petition, Mona Baker, a professor of translation studies from the University of Manchester, believed she had a decision to make. She ran what *The Guardian* newspaper called a "pair of obscure journals," *The Translator* and the *Translation Studies Abstracts*. Gideon Toury, from Tel Aviv University, was on the advisory board of the former, and Miriam Shlesinger, from Bar-Ilan University, was on the editorial board of the latter. On 8 June 2002, Baker wrote to Toury:

> Dear Gideon, I have been agonizing for weeks over an important decision: to ask you and Miriam, respectively, to resign from the boards of the Translator and Translation Studies Abstract. I have asked Miriam and she refused. I have "unappointed" her as she puts it, and if you decide to do the same I will have to officially unappoint you too. I do not expect you to feel happy about this ... My decision is political, not personal ... I do not wish to continue an official association with any Israeli under present circumstances.[3]

Gideon Toury responded: "I would appreciate it if the announcement made clear that [I] was appointed as a scholar and unappointed as an Israeli."[4]

Some members of her boards resigned in protest. Academics weighed in, both supporting her decision and condemning it. Apparently, for some professors, the idea of blacklisting Israeli academics, simply because they were Israeli, seemed so benign, maybe even just, that they were open about their motives. In June 2003 Andrew Wilkie, a professor at Oxford University, rejected an Israeli for a position in his laboratory. He wrote:

> Thank you for contacting me, but I don't think this will work. I have a huge problem with the way that Israelis take the moral high ground

from their appalling treatment in the Holocaust, and then inflict gross human rights abuses on the Palestinians because the Palestinians wish to live in their own country.

I am sure that you are perfectly nice at a personal level, but no way would I take on somebody who has served in the Israeli army. As you may be aware, I am not the only UK scientist with these views but I'm sure you will find another suitable lab if you look around.[5]

Of course that caused an uproar too. That Wilkie discriminated against an Israeli academic simply because of his nationality didn't surprise me at the time; that he felt license to put his reasons in an email did. I thought it was carelessness or stupidity, but in retrospect perhaps it was something else.[6]

If you take a scenario and change the players around, you can see if the same rules apply; if they don't, bigotry might be involved. Would Wilkie have sent such an email simply on the basis of the nationality and a presumption of military service to an academic from any other country? Sudan? China? North Korea? The United States?

Perhaps for Wilkie, the only moral parallel to Israel was Nazi Germany. Now the morality becomes a bit murkier, if we do a thought experiment and enter into the mind of someone who honestly believes this equation. Would a British academic in 1939 have taken a German student who had served in Nazi Germany's military? My guess is even in that scenario, someone in Wilkie's position might have inquired more about the individual's credentials, and perhaps wondered if the applicant was an opponent of his government. But an Israeli, apparently, was beyond the pale, no further inquiry required.

It seemed odd to some at the time that British and other academics (some Jewish) were the ones calling for an academic boycott, when the Palestinians were not. Then in 2004 the Palestinian "call" arrived, from the Palestinian Campaign for the Academic and Cultural Boycott of Israel, stating in part:

Whereas Israel's colonial oppression of the Palestinian people, which is based on Zionist ideology, comprises the following:

- Denial of its responsibility for the Nakba ...
- Military occupation and colonization of the West Bank ... and Gaza ...
- The entrenched system of racial discrimination and segregation against the Palestinian citizens of Israel, which resembles ... apartheid ...;

Since Israeli academic institutions ... and the vast majority of Israeli intellectuals and academics have either contributed directly to maintaining, defending or otherwise justifying the above forms of oppression, or have been complicit in them through their silence ...

Recognizing that the growing international boycott movement against Israel has expressed the need for a Palestinian frame of reference outlining guiding principles ...

We, Palestinian academics and intellectuals, call upon our [international] colleagues [to] boycott all Israeli academic and cultural institutions ... [by] the following:

1. Refrain from participation in any form of academic and cultural cooperation, collaboration or joint projects with Israeli institutions;
2. Advocate a comprehensive boycott of Israeli institutions ... including suspension of all forms of funding and subsidies ...;
3. Promote divestment and disinvestment from Israel by international academic institutions;
4. Work toward the condemnation of Israeli policies by pressing for resolutions to be adopted by academic, professional and cultural associations and organizations;
5. Support Palestinian academic and cultural institutions directly without requiring them to partner with Israeli counterparts ...[7]

A close look at the language of the call showed it objected to Israel's existence (it seemed to suggest that the entirety of the nation was illegitimate, because the objection is not to Israel's behavior but to its founding principle rooted in Zionism). Activists in the UK nevertheless (or perhaps because of this) used the Palestinian Call to justify a larger effort to institutionalize an academic boycott.

At the time there were two UK academic unions, the Association of University Teachers (AUT) and the National Association of Teachers in Further and Higher Education (NATFHE). Both were essentially trade unions. A resolution had been introduced at AUT in 2003 calling for members to "sever any academic links they may have with official Israeli institutions, including universities."[8]

But in 2005, AUT decided to institute a formal boycott. It was limited and specifically targeted the University of Haifa and Bar-Ilan University. Bar-Ilan allegedly had too close a relationship with Ariel College (an institution in the West Bank), and the University of Haifa had, allegedly, been unfair to one of its professors, Ilan Pappé, an Israeli historian who had taken up the Palestinian cause.

At the time I was at AJC, and had close relationships with many leaders in the UK Jewish community, largely from my role in 1999–2000 as part of Deborah Lipstadt's defense team, when she won a defamation lawsuit brought against her in London by David Irving, the British Holocaust denier. Anthony Julius, who had been Dr. Lipstadt's lawyer (and more famously Princess Diana's before that), now worked with Jewish members of the AUT and then the University of Haifa, threatening litigation given the violation of the AUT's own rules, as well as provisions of UK anti-discrimination law. It seemed wrong that the University of Haifa should use its funds to pay Julius (who even at his discounted rate was expensive), rather than educate its students, so AJC raised money to defray the legal costs. The irony was that Pappé was still being paid by his university, despite publicly calling for its boycott. The university's protection of Pappé was the essence of what academic freedom meant.

Meanwhile Jewish and non-Jewish academics pushed back against the AUT. Sociologist David Hirsh founded a group called Engage, which was the central address for organizing against the AUT and subsequent academic boycott attempts.

The unfairness of the boycott was hammered home. Why only Israel? And to the extent that a trade union of academics had an interest in the Israeli/Palestinian conflict, why was it trying to push the sides further apart, rather than find initiatives to bring Israeli and Palestinian academics together on joint projects that might actually help build the foundations for peace?

Sari Nusseibeh, then head of Al-Quds University, spoke out against the boycott (and received death threats in return). He said:

> Bridging political gulfs – rather than widening them further apart – between nations and individuals thus becomes an educational duty as well as a functional necessity, requiring exchange and dialogue rather than confrontation and antagonism. Our disaffection with, and condemnation of acts of academic boycotts and discrimination against scholars and institutions, is predicated on the principles of academic freedom, human rights, and equality between nations and among individuals.[9]

The American Association of University Professors issued a statement against the academic boycott.[10] Eventually, under threat of political pressure and of a lawsuit, the AUT canceled its boycott. But that was just the beginning. The other academic union, NATFHE, soon took up the academic boycott baton.

So, what do you do if you want to impose a boycott on Israeli academics, but as many pointed out at the time, Israeli academics were, as a group, on the political Left and among the most vocal opponents of Israeli policy?

NATFHE's resolution stated:

> The conference invites members to consider their own responsibility for ensuring equity and non-discrimination in contacts with Israeli educational institutions or individuals, and to consider the appropriateness of a boycott of those that do not publicly dissociate themselves from such policies. The conference notes continuing Israeli apartheid policies, including construction of the exclusion wall, and discriminatory educational practices. It recalls its motion of solidarity last year for the AUT resolution to exercise moral and professional responsibility.[11]

So, now there was to be a McCarthy-like litmus test. It didn't matter if you were an agrarian economist working to stop famine and were collaborating with an Israeli academic partner to help save lives around the world. It was more urgent to find out the Israeli academic's politics and determine that they were not only sufficiently critical of his/her government, but that he/she also took the affirmative step of stating so publicly.

As Jane Ashworth, David Hirsh's Engage colleague, repeatedly pointed out to me, the whole academic boycott movement's impact was simple, even if that was not its intent: the hunting of Jews in the academy. Jews who were Israeli, Jews who might be working with Israelis. These were the people who were disproportionately going to be vilified, ostracized, and isolated.

The AUT, having withdrawn its boycott, now spoke out against NATFHE's version. This was significant, because the two unions were about to merge.

In March of 2007, I convened a two-day meeting at the American Jewish Committee headquarters in New York. Following the Durban conference of 2001, the divestment petitions on American college campuses starting in 2002, and the various proposals for academic boycotts of Israel, a new equation was gaining traction among some opponents of Israel. Beyond Zionism = racism and Israelis are acting like Nazis, now it was Israel is practicing Apartheid. The charge was leveled by some significant people, most prominently Archbishop Desmond Tutu, a hero of the struggle against South African Apartheid. And while former US president Jimmy Carter's 2006 book *Peace Not Apartheid* was mischaracterized by many in the Jewish community (he only used the word "Apartheid" a few times in the book, and his point was that if peace did not materialize, Apartheid would be the result), his provocative title added fuel to the equation.

I wanted people who were engaged with the political Left to better understand this linkage – why it was being used, the impact it had, where it was totally wrong, and where there were some troubling similarities.

I invited Columbia University president Lee Bollinger to give a keynote address. In 2002, when this equation was used to promote a divestment resolution at Columbia, Bollinger had called the parallel "grotesque" and "offensive." But I had an ulterior motive for inviting him. The UK's AUT and NATFHE had indeed merged into the newly formed University and College Union (UCU). It was set to meet in May. The anti-Israel boycott issue was almost certain to appear.

After Bollinger spoke, I mentioned the upcoming UCU meeting, and the likelihood that a resolution calling for an academic boycott of Israel would be introduced. If it passed, global academic freedom, no matter how one quantifies it, would be diminished. I asked Bollinger, "What then is the responsibility of other academics to replenish it?" He said that should the UCU do such a thing, he would issue a statement condemning it, and encourage other university presidents to do so too.

The UCU passed a resolution advancing a boycott of Israel. Bollinger issued a statement:

> As a citizen, I am profoundly disturbed by the recent vote by Britain's new University and College Union to advance a boycott against Israeli academic institutions. As a university professor and president, I find this idea utterly antithetical to the fundamental values of the academy, where we will not hold intellectual exchange hostage to the political disagreements of the moment. In seeking to quarantine Israeli universities and scholars this vote threatens every university committed to fostering scholarly and cultural exchanges that lead to enlightenment, empathy, and a much-needed international marketplace of ideas.
>
> At Columbia I am proud to say that we embrace Israeli scholars and universities that the UCU is now all too eager to isolate – as we embrace scholars from many countries regardless of divergent views on their governments' policies. Therefore, if the British UCU is intent on pursuing its deeply misguided policy, then it should add Columbia to its boycott list, for we do not intend to draw distinctions between our mission and that of the universities you are seeking to punish. Boycott us, then, for we gladly stand together with our many colleagues in British, American and Israeli universities against such intellectually shoddy and politically biased attempts to hijack the central mission of higher education.[12]

I spent the next weeks asking other presidents to endorse Bollinger's statement and apply it to their campuses. This was not as easy an ask as you might think. No one disagreed with Bollinger's views. Some were reluctant to sign another's statement, suggesting that they would prefer to write their own. Some wanted to see if a word or two or more might be changed. Some had a general reluctance to signing statements, for fear it would set a precedent. Some were concerned that they were getting ahead of their faculty.

When AJC published Bollinger's statement in the *New York Times*, over 400 of Bollinger's colleagues had signed on. After the ad appeared, presidents who had not received or had not noticed the emails inviting their participation asked to be part of the effort.

What Bollinger captured was the essence of academic freedom, in contrast to the first instincts of the mainstream Jewish community. In 2005 the Anti-Defamation League (ADL) had suggested the way to fight the UK's academic boycott of Israel might be US academics counterboycotting the UK's universities.[13] At the time, Antony Julius, David Hirsh, and I pushed hard against this approach. Even on a tactical level, it made no sense. The key argument against the academic boycott was that it violated a core principle of the university: it exists to increase knowledge, not to discard ideas because they come from academics of particular countries. The ADL's stance gave up that key argument, and changed the debate to "who should be boycotted?" Bollinger said that if the UK's UCU was intent on dividing the academic world into two – Israelis who should be shunned and everyone else – count Columbia in the Israeli academic world. He would never have endorsed a counterboycott, and no other university president would have either.

With some minor exceptions here and there, the push for a boycott of Israel stalled after this clear statement from American college presidents in 2007. The focus on American campuses remained on divestment, despite the 2009 formation of a US group supporting PACBI – the US Campaign for the Academic and Cultural Boycott of Israel.

In the spring of 2013, to the surprise of most in the Jewish community, the small Association for Asian American Studies (AAAS) passed a resolution supporting a boycott of Israeli academic institutions. Approximately 10 per cent of the association had been present at the meeting, and in a secret ballot "resolved that the

Association for Asian American Studies endorses and will honor the call of Palestinian civil society for a boycott of Israeli academic institutions ... Be it also resolved that the Association for Asian American Studies supports the protected rights of students and scholars everywhere to engage in research and public speaking about Israel-Palestine and in support of the boycott, divestment and sanctions (BDS) movement."[14]

No Jewish professional knew much about the AAAS, but those with contacts in the Asian American community and/or in the academic community tried to figure out what had happened, if it could be reversed, and whether this resolution was an anomaly, especially given the strong anti-boycott statements of the American Association of University Professors, or the beginning of a trend.

We received an answer to that last question first. Although not an academic organization, the American Public Health Association (APHA), a much larger and much more important group, was set to consider a divestment resolution at its upcoming meeting.

One of my AJC colleagues was friends with someone active within the APHA, and with that person's background information as a starting point, the community (AJC working along with a few colleagues in other organizations who were committed to collaborating on a common approach) developed an organizing plan. We identified people inside the APHA who were opposed to the resolution, and were eager to work against it, and helped them come together as a group.

The resolution was based on incomplete, false, and misleading information about Israel in general and the public health of Palestinians in particular. Pro-Israel APHA members exposed those misstatements, emphasizing that a concern for public health should lead to APHA members wanting to find ways to improve public health for people in the region, not harm it in service of a partisan political agenda.

It also turned out that BDS activists had been attempting to pass an anti-Israel resolution at APHA before, but that the APHA's leadership had thwarted these efforts. The BDS proponents had worked to change the organization's rules and its leadership, increasing their likelihood for success.

That BDS supporters were doggedly committed and now tactically more sophisticated was not surprising. In 2002, at an AJC conference about the anti-Israel movement on the Left in the aftermath of Durban, Jewish labor leaders from the United States and Canada gave a warning that seemed more generally applicable. They said, for many years, Jews had been in the leadership of the trade union movement and had managed to quash anti-Israel proposals. This was an exercise in power, not union democracy, but they were determined not to let their unions be sidetracked by the Israel/Palestine issue. Their warning was about demographic change, both in the membership and the leadership of the unions. Over time, they said, anti-Israel positions would be more palatable to their membership, and leaders who could block such efforts would be fewer and fewer.

That's essentially what happened at APHA. But with energetic organizing, the anti-Israel resolution was defeated. Nonetheless, working against boycott resolutions in late 2013 soon felt like a game of "whack-a-mole." That same summer (2013) a petition of American Studies Association (ASA) members had been circulating, supporting the Association for Asian American Studies boycott. It seemed clear that some key ASA leaders were in favor of the boycott, and that it was likely that the ASA's executive committee would approve a resolution to be decided at its fall conference. A campaign of ASA members opposed to the resolution began, with organizational support from the same Jewish communal professionals who had worked with the APHA members. The ASA members analyzed whether a resolution could best be prevented, defeated, or modified, or an alternative proposed, what the process should be, who were the key people to contact, what materials (detailed and brief) should be prepared, who should track assignments, what were the strategies and plans for finding key people inside ASA to help, and other tasks.

American Studies scholars circulated two letters – one for ASA members and the other for non-members who identified themselves with the field – opposing all academic boycotts, and noting that this one "would set a dangerous precedent by sponsoring an inequitable and discriminatory policy that would punish one nation's universities and scholars and restrict the free conduct of ASA members to engage with colleagues in Israel."[15]

The AAUP also sent a message to the ASA leadership, underscoring its opposition to academic boycotts, and its belief that academic associations shouldn't endorse them either. The letter called on the ASA to reject the proposal, noting that "[m]embers of the ASA who oppose Israeli policies are, of course, entitled to their views and to act on them, but they should find other means than an academic boycott to register their opposition."[16]

An "Open Discussion" was scheduled for a Saturday. By Thursday over fifty scholars had signed on to the opposition letter, among them five former ASA presidents. But just as opponents organized against the resolution, proponents inside the ASA had too, and they clearly held the upper hand.

On Friday there was a "town hall" on ASA and Israel/Palestine, which included Angela Davis and Steven Salaita. This was an entirely one-sided, anti-Israel program. Angela Davis reportedly said the resolution marked a turning point, one that would normalize anti-Israel sentiment.[17]

About 500 people attended the Saturday forum entitled "ASA Open Discussion: The Israeli Occupation of Palestine."[18] Those who wanted to speak put their names in a hat, to be selected. About forty-five people spoke in favor of the boycott, seven against.

Sharon Musher, a history professor at Stockton University, reported on the atmosphere:

> People described themselves as having recently been drawn to the ASA precisely because of this resolution and the match between it and their politics. They clearly viewed this meeting as a "safe" place where they could articulate their anti-Israel views without reprisal, which they claimed to experience in other contexts. I think signing the resolution became synonymous for many of them with affirming their own radical politics, BUT it also confirmed that American Studies was a proper fit for their ideology.[19]

The resolution would be voted upon the next month by the membership of between 4,000 and 5,000 people. Neither the AAUP statement nor the additional material prepared by those opposed to the resolution would be circulated by the ASA leadership, while pro-boycott material was promoted.[20] In the end, 820 members voted for a boycott, 420 either voted against or abstained.[21]

Scores of college presidents, the prestigious Association of American Universities,[22] and the American Association of University Professors[23] denounced the ASA's action, and many withdrew their institutional affiliations.[24] The fear, however, was that Angela Davis was right, that the floodgates were opening. More concerning than the small ASA or even smaller AASA[25] was the Modern Language Association, with about 25,000 members. One of the most important academic associations, it was meeting in Chicago in January 2014.

The resolution under consideration called on the US Department of State "to contest Israel's denial of entry to the West Bank by US academics who have been invited to teach, confer or do research at Palestinian universities."[26] While not a boycott resolution, proponents and opponents both viewed the anti-Israel text under consideration as the opening round in a battle that would ultimately lead to such a resolution.

The ASA boycott vote, however, made it more difficult for the staff of the few Jewish organizations focused on the academic boycott to cooperate as effectively as before, despite the professionals' determination to work together to help the MLA members opposed to the resolution. The upcoming MLA meeting was now a front-burner issue in the Jewish community. Each Jewish agency, including those not directly involved supporting pro-Israel members of APHA and ASA in their fights, now felt an institutional need to show they were doing the most important work to stop the MLA's resolution. The problem wasn't that each group wanted to highlight its work and communicate that to its members. That was natural and logical. The challenge was that with so many more players (Hillel, Federations, etc.) involved, groups that saw themselves as competitors, a cooperative strategy to help those on our side in the MLA became difficult, if not impossible, to implement.

That's not to say important work wasn't done by those committed to collaboration. Led by a group of MLA members directly involved (which named itself MLA Members for Scholars' Rights), the professionals helped divide tasks, conducted research to refute the errors in the documents supporting the resolution, helped prepare fact sheets, and identified MLA members who would likely attend the meeting. The academics leading the effort against the resolution didn't have a staff and needed to rely on these professionals, particularly for administrative support.

Because no opponents of the resolution had had sufficient notice that the anti-Israel resolution was to be discussed, the deadline to organize an official session was missed. Proponents had already had theirs scheduled. It was, of course, one-sided in their favor.

Hillel and the Israel on Campus Coalition (ICC) wanted to organize an alternative forum (against academic boycotts) under their agencies' brands[27] during the MLA meeting. The Jewish Federation of Metropolitan Chicago's leadership and the MLA members organizing against the resolution opposed that idea, for good reasons. First, scholars listen to other scholars in settings organized by other scholars, not communal advocacy groups. Second, we all thought the focus should be on exposing the one-sided "debate" in the official MLA session, not on organizing a side event. Third, the vote that mattered was that of the MLA's Delegate Assembly, and it was already a labor-intensive operation to identify each member, and figure out the best person to approach each one, hoping to persuade them to vote against the resolution. The few Jewish communal professionals on the ground in support of the MLA Members for Scholars' Rights had their hands full, and pulling some off to help organize a side event didn't seem like a wise choice.

Hillel's leadership eventually agreed to scrap the idea. However, the ICC insisted on going forward, and the decision having been made, there was no choice but to support the event, especially since it featured three MLA members (including Russell Berman, a former MLA president). The program, held in a nearby hotel, turned out to be a good idea. Yes, staff time was diverted, and most attendees were those already committed to opposing the resolution. But it was helpful for MLA members eager to fight the resolution to meet each other, and develop the sense of a group on a mission, particularly those who had worked hard in the preceding weeks, but who had only communicated through email and conference calls.

I was distressed, though, that some agencies, including my own, refused to send local staff to help the handful of Jewish communal professionals in Chicago who were eager to assist the MLA members with tedious, but necessary, tasks such as copying documents, keeping track of which MLA members with votes had been approached, and handing out information sheets. Rather than focus on the goal, it was seen as wasteful to help when staff from other organizations were taking the lead on a specific task.

During a lengthy and contentious meeting, the Delegate Assembly voted, 60–53, to send the resolution to the MLA membership for a vote.

After months of lobbying by both sides, the resolution failed when the membership cast their ballots. The result was announced in June 2014: 1,560 votes in favor and 1,063 against. But MLA's rules required that 10 per cent of the membership, calculated at 2,390, would have to have voted yes for the resolution to succeed. It fell short.[28]

Despite the good work of academics such as Cary Nelson and Sharon Musher, who tirelessly opposed the rash of anti-Israel resolutions, I was worried that the strategy was too ad hoc and reactive. More broadly, I was concerned that the anti-academic boycott effort was coming from a defective organizational and political approach.

This was a battle inside the Left, just like it was in 1977 and 1982. On one side, there were progressives who saw pro-Palestinian activism as incredibly important for social justice, and pointed to the difficulties facing faculty and students living under occupation. On the other, there were progressives who were also concerned about Palestinians, but saw unfairness, perhaps bigotry, in the reflex to demonize Israel, and were also concerned with maintaining academic freedom.

With the Jewish communal focus on the campus ratcheted up after the ASA vote, funding for programs was likely to go to those groups that appeared the most pro-Israel, in other words on the political Right. You don't win a battle within the political Left by empowering the political Right, in fact, you decrease your chances of winning. For the pro-boycott movement to be slowed, progressive faculty had to be organized.

The UK experience was the model. Despite the structural differences (the boycott resolutions in the UK were inside traditional trade unions of faculty; in the US, these resolutions were being considered in associations based on scholarly disciplines), progressive academics in the UK had taken the lead, organized under the group Engage, headed by David Hirsh. There was no analogous group of progressive academics in the US. But there needed to be.

On a snowy February day in 2014 I met with Kenneth Bob, president of AMEINU, a progressive Zionist group that had just launched a program called "The Third Narrative," trying to find ways around the seemingly irreconcilable two narratives, pro-Israeli or pro-Palestinian. Joining us were progressive scholars I had invited to discuss the idea of an organization, people I had worked with over the years, or who David Hirsh had suggested. Among them were Todd Gitlin of Columbia, Chad Goldberg of Wisconsin, Eric Alterman of Brooklyn College, and independent scholar Jeff Weintraub.

Kenneth Bob wanted academics linked to his Third Narrative project, and I was eager to have an organizational home for this enterprise, because faculty needed the logistical support in order to organize and develop programs and strategy. The "Academic Advisory Council" to The Third Narrative was born. Eventually, it would be rebranded the Alliance for Academic Freedom.

The group's founding document states:

> We are progressive scholars and academics who reject the notion that one has to be either pro-Israel or pro-Palestinian. We believe that empathy for the suffering and aspirations of both peoples, and respect for their national narratives, is essential if there is to be a peaceful solution. Scholars and academics should play a positive role in asking difficult questions, and promoting critical thinking, about the Israel-Palestinian conflict. To achieve this goal we insist on the importance of academic freedom and open intellectual exchange, and so reject calls for academic

boycotts and blacklists, as well as efforts to punish academics for their political speech, including even those who support the academic boycotts that we oppose.

The group's Statement of Principles reads:

a) We respect the humanity of Israelis and Palestinians alike, and believe that all political analysis of the Israeli-Palestinian conflict must be grounded in empathy for both peoples.

b) We believe in two states as the only way to avoid perpetual conflict, and recognize that since both peoples require national self-expression, the struggle will continue until this is achieved.

c) We believe the Israeli occupation of the West Bank not only deprives Palestinians of their fundamental rights, but is also corrosive to Israeli society and is incompatible with the democratic principles upon which the State of Israel was founded.

d) We accept the obligation to actively oppose violations of human rights, but cannot condone the use of violence targeting civilians as a tool to address grievances, or to promote strategies that would undermine the future viability of each nation.

e) We strongly oppose the rhetoric used by both sides which demonizes and dehumanizes the other, or distorts the history and national aspirations of each people, to promote violence and hatred.

f) We reject the all-too-common binary approach to the Arab-Israeli conflict that seeks to justify one side or the other as all right or all wrong, and sets out to marshal supposed evidence to prove a case of complete guilt or total exoneration. Scholarship and fairness require a more difficult and thoughtful approach. As academics we recognize the subjective perspectives of individuals and peoples, but strive to apply rigorous standards to research and analysis rather than to subsume academic discipline to political expediency.

g) We reject all attempts to undermine or diminish academic freedom and open intellectual exchange, including those cases associated with the Israel-Palestine debate. Academic boycotts and blacklists are discriminatory per se and undercut the purpose of the academy: the pursuit of knowledge. Likewise, we are against legislative and other efforts by domestic or foreign interests that seek to diminish the academic freedom of those scholars who might propose, endorse, or promote academic boycotts, even if we strongly disagree with these tactics.[29]

In addition to the people at the lunch, there were close to fifty other founding members, many top academics (including ones from Jewish studies) among them: Sharon Musher and Cary Nelson, joined by Peter Beinart, Hasia Diner, Shelley Fisher Fishkin, Sam Fleischacker, David Greenberg, Harold Hellenbrand, Susannah Heschel, Ira Katznelson, Michael Kazin, Alice Kessler-Harris, Steven Lubet, Jeffry Mallow, Maud Mandel, Deborah Dash Moore, David N. Myers, Derek J. Penslar, Riv-Ellen Prell, Judith Shulevitz, Mira Sucharov, Kenneth Waltzer, Michael Walzer, and Steven Zipperstein.

There were two cornerstone principles in play here. First, that academic boycotts violate academic freedom, period. The distinction that proponents tried to make – boycotting Israeli institutions rather than individual academics – made no sense and in fact was disingenuous. As we saw in the UK's NATFHE case, there have been attempts to isolate Israeli academics based on whether they vocally rejected their government. More fundamentally, scholars are inextricably linked to, and dependent upon, their institutions: they are paid by their universities, which also frequently provide funds for its academics to attend conferences, for example.

The second point is more important. In order to be credible when asserting a position or principle, you have to be consistent. You have to go out of your way to demonstrate that you are refuting "my side bias." As Jonathan Haidt pointed out, partisanship is addictive. Part of that addiction is refusing to acknowledge bad behavior of "our side," while hunting examples of such behavior from the "other side" to weaponize.

If academic boycotts are a violation of academic freedom, as we asserted, then efforts to combat the boycott that violate academic freedom have to be called out too. The Alliance for Academic Freedom not only worked against proposed boycott initiatives (such as at the American Anthropological Association), it also called out pro-Israel groups that used similar tactics against pro-boycotters. Most importantly (as will be discussed in chapter 6), it strongly condemned a group called Canary Mission for creating a McCarthy-like blacklist of pro-Palestinian students and faculty. It also objected to the Antisemitism Awareness Act for its corrosive effect on academic freedom (see discussion in chapter 7).

Because this group of progressive academics was seen as promoting a principle more than a political agenda, and because it was made up of faculty – insiders, not outsiders like the various Jewish agencies – it had credibility. Its members led the successful fight against anti-Israel resolutions in the American Historical Association,[30] the Modern Language Association, and in other groups. And they were able to go on the offensive, making it less likely that boycott resolutions would be introduced year after year by those who wanted their organizations to boycott Israel. In fact, in 2017, the MLA would pass a resolution refraining from endorsing the academic boycott because it contradicts the MLA's purpose.

While it is certainly possible that academic boycott motions will again appear,[31] they have not been as frequent since 2015, as those of us working against them feared at the time. That said, it is hard to gauge how widespread the subterranean, shadow boycott of Israeli academics is. Not everyone who decides they are going to treat Israelis by a different standard, or avoid them as colleagues entirely, is stupid enough to memorialize their intentions in an email.

When I was at AJC I tried, but failed, when I asked the Israelis to find data, even by approximation, of this personal boycott. Were fewer of its graduate students invited to participate in programs abroad? Were more being rejected for fellowships, and so forth? The Israelis either weren't interested in figuring out how to find the data, or simply didn't have a way to do it.

But there is anecdotal evidence showing that there is an ongoing, personal, "micro-boycott" of Israeli academics, as former AAUP president Cary Nelson coined the practice. He tells of a "University of Haifa faculty member in the sciences [who] shared with me the story of his Oxford University lecture being cancelled with an email stating that his government's policies did not make it easy to bring Israelis to campus."[32] Nelson also collected other pieces of evidence, among them an email that a religious studies professor sent to a recent Israeli PhD:

> Thanks for your inquiry. If I understand you correctly, you wish to apply for funding to pursue a post-doc at Yale University and ask for a letter that would clarify a possible post-doc period at Yale, right?
>
> ... I should say right away that there are two things that trouble me: First, you[r] research project might not exactly be matching to my research profile ... Second, your ties with the IDF. I generally think that research and war should be two things kept apart from each other (by miles!).[33]

In 2014 PACBI issued updated boycott guidelines, and despite the throw-away language about academic freedom and institutional vs. personal boycotts, the guidelines not only set up the intellectual argument for making Israeli academics second or third class members of the academy (if that) but also provided a blueprint on how to engage in a personal boycott. The guidelines note that Israelis "cannot be exempt from being subject to 'common sense' boycotts ... that conscientious citizens around the world may call for."[34] The guidelines' purpose is to urge academics "to boycott and/or work towards the cancellation or annulment of events, activities, agreements, or projects involving Israeli academic institutions or that otherwise promote the normalization of Israel in the global academy." Individual Israelis can participate in a project with financial support from their government or academic institution (the usual way academics get to conferences) as long as the funding "is not conditioned upon serving Israel's policy interests in any way, such as public acknowledgment" of this support. In other words, to participate you likely have to take affirmative steps to deny your nationality or even thank your institution for the funding it gives you.

The guidelines continue to say that people cannot work with Israeli academics on "events, projects, or publications that are designed explicitly to bring together Palestinians/Arabs and Israelis so they can present their respective narratives or perspectives ... [unless] the project/activity is one of co-resistance rather than co-existence." Of course, "[p]ublishing in or refereeing articles for academic journals based at Israeli universities or published in collaboration with Israeli institutions, or granting permission to reprint material published elsewhere in such Israeli-based journals" is a violation of the guidelines. Likewise, "[a]ccepting to be on a dissertation, referee or review committee appointed by or serving an Israeli university … directly conflicts with the institutional boycott of these universities, as it legitimates Israel's academic standing around the world."[35]

After the ASA passed its boycott resolution, a Tel Aviv doctoral student could not find an American faculty member willing to be an external examiner for his thesis. Ironically, this student victimized by the boycott was Palestinian.[36]

Nelson provided other examples of Israelis not allowed to participate in normal academic activities because of the micro-boycott. And then there are those who try to avoid the damage by hiding their ethnicity or nationality. He wrote:

> Still other academics self-censor to avoid paying a price for being Jewish or Israeli. As Ya'arit Bokek-Cohen of Israel's Academic College of Management Studies wrote to me, "After learning that colleagues have been summarily turned down for professional opportunities like giving a scholarly presentation or publishing a paper because they are both Jewish and Israeli, many of us have had to adapt to this highly stressful working environment. I sometimes omit 'Cohen' from my hyphenated name or refrain from giving the name of my country. That is what the BDS movement has driven us to do if we want to sustain our careers."[37]

But hiding your ethnicity won't work, and indeed won't matter, if you are an American college student who wants to study abroad in Israel and needs a letter of recommendation from a professor who puts his politics above his students' interests. On 5 September 2018, University of Michigan professor John Cheney-Lippold emailed a student that he had made a mistake when he had agreed to write a letter of recommendation for her. He hadn't noticed that the program was in Israel, and explained, "[a]s you may know, many university departments have pledged an academic boycott against

Israel in support of Palestinians living in Palestine." He offered to write recommendations for study elsewhere.[38] The university's president and provost issued a statement saying, in part, "[w]ithholding letters of recommendation based on personal views does not meet our university's expectations for supporting the academic aspirations of our students. Conduct that violates this expectation and harms students will not be tolerated and will be addressed with serious consequences. Such actions interfere with our students' opportunities, violate *their* [emphasis in original] academic freedom and betray our university's educational mission."[39]

Some faculty signed a petition supporting Cheney-Lippold, saying they too refused to write recommendations for students wanting to study in Israel, and this was a faculty "right." An online petition demanded Cheney-Lippold be fired. He received death threats. The Alliance for Academic Freedom issued a statement criticizing the refusal to write the recommendation, condemning the death threats, upholding the professor's right to keep his job, and stressing that universities must have clear policies in this area. Faculty can refuse to write recommendations for many valid reasons, but prioritizing their politics over their students' interests isn't one of them.[40] The university, underscoring this responsibility, disciplined the professor (refusing his normal raise and postponing his sabbatical).[41]

You would think that Israelis would be doing all they could to encourage regular and routine collaboration between foreign and Israeli faculty and students, and between Palestinian and Jewish academics, as a way to undercut the effectiveness of the boycott. You'd think they'd be concerned, as I am, about the difficult-to-document micro-boycott too. The best way to fight the effort to marginalize Israeli academics is to increase the volume of work being done with Israelis, in Israel.

This is not rocket science. When the "cultural" part of the boycott started to get traction in the mid to late 2000s, with some performers and artists deciding not to set foot in Israel, I reached out to people I knew in the entertainment industry. Rather than getting into a public relations battle with individual performers, or with BDS promoters, they noted that many of the agents who sent performers to the rich Middle East states were Jewish, and it would be easy to add a stop in Tel Aviv along the way. Some performers skipped Israel, yet many others came, undercutting the boycott.

But Israelis have done the opposite. During the height of the UK fights, they had a talented person tasked with finding ways to increase contacts between Israeli and UK academics. That position was eliminated. Worse, the Israelis decided on a strategy that will likely help the boycott more than anything the boycotters can do.

I'm not sure of the Israelis' thinking process, because the Israeli approach to BDS has been erratic. When I first started writing about BDS and reached out to Israeli officials suggesting it be taken seriously, they didn't do so. Part of the reason was structural. The Ministry of Foreign Affairs, I was told, was set up for country-to-country relations. It had little capacity to focus on specific issues. Ultimately, it appointed a person to focus on BDS, but the country's pronouncements seemed more about internal politics than effective strategy. From not being a concern, it became a "strategic threat" according to Prime Minister Netanyahu in June 2015.[42] Thirteen months later, in July 2016, Netanyahu announced that BDS had been "beaten."[43]

In early 2017 Israel passed a law that barred entry to BDS advocates.[44] As Rabbi Rick Jacobs, head of the Union for Reform Judaism, said, "It's going to be a giant sign up by the door of the Jewish state: 'Don't come unless you agree with everything we're doing here.' I don't know what kind of democracy makes that statement."[45]

Years ago, when organizing against anti-Israel efforts, I emphasized the robust nature of Israeli democracy, and pointed to the press, which frequently aired opinions critical of the state and its policies and leadership that were far beyond how the mainstream American press criticized American leaders and institutions. Whatever its failings, Israel seemed mature enough to value dissent.

Now its decision to bar people who support BDS (including people whose BDS-advocacy is limited to things relating to the territories) is the sign of an emerging "illiberal" democracy. Since when do ideas (as opposed to actual incitement of violence or terrorism) become such a threat that you can't have people who possess the "wrong" idea visit your country?[46]

Politically, Israel's actions remind me of an era when communists were excluded from visiting the US, among them Pablo Neruda (a Chilean poet and politician who would later win the Nobel Prize for literature). "The United States is the only Western democracy that excludes a foreign visitor simply on the basis of belief or association without the allegation that he will harm the country," said Morton Halperin of the American Civil Liberties Union's Center for National Security Studies at the time.[47]

But aside from the weakness the recent anti-BDS law reveals about Israeli democracy and its radically different approach to dissent, the law is a strategic blunder. First, while the objective reality is that BDS has had marginal if any success – the Israeli economy is booming, no colleges have divested from Israel – refusing entry to BDS proponents tells BDS supporters they are having such an impact that Israel has to bar them.

Second, Israel has announced a list of twenty organizations whose members are to be kept out.[48] This is a blacklist. The academic boycott is a blacklist. You don't make the case that blacklists (especially of academics) are proper if your goal is to oppose blacklists. You are conceding the argument.

Third, and most importantly, imagine you are an academic leader who either opposes the boycott or doesn't care about it. Imagine your association or discipline has strong connections with Israeli academics and academic institutions, because of cutting-edge work being done in your field. Imagine you are thinking about holding a conference in Israel. You'd have to worry that one of your members might have signed a BDS petition, or is somehow associated with one of the groups on the Israeli blacklist.[49] Why would you choose to hold your event in Israel, fearing one of your members would be refused entry at the airport?

This isn't a hypothetical concern. Lara Alqasem, an American student of Palestinian background, graduated from the University of Florida. She had a visa to go to Israel, where she had been accepted in a master's program in human rights at Hebrew University. She was detained at the airport, and refused entry, because she had apparently been part of a small Students for Justice in Palestine chapter, which had called for the boycott of Sabra Hummus (an American brand, but jointly owned by PepsiCo and an Israeli company). Apparently, the Israelis used the Canary Mission website's blacklist (see discussion of Canary Mission in the next chapter) as its source. Israel's strategic affairs minister Gilad Erdan said, "We don't want to see their activists coming to Israel and trying to use our infrastructure to harm us and destroy us," but Israel would let Alqasem into the country if she spoke out against BDS and called it "illegitimate."[50] After two weeks, the Supreme Court of Israel ruled that Alqasem couldn't be deported, noting that she was no longer a pro-BDS activist (which you think Israeli officials would have realized by the simple fact that she was coming to study in an Israeli university, an act irreconcilable with the PACBI guidelines).[51]

It would be funny if it weren't so alarming that Israel had detained and tried to deport an American student because she was involved in a protest over hummus, and that it happened shortly after the University of Michigan professor Cheney-Lippold was taken to task for refusing to write a recommendation for a student who wanted to study in Israel.

Many Jewish studies professors are active members of the Alliance for Academic Freedom listserv. The AAF executive committee, urged by its members, wrote an op-ed condemning Cheney-Lippold's actions. Some of these same Jewish studies professors now face an ethical dilemma because of Israel's anti-BDS law and its treatment of Alqasem. One noted that her institution had an exchange program with Hebrew University. "How can we offer a program that is limited to students with the 'correct' political views?" she pondered.[52]

chapter six

Stopping and Chilling Speech; Heckler's Veto, Legal Threats

[W]e oppose [Israeli Ambassador to the United States] Michael Oren's invitation to our campus. Propagating murder is not a responsible expression of free speech.

> Statement by University of California, Irvine's Muslim
> Student Union, before it disrupted Oren's talk[1]

[M]ore than half of the speakers at [a campus event at a law school] ... are also affiliated with the anti-Israel Boycott, Divestment and Sanctions campaigns, and at least one talk will be devoted to finding legal strategies for defending these campaigns ... This leaves no doubt that the conference was organized for the purpose of harming the Jewish state. Your law school has provided funding and is therefore complicit in this effort ... [W]e believe that this event may be in violation of Title VI of the 1964 Civil Rights Act.

> Tammi Rossman-Benjamin et al.[2]

Political struggles are usually fought by deploying whatever weapons are available. That has never been the best strategy in higher education.

> Cary Nelson[3]

On 8 February 2010, Michael Oren, a former AJC colleague who was then Israel's ambassador to the United States, spoke, or at least he tried to, at the University of California, Irvine. To the pro-Israel groups on this campus, Oren was not only a respected representative of the Israeli government but also a scholar, having written a well-received book on the 1967 War. He was also a former visiting professor at Harvard, Georgetown, and Yale. To the Muslim Student Union (MSU), he was complicit in mass murder. MSU released a statement before the event:

> [We] strongly oppose the presence of Michael Oren on our campus ... We strongly condemn the university for cosponsoring, and therefore, inadvertently supporting the ambassador of a state that is condemned by more UN Human Rights Council resolutions than all other countries in the world combined.
>
> A year after the war on Gaza, in which 1,400 people were massacred ... Israel attempts to hide [its] war crimes behind the deceitful facades of so-called "academics" and "diplomats" ... The United States is going through the worst economic recession since the great depression, our tuition as UC students is increasing by more than 30% ... and yet we continue to supply Israel with billions of dollars worth of brutal and illegal weapons used to oppress and inflict further suffering upon the Palestinian people.
>
> To further understand why we oppose Michael Oren's visit to UCI, one must consider his professional and military background. Oren personally participated in the Israeli Defense Force in wars that took place in Lebanon and Palestine. Oren took part in a culture that has no qualms with terrorizing the innocent, killing civilians, demolishing their homes, and illegally occupying their land ...
>
> As people of conscience, we oppose Michael Oren's invitation to our campus. Propagating murder is not a responsible expression of free speech. Oren and his partners should only be granted a speakers platform in the International Criminal Court and should not be honored on our campus.[4]

After Oren began to address a packed audience in a speech entitled "US Israeli Relations from a Political and Personal Perspective,"[5] protestors, one by one, interrupted him. Osama Shabaik yelled, "Michael Oren, propagating murder is not free speech."[6] Others then joined in, shouting, "Michael Oren you are a war criminal," and "[I]t's a shame this University has sponsored a mass murderer like yourself."[7]

One by one, protestors stood, interrupted, shouted, and left, ushered out by campus police.[8] Each interruption was applauded, and those upset by the protestors were also vocal. School officials went to the podium and told the students that their actions were consistent with neither free speech norms nor conduct expected of them. After the eleventh student interrupted Oren, and left, their supporters departed en mass, loudly.

Although Oren eventually was able to finish his speech, there was no time left for questions. According to the Jerusalem Center for Public Affairs, Oren was able to talk for only two minutes and twenty-one seconds during the first thirty-five minutes of his presentation.[9]

The university investigated. Despite claims to the contrary, the Muslim Student Union had actively organized the heckling. MSU was suspended for a quarter, and placed on probation.[10] The following year, the eleven (eight students from Irvine, the others from UC, Riverside)[11] were charged with misdemeanors in the California criminal court system, and ultimately convicted.[12]

Students have the right to protest a speaker, and to interrupt minimally. But this disruption was too much – a slow motion, rolling, heckler's veto[13] – depriving the audience of an opportunity not only to ask questions but also to hear Oren lay out his thoughts. Yet the Irvine faculty and many others who criticized the criminal case as overkill were right – the discipline the university had administered (including putting MSU on probation) was sufficient.

For the most part, outside groups had strongly divergent views of both the disruption and the wisdom of bringing criminal charges, based largely on their political positions.[14] Many pro-Israel advocates saw the prosecution as defending democracy and free speech – the idea that an Israeli representative should be able to speak on a campus and be heard. Many pro-Palestinian advocates saw the opposite – arguing that "Irvine 11's" actions, inspired, they said, by the same quest for justice that motivated Martin Luther King Jr. and anti-war protestors, deserved respect, and that they were being singled out for punishment because of their pro-Palestinian views.[15] Likewise, when the students were convicted, each side claimed the mantle of free speech.[16]

There have been other incidents of Israel-related speakers shouted down on college campuses. Recall (in chapter 4) the 2002 riot at Concordia University in Montreal, where Benjamin Netan-yahu was prevented from speaking. Data from 2010 to spring 2019 collected by the Israel on Campus Coalition[17] show that pro-Israel events have been interrupted (or have been cancelled after pro-tests) 117 times. All but sixteen programs, on a total of twelve dif-ferent campuses, were able to be completed.[18] Over nearly a decade that's hardly ubiquitous, as some pro-Israel activists suggest. But it is still too frequent and disturbing. Students and faculty who invite a partisan speaker should be prepared for controversy, even protest, but shouldn't have to fear that their event will be stopped.

Go back to the social and moral psychology we reviewed in chap-ter 1, and the conversation with J Street students about "no platform-ing" in chapter 3. Each side defines itself as a group, fighting for justice, equality, and freedom. Freedom for Jews to have their right to self-determination, safe from existential threat and terrorism; free-dom for Palestinians to have the same. Each in their own land. The same land. Rather than seeing these rights as difficult and in conflict, maybe irreconcilably, each side is addicted to the partisanship of its own narrative. With partisanship comes intellectual blinders, and too often a desire to censor those with opposing views.

The pro-Israel side hasn't made it a practice to shout down pro-Palestinian speakers,[19] but that doesn't mean it hasn't tried to thwart, rather than merely speak out against, pro-Palestinian cam-pus programming.

The University of California Hastings College of Law funded and co-sponsored a conference entitled "Litigating Palestine: Can Courts Secure Palestinian Rights?" which was scheduled for 25 and 26 March 2011.[20] On 24 March 2011, Tammi Rossman-Benjamin, a lecturer at the University of California, Santa Cruz (and a co-founder of the AMCHA Initiative, which advocates for pro-Israel students and faculty), co-wrote a letter to Chancellor Wu, sending copies to Jewish leaders, politicians, and many others, saying:

> [T]he authorized description of this event makes it clear that conference participants will be … seeking to exploit Western courts in order to agi-tate against Jews and the Jewish state …

[W]e believe that this event fits within the Working Definition of Anti-Semitism issued by the European Monitoring Centre on Racism and Xenophobia ... [The definition] identifies the following practices as anti-Semitic and distinguishes them from acceptable forms of criticism of a sovereign nation's policies [including] [d]enying the Jewish people the right to self-determination [and a]pplying double standards by requiring of Israel behavior not expected or demanded of any other democratic nation.

... [W]e believe that this event may be in violation of Title VI of the 1964 Civil Rights Act ... The Office of Civil Rights has already opened two investigations of possible Title VI violations at the University of California. One of the complaints ... argues that university funded/ sponsored events that are virtually anti-Israel have created a hostile environment for Jewish students ...

... [W]e urge you to publicly announce that you are withdrawing all Hastings College of Law funding and sponsorship of this event, as well as your own participation in it.[21]

The week before Rossman-Benjamin's email, AJC's San Francisco area director shared news about the Hastings program with me and AJC's (then) associate general counsel, Marc Stern (no relation). I wrote a memo to AJC leadership that said what Rossman-Benjamin was doing was "not unlike what the Muslim student group did with Oren – she is trying to prevent academics from uttering a word ... [I]f we take the position that it is okay to censor views we disagree with, but not views we endorse, we lose all credibility, especially with the college presidents we have collected around AJC."[22] David Harris, AJC's executive director, wrote back, approvingly.[23]

The Hastings board had an emergency meeting following Rossman-Benjamin's email and decided to remove its name from the conference. While the event would proceed, the dean's remarks were cancelled, and a private foundation withdrew its funding.[24]

The AJC letter Marc Stern and I proposed (which would have come from him) said, in part:

We do not share [Rossman-Benjamin's] view that the College's sponsorship of the event would in any way have violated Title VI of the 1964

Civil Rights Act ... No doubt, the participants in this conference are critical of Israel, and many may believe there should not be a Jewish state. However, the mere existence of this event at UC-Hastings College of Law does not in any way interfere with the rights of Jewish or other supporters of Israel to express their views or be present comfortably on campus, a sin qua non of a Title VI claim. Profound disagreement with what is said is not to be identified with discrimination.

The "working definition" of antisemitism, of which an AJC staff member was the lead drafter, was intended as a means for data collectors and others to identify anti-Semitism, including anti-Semitism which appears in the guise of criticism of Israel. It was never intended, and should not be used, to silence academic discussions – even unbalanced ones ...

Rather than make prior assumptions and prohibit speech, a college administration should speak out and use its own voice to educate, if anti-Semitism or other forms of bigotry appear.[25]

The letter required the approval of AJC's executive director. It was a Friday, and the draft was sent to him around 2:30 p.m. By Friday evening it was not sent, and supposedly because of a reluctance to send letters after the Sabbath began, it was never issued.

When I talk to Jewish audiences about the campus and the impact of the Israel/Palestine debate, I usually start off asking for a show of hands.

How many think there's a crisis of antisemitism on American college campuses?

That it's at an all-time high?

How about anti-Israel animus?

Many, if not most, agree with these sentiments.

I tell them that the divestment petitions first appeared in 2002, and ask how many colleges have divested. Many seem surprised when I say "zero." Just like they seem surprised when I tell them that the data are consistent – there are relatively few campuses where Israel is a burning issue, and every year the number of pro-Israel programs (3,155 in 2016–17) is usually at least double the anti-Israel ones (1,172 in 2016–17).[26] There are over 4,000 campuses in the US – in the 2017–18 academic year, 149 had anti-Israel activity.[27] The year 2017 was the fiftieth anniversary of the Six-Day War, and 2018 was the seventieth anniversary of Israel's War of Independence and the Nakba. Yet only nine student anti-Israel resolutions passed.[28] So the campuses aren't burning. In fact, historically, they are very welcoming to Jewish students. In my parents' and grandparents' generations, there were quotas keeping Jews out of elite colleges. Today, many colleges have Jewish presidents.

That's not to say, as we've seen, that there aren't great tensions on some campuses over Israel, with speech and actions that students and faculty on both sides find disturbing, even hateful. What student, whose Jewish identity is largely shaped by a connection to Israel, wants to hear that Israel should, in one way or another, be destroyed? You plan to bring someone from Israel or an expert about Israel to your campus, and you may fear a disruption, rather than a dialogue. While, as noted before, there were 117 disruptions (or cancellations because of protests) of pro-Israel events from 2010 through the 2018–19 academic year, of which all but sixteen were able to be completed,[29] who wants to hear people chanting "From the river to the sea Palestine will be free!" or "Israel, Israel, what do you say? How many people have you killed today?"[30] Who wants to see signs saying "End Israeli Apartheid,"[31] or their classmates conducting a "die-in,"[32] or holding banners proclaiming "Zionism Is Racism," or even "Israel Is a Genocidal White Supremacist Ethno State."[33]

The pro-Palestinian students, like many pro-Israel students, are ginned up on righteousness. Playing "fair" with your schoolmates on this issue doesn't seem as important as winning. So there have been times when anti-Israel student resolutions were to be considered on a Friday afternoon or around a Jewish holiday, further aggravating pro-Israel students because the scheduling seemed designed to deny them an opportunity to be heard.[34]

Israel Apartheid Week (IAW) is an event at some colleges. The perception is that it is ubiquitous, but in the United States, it is not, perhaps appearing on a few dozen campuses.[35] Sometimes speakers can be incendiary, but frequently this is a theater of the absurd. When I was at AJC, someone called me, alarmed, that an

IAW event was happening that day at Columbia University. I saw about half a dozen pro-Palestinian students handing out literature by a cardboard mock wall. About fifty feet away there were pro-Israel students, draped in Israeli flags, handing out literature too. Us/Them – each marking their spot on the quad, with symbols. Social psychology in practice.

Sometimes political theater edges up to the possibility of intimidation or discrimination. The occasional mock check point is a permissible expression; actually obstructing students from exercising their freedom of movement, or specifically targeting particular students (such as Jewish ones) would likely not be. Likewise, there have been incidents when pro-Palestinian students have put mock eviction notices in dorms, suggesting that their classmates get a taste of what they allege is Israeli practice since 1948.[36] These notices might violate a content-neutral campus policy of what can be distributed in dorms, and certainly could be discriminatory if specific students were targeted because of their religion, ethnicity, or other such characteristic.

There have been instances where campus anti-Israel protests have been discriminatory. For instance, four Hillel-affiliated Jewish student activists were removed from a pro-BDS talk at Brooklyn College.[37] After an investigation, it was determined that the school had handled the situation poorly and the four should not have been excluded. But they were almost certainly not asked to leave because they were Jewish, but because of their pro-Israel stance.[38] For legal purposes, that's an important distinction; for practical purposes, it was horrid nonetheless. The whole point of hosting contentious speakers on campus is that any member of the student body or faculty should be able to attend.

So how bad are things for Jewish students on campus? In 2015, the Cohen Center for Modern Jewish Studies at Brandeis University released a report entitled "Antisemitism and the College Campus: Perceptions and Realities."[39] The report posed several different questions to the students and reported the key findings. One-quarter of the students surveyed said there was a "fairly" or "very big" problem of hostility on their campus against Israel. Fifteen per cent said there was a similar problem of hostility against Jews.

Three-quarters reported being "exposed to" some form of antisemitic statement (examples of antisemitic statements were provided in the survey). It was widely cited to claim that antisemitism and anti-Israel animus were rampant on campus.

The problem with the Cohen Center survey was that it focused on students who were participating in Taglit-Birthright Israel, a program that sends Jewish college students and young adults on a free trip to Israel. They are hardly representative of Jewish students generally, and would be expected to have a closer connection to Israel. Nor was it comparative. Is hearing something considered antisemitic a problem Jewish students experience more than women hear something sexist, gay students something homophobic, Muslim students something Islamophobic, and so forth?

Another 2015 survey – this one by the advocacy group the Brandeis Center (the organization Kenneth Marcus founded, which is not associated with Brandeis University) in conjunction with Trinity College – concluded that about half of Jewish students during the first half of the 2013–14 academic year "witnessed or [were] personally subjected to anti-Semitism." Antisemitism was not defined, students just answered yes or no. There was no indication of whether they had experienced it or witnessed it (perhaps they read a story in the student newspaper that they believed was antisemitic, however defined).[40]

Two years later, Brandeis University issued another study, looking closely at four campuses, and concluded that "Jewish students are rarely exposed to antisemitism on campus ... Jewish students do not think their campus is hostile to Jews ... Jewish students are exposed to hostile remarks toward Israel on campus ... The majority of students disagree that there is a hostile environment toward Israel on campus ... Support for BDS is rare ... Israel and Jews are not a top concern for students."[41]

What can one conclude, from these inconsistent and somewhat suspect data? That for the most part Jewish students are not in a hostile environment, but that on some campuses where anti-Israel activity is prominent, pro-Israel Jewish students may feel marginalized, dismissed, or vilified, sometimes with antisemitic tropes. And, of course, these incidents reverberate through both the Jewish community and the academic world. When academics vote to segregate Israeli academic institutions from every other country's institutions of higher education, or when pro-Israel groups are trying to use instruments of the state to chill and suppress political speech they don't like (as we'll discuss in chapter 7), academic freedom and free speech are jeopardized, poisoning the culture required for students and faculty to pursue knowledge.

Part of the challenge for pro-Israel students has nothing to do with Israel and more to do with social psychology: ingroups and outgroups. Clearly American society discriminates against people of color. Yes, there's been great progress since the civil rights era. But the notion of white privilege is not a fantasy. How many young black men have feared a traffic stop becoming a deadly encounter with a police officer? In comparison, a young white man might fear getting a ticket. How many white people, if given the choice, would choose to be black, to have their children grow up as black, in a society where, still today, racism is inescapable, knowing their children will be discriminated against and may even endure the physical harm of hate?

But that reality of discrimination becomes a mythology of group. The world becomes divided into whites who oppress and people of color who are oppressed. In the too easy, simplistic, fashionable desire to split the world into these two categories, Jews are nowadays defined as white.

There's some truth and some unreality to this categorization. Jews certainly know the historic sting of prejudice and worse,[42] as do people of color (and there are Jews of color as well). But the historic structural discrimination against Jews in American society – college admissions, board rooms, hotel accommodations, real estate purchases – is now essentially a thing of the past. For the last few decades the crisis in the Jewish community has not been antisemitism but Jewish continuity. Families that would not welcome a Jew now do. Jews are, perhaps, being loved to death, at least from the demographic perspective, given the rate of intermarriage.

But on the other hand, the labeling of Jews as white becomes a problem when shared victimhood becomes a sacred symbol, a badge of honor, a precondition to enter a club of the oppressed. Antisemitic discrimination is rendered invisible. When Jewish students hear antisemitism, they are doubly stung when others dismiss their concerns, because as whites they could not possibly, it is alleged, have a problem. This despite the increase of antisemitism on campus from white supremacists, following the 2016 presidential campaign and election of Donald Trump. White supremacists generally view Jews as not only non-white, but anti-white.[43] For example, a poster with a stylized swastika at Cornell University in 2017 showed a snake with a Star of David constricting the world. It said "JUST SAY NO TO JEWISH LIES! ... JOIN THE WHITE GANG."[44] Historically, antisemitism has been expressed in contradictions – Jews as capitalists and communists, tribalists and globalists, landless cosmopolitans and Jewish nationalists. Now Jews are being seen as white (on the Far Left) and as anti-white (on the Far Right, which blames Jews as a conspiratorial force promoting integration, affirmative action, immigration, and other alleged assaults on white people).

Sometimes the Jewish-whiteness claim becomes overtly antisemitic. Posters at the University of Illinois at Chicago proclaimed "Ending White Privilege ... Starts with Ending Jewish Privilege."[45] Jews are white, whites have power, the powerless are not white, and only people without power can be oppressed, or so it is claimed. And in this club of non-white oppressed folk, into which Jews are not allowed, is the added claim of intersectionality. The idea is that there are relationships between different types of oppression. The discriminatory experiences of white women and black women, for example, are not identical, as racism and sexism both have a role. The politics that is anti-Muslim is related to that which is anti-Hispanic or anti-gay or anti-woman, for instance. But this valuable observation has now too often been twisted into an overly simplistic ideological formula in which if you are a supporter of the Movement for Black Lives some believe you *must* be anti-Israel (the platform of the movement accuses Israel of committing "genocide" against the Palestinians).[46] Kenneth Waltzer of the Academic Engagement Network quipped: "If at Charlottesville neo-Nazis carried signs avowing '*Jews will not replace us*,' progressive students in SJP and in other allied groups seem now to say: '*Jews will have no place among us* [emphases in original].'"[47] (Presumably Waltzer means pro-Israel Jews.) Social psychology: the world is easier if there is an "us" and a "them." Our primitive instincts may be on display, we know who to fear if we do not have to take the time to think, perhaps.

Part of the anti-Israel animus on some campuses is due to reasonable concerns with Israel's actions, and the complex and conflicting equities of its founding. But part is simply political fashion; what Morty Stavis saw at the National Lawyers Guild in 1977 still applies today. As difficult as these attitudes may be for Jewish students who define their Jewishness as grounded in love for Israel, this remains a battle of ideas. The overtly antisemitic expressions should be called out, and the ones that play on antisemitic tropes (Jews and money, Jews and power, and so forth) should be exposed too – indeed, it should be asked why these tropes are referenced at all. But when each side sees the other as so hateful that allowing it to speak is deemed an act of immoral complicity, the instinct to censor comes to the fore. Pro-Palestinian students might try to censor by shouting, disrupting, and heckling; Jewish organizations tend to work through connections to administrators and donors, with phone calls and emails. But the goal – diminishing the other side's ability to speak – is the same.

Sometimes I wonder if colleges should fight this tendency – the "you wouldn't have a Nazi on campus, and the view I detest is a Nazi equivalent" – by bringing in at least one speaker a year whom most would view with contempt, perhaps even a neo-Nazi. Jewish groups, African American groups, and others would probably protest such a program. But the benefit of establishing the principle that students should be able to hear even the most reprehensible idea on a campus, where the point after all is to study and wrestle with ideas, might well be worth the cost. What value would there be in hearing a neo-Nazi firsthand? There are thousands of people around the world who consider themselves neo-Nazis, or agree with some of their ideas. Why shouldn't students hear them firsthand rather than only filtered through speakers like me who study and detest their point of view?

Regardless of whether schools might ever cultivate the study of hateful views firsthand, outside pro-Israel and pro-Palestinian groups are pumping steroids into this impulse to censor and suppress speech they don't like. Pro-Israel Jewish groups, by trying to match or beat their pro-Palestinian competitors in the silencing game, are actually hurting their own cause. Israel's case is best understood as inherently complex and difficult; playing into the "all bad" and "all good" binary of the other side renders those complexities invisible.

Canary Mission is a shadowy online group. It doesn't list a board of directors or staff. It has long been said that antisemitism is the "miner's canary" for a society, meaning just as miners of old took canaries into the mines to see if the air was safe to breathe, tolerance of antisemitism is a measure of a society's health.

The group's website is a distortion of that notion. It seeks to expose, and punish, those students and faculty whose views, it believes, "promote hatred of the USA, Israel and Jews on North American college campuses." "If you're racist," its website said for a long time, "the world should know."[48]

Its site proclaimed:

Today college campuses are filled with anti-Semitic and anti-American radicals waving Palestinian flags and placards and screaming "Apartheid" and "Murderer." A few years later these individuals are applying for jobs within your company. There's no record of their membership of [sic] radical organizations. No one remembers their yelling profanities on campus or attending Jew-hating conferences and anti-American rallies. All evidence has been eradicated, and soon they will be part of your team. We are Canary Mission, an organization dedicated to documenting these acts of hate, exposing them, and holding these individuals accountable.

"It is your duty," the site said, "to ensure that today's radicals are not tomorrow's employees."[49]

The Alliance for Academic Freedom[50] spoke out against Canary Mission, terming it "McCarthyite."[51] Suzanne Nossel, the executive director of PEN America testified, "Students are supposed to be able to experiment with ideas and expressions and should not live in peril that an errant chant or remark could be the beginning of the end of an academic career."[52] But most Jewish groups and leaders stayed silent about Canary Mission, perhaps not wanting to be seen as criticizing an approach that chilled anti-Israel speech, despite the tactic's immorality. When I pressed Kenneth Marcus at the Arendt Center event at Bard (see chapter 1, page 16) to condemn Canary Mission, he did not. Worse, the mainstream pro-Israel group Israel on Campus Coalition praised Canary Mission, and there is evidence it has received significant funding from mainstream Jewish communal foundations.[53] (The website has changed its self-description, now saying it "investigates hatred ... [and is] motivated by a desire to combat the rise in anti-Semitism on college campuses." It says it has an "ethics policy."[54] What is ethical about the blacklist of students, which it remains, is difficult to fathom.)

It is hard to imagine mainstream Jewish groups willingly accepting, endorsing, or funding blacklists, other than ones that target opponents of Israel. When I was at AJC, the website known as the "Nuremberg Files" listed people who were pro-abortion in an attempt to threaten and silence them, and we worked against it. The academic boycott of Israel is a blacklist, and we worked against it. But a blacklist of boycott proponents? That's apparently unobjectionable, even laudable.

I don't know who the people are behind Canary Mission, but I recall a conversation I had with the leader of an activist right-wing group during the controversy over the charges contained in the film *Columbia Unbecoming*. AJC had put out a press release that, on balance, complimented the university on how it was handling the inquiry. The activist called me to complain. I said, let's review the text line by line, and tell me what you think we got wrong or was unfair. "This isn't about fairness," he said, laughing. "We're in a war. We have to keep on the attack."[55]

Sometimes, when you view the campus as a war zone, you make tactical mistakes. In the 2017–18 academic year, there were twenty-five student BDS campaigns (usually urging divestment – and no campus has yet divested from Israel). Of these, nine were passed[56] –

a very small number, considering that there are over 4,000 institutions of higher education in the United States.[57] One was at the University of Michigan. Students who opposed the divestment petition believe it passed in large measure because of Canary Mission. The potential threat to students who might vote in favor of the resolution resulted in the ballot being taken in secret. If the vote had been open, and student government members had had to justify their position, it was believed the resolution might have failed.[58]

The Anti-Defamation League describes Students for Justice in Palestine this way:

> Students for Justice in Palestine (SJP) is a network of pro-Palestinian student groups across the US which disseminate anti-Israel propaganda often laced with inflammatory and at times combative rhetoric. They are a leading campus organizer of Boycott, Divestment and Sanctions (BDS) campaigns against Israel, and specialize in using confrontational tactics such as disrupting student-run pro-Israel events, constructing mock "apartheid walls" and distributing fake "eviction notices" to dramatize what they consider Israeli abuses of Palestinians. As proponents of "anti-normalization" between pro-Palestinian and pro-Israel advocates, they make it more difficult for groups with diverging views on the Israeli-Palestinian conflict to work together and achieve mutual understanding.
>
> Although many SJP chapters state that they reject anti-Semitism, they also regularly demonize Jewish students who identify as Zionists or proud supporters of the State of Israel, despite the fact that a more nuanced understanding of Zionism shows that a connection to the state of Israel is an important part of many Jews' religious or cultural identities. SJP's insistence that one cannot be a good Jew while still being a Zionist is a blatant effort to constrain the Jewish identities of their fellow students and can turn campuses into hostile places for Jewish students.[59]

Chapters of student organizations vary, depending on the culture of the campus and the personalities of the students. When I was at AJC, it would not have been politically wise to have a private conversation with an SJP member. But when an SJP activist read some of my post-AJC op-eds about academic freedom and reached out to me, we found, despite deep disagreements, we could not only have a civil conversation but that we could also agree that efforts to restrict student speech were damaging, to both sides. Yet some SJP chapters have engaged in advocacy that challenge academic freedom.

Jill Schneiderman and Rachel Friedman are professors at Vassar College. They co-taught a class called "The Jordan River Watershed," which included a field trip to study the scientific and geopolitical issues affecting Israel, the West Bank, and Jordan. SJP organized against the course, and asked students to drop it. The group said the class would "greenwash" the political situation – focusing on an environmental issue when the only issue of importance was the oppression of Palestinians by Israel. While not blocking access, SJP formed a sort of picket line outside the classroom so that students taking the course had to pass through them and their "loud ululating sounds."[60]

A flyer addressed to the students in the course said:

> You are not just taking a class, you are making a political choice! The simple act of entering and moving within the state of Israel is a freedom denied to over five million Palestinian refugees who were ethnically cleansed from their homes by the Israeli state. Your participation in the class financially and symbolically supports apartheid and degradation of Palestinians. You may be critical, but your physical presence in the occupied country of Palestine is an endorsement of the systematic violation of human rights …
>
> The indigenous people of Palestine do NOT want you to come!
>
> Do your research, engage with the realities of settler colonialism, and support BDS by opting out of this class![61]

School officials, faced with a crisis, called a community meeting. Pro-Palestinian blogger Phillip Weiss attended and wrote about it. It is worth reading a substantial part of his post:

> Over 200 students and faculty jammed a large room of the College Center, and torrents of anger ripped through the gathering. Most of them were directed at Israel or its supporters …

"What crossed the line," Friedman said, was when she walked in to her class February 6 and was greeted by posters telling people to "drop the class, it's not too late," and "Indigenous Palestinians don't want you to come." Her students felt harassed and bullied by the reception ... "The protest shocked me frankly. In 17 years of teaching at Vassar, I've never witnessed anything like this ... My students were upset and shaken up ... We're in a dangerous place, if suddenly classrooms are being picketed and students made to feel harassed when they are going to [a] class that they've chosen."

... When a Jewish sophomore said that he had come to Vassar in part because there was a large Jewish student body and he felt that he would not face anti-Semitism, till he saw the words "Israeli apartheid" – "and that's charged language" – people on the other side laughed ...

The last portion of the meeting was dominated by an SJP member, a slender woman wearing a keffiyeh who stood two or three times and spoke in an earnest manner. As one of only 8 or 9 Arabs at the school, she said, she sees her college putting thousands of dollars into supporting a government that oppresses people who are like her. There were so many flaws with the trip no one could say it was neutral: it was going to a discriminatory national airport and would travel on apartheid roads. She could not go on this trip because she would be stopped at Ben-Gurion airport on account of the Lebanese stamps in her passport, and because her going would prevent her from traveling to Arab countries.

"How am I to feel when my university is funding a trip going to a place that discriminates against people based on my ethnicity? They are leading a trip that is inherently discriminatory, and no one at this college has spoken out against that except the SJP."

...

Both sides had now expressed sincere feelings of being bullied ... I left feeling some empathy for Schneiderman and Friedman. The atmosphere was more intimidating to pro-Israel speakers than pro-Palestinian speakers ... Being for Israel makes you a clod.

... [T]he spirit of that young progressive space was that Israel is a blot on civilization, and boycott is right and necessary. If a student had gotten up and said, I love Israel, he or she would have been mocked and scorned into silence. Or bedevilled by finger-snapping – the percussive weapon of choice among some students, a sound that rises like crickets as students indicate their quiet approval of a statement.

I left the room as soon as the meeting ended. The clash felt too raw, and there was a racial element to the division (privileged Jews versus students of color). Vassar is not my community, and I didn't want to say anything to make things worse.[62]

The SJP students expressed opinions, which I both understand and reject. From their perspective, the mere fact of the field trip harms Palestinians and discriminates against students who might not be welcome on the trip. They have a right to express this point of view, and while the forum might have been better conceived and executed, their protest allowed the campus to learn more about their perspective (and why pro-Israel Jewish students saw the singling out of Israel as discriminatory if not antisemitic).

It's likely true that the young Arab student might have had difficulties that some of her Jewish classmates might not if she wanted to go on the trip. But the logic of that objection fades when one considers it is likely easier for her to go on a school field trip to Saudi Arabia than one of her Jewish classmates, or that it was easier for white law students to go Mississippi during the civil rights struggles. I'm confident if she had wanted to go on that trip, the Vassar administration would have done all it could (with the State Department's help if necessary) to make it happen.

If the ability to learn from firsthand experience is to be abandoned because of the potential discriminatory policies of the country visited, or because of questions of injustice, the limitations on academic inquiry would be stark. Either students are allowed to go anywhere to learn or we can start creating lists of where they should not go.[63] In this sense Israel would be the miner's canary, and the mines to be added would include most of the other Middle Eastern countries, Burma, China, Hungary, Russia, and probably most other nations.

While it's probable that, in colleges where Israel/Palestine is an issue, pro-Palestinian students feel more supported by their classmates than do pro-Israel students, some pro-Palestinian students have been threatened and vilified too. At New York University, pro-Palestinian students have received anonymous death threats:

WE WILL KILL ALL OF YOUR TROLLS WITH GUNS AT YOUR NEXT PROTEST YOU WILL ALL DIE WE WILL MURDER YOU ALL THE BLOOD WILL RUNS SLOWLY ON THE STREETS OF NYC.[64]

You will all be shhot [sic] at your next protest SJP members. It will be a family affair ... WE WILL PAINT THE STREET WITH PALESTINIAN / MUSLIM / BLACK LIVES MATTER / STUDENTS FOR JUSTICE IN PALESTINE / BLOOD.[65]

In 2015 students at Columbia University planning an Israel Apartheid Week event received this tweet from @ProudJewYr3833: "all you neo-nazis in one place makes a good target for an IED. ;)."[66]

Students have not only received threats for their political advocacy but also for their teaching. In 2015 a student-run course entitled "Palestinian Voices" was scheduled to be taught at the University of California, Riverside. According to Palestine Legal, "The course sought to explore Palestinian voices through contemporary literature and media ... Assigned reading materials, from Palestinian authors such as Edward Said and Rashid Khalidi and a spectrum of Israeli Jewish writers from Benny Morris and Eyal Weizman to David Grossman and Neve Gordon, focused on Palestinian historical narratives, literature, and cultural production."[67] The AMCHA Initiative tried to get the course cancelled. AMCHA said, in a letter to the university leadership, that "while the website description of 'Palestinian Voices' already makes clear that the course will focus on only one side of the Palestinian-Israeli conflict, the full [syllabus shows the] extent of the course's anti-Israel bias, and its clear intent to politically indoctrinate students to hate the Jewish state and take action against it."[68] AMCHA alleged:

According to the syllabus, the title of the course is *not* "Palestinian Voices," but rather "Palestine & Israel: Settler-Colonialism and Apartheid." Not only does the course's actual title reveal the student instructor's unambiguous anti-Israel bias, it includes a patently false canard about Israel frequently used to delegitimize the Jewish state, language which meets the US State Department's definition of antisemitism. Perhaps even more troubling, however, is the fact that there was a clear attempt to obfuscate the extreme anti-Israel bias of the course by re-titling it for the R'Course web page and including a graphic of Israeli and Palestinian flags that falsely suggests a modicum of even-handedness about the conflict which is sorely lacking from the syllabus and, presumably, from the course itself.

In the syllabus, Ms. Matar identifies herself as a member of the UCR chapter of Students for Justice in Palestine (SJP) and implies that her work with that group forms the basis for the development of the course. Indeed, Matar is a leader of UCR's SJP group, whose primary mission is to engage in activism to demonize and delegitimize the Jewish state and work towards its elimination, especially through anti-Israel boycott, divestment, and sanctions (BDS) campaigns. Matar herself was an author and proponent of the extremely contentious anti-Israel divestment resolution passed by the UCR student senate last April.[69]

A review by the university determined that this class could be offered and that it didn't violate a policy against "political indoctrination." But Matar started receiving menacing messages, including an email saying, "Since the Palestinians weren't a people, but an islamo-nazi invention for the annihilation of Jews, then anything can be taught in colleges. Like hamas baby shields, college baby brains are a great weapon."[70]

Right-wing Jewish groups have tried to get other classes cancelled too; courses that approach Israel in what to them appears as a one-sided or demonizing fashion. I agreed with them only once, limited to finding fault with a course's description. I disagreed with the course's framing, but academic freedom protected this summary: "The brutal Israeli military occupation of Palestine, an occupation that has been ongoing since 1948, has systematically displaced, killed, and maimed millions of Palestinian people … yet, from under the brutal weight of the occupation, Palestinians have produced their own culture and poetry of resistance." The problem with the course description was the final line: "Conservative thinkers are encouraged to seek other sections."[71] It should go without saying that regardless of a teacher's point of view, students from all perspectives should be welcome in a class – in fact, differences of opinion help make a class worthwhile.

And while pro-Palestinian groups have sometimes disrupted pro-Israel events, right-wing pro-Israel groups have frequently tried to use public letters and other pressure tactics to stop or chill speech from people with whom they disagree, including Israelis who are harsh critics of their country. For example, the AMCHA Initiative wrote to the leadership of three California State University campuses, objecting to the appearances of Israeli academic Ilan Pappé because the events were being

> organized and promoted by faculty and administrators of the California State University system, using the name, resources, and imprimatur of CSU, in order to vilify and harm the Jewish state and its supporters. As you may know, Ilan Pappé is an Israeli Jew who harbors deep animus towards the Jewish state, has publicly called for its elimination, and engages in activities to harm its citizens, such as a campaign to boycott Israeli academics, which he helped to found. In addition, he openly supports the terrorist organization Hamas and falsely accuses Israel of "crimes against humanity," including "genocide" and "ethnic cleansing" ... [M]uch of the rhetoric Pappé uses to demonize and delegitimize the Jewish state is anti-Semitic according to the working definition of anti-Semitism employed by the US State Department, as is the academic boycott which he promotes in his talks and writings.[72]

Despite AMCHA's objections, Pappé spoke.

In 2015 the Zionist Organization of America (ZOA) wrote to Professor Lila Abu-Lughod of the Middle East Institute at Columbia University, objecting to a proposed teacher workshop on "Citizenship and Nationality in Israel/Palestine." "Indeed," the ZOA wrote, "the very title of the workshop is inaccurate and would mislead teachers and instructors since there is presently no country called 'Palestine ...'"[73] The ZOA also had a legal objection. Title VI of the Higher Education Act (not to be confused with Title VI of the Civil Rights Act, which we will examine in chapter 7) funds educational programs to "develop and maintain capacity and performance in area/international studies and world languages."[74] The ZOA wrote: "The Middle East Institute is a recipient of funding from the Department of

Education, pursuant to Title VI of the Higher Education Act. As you surely know, the law requires that Title VI programs 'reflect diverse perspectives and a wide range of views and generate debate on world regions and international affairs.'"[75]

For years the Jewish community had concerns that many classes funded under such programs were hostile towards Israel, and in 2014 right-wing Jewish groups wrote an open letter advocating major changes to the program, including more active ensurance of a balance of political views about Israel.[76] This is a complicated issue. Pro-Palestinian groups object to the attacks on these programs from Jewish organizations, accusing them of violating academic freedom and trying to deny teaching anything critical about Israel. But the pro-Palestinian groups frequently neglect to note that this is not a general academic activity, but one funded by Congress for the specific purpose of increasing Americans' ability to engage the world effectively (such as by students who might grow up to become State Department employees).[77]

Yet the insistence on "balance" by the Jewish Right is troubling. Students should not be treated like scales – that they'll somehow become off-kilter if the right collection of pro- and anti- positions on Israel are not covered in a training.

Deeply disturbing in the ZOA's letter was a demand made after it attacked a professor for her views on Israel, including her support of BDS:

> We ask that you provide us with the information that shows that this upcoming workshop will comply with Title VI, including in your response the following information:
>
> 1. The name(s) and professional affiliation(s) of all additional speakers besides Katherine Franke;
> 2. The names of any films that will be screened; and
> 3. A copy of all the readings and other materials that will be used and distributed to the participants in the workshop.
>
> We take the fair, accurate and unbiased education of teachers and students very seriously. Our members and supporters, who include many alumni of and donors to Columbia, do as well – especially when taxpayer money is at issue and might be used wrongfully to indoctrinate rather than educate, with propaganda that is false, one-sided and hostile to Israel.[78]

The ZOA, of course, has the First Amendment right to articulate its point of view and make such demands. But the chilling effect is damaging to academic freedom. Why should any professor have to fear having her program sent in advance to an outside advocacy agency, which is hunting for reasons to sue? The ZOA's demands were rejected, and the training went on.

The instinct to chill and suppress, rather than promote other programs or engage in public debate, is anathema to academic freedom. And it made for one of my worst days at AJC.

Rashid Khalidi is the Edward Said Professor of Modern Arab Studies at Columbia University. He is Palestinian American, and like the late Said, he is undeniably a public intellectual (even though one might disagree forcefully with what he has to say). In February 2005, a news story appeared in a New York newspaper; Khalidi was to play a key role in a professional development course about the Middle East for teachers in New York City. People immediately pressed NYC's school chancellor Joel Klein to fire Khalidi and his group from this program, for fear that he would turn the teachers into Israel haters. I was told that AJC was going to call on Klein to do just that, and that I should draft a press release as soon as possible.

Before writing it, I quickly researched why people were calling for Khalidi's removal. The key charge was that he said Israel was practicing Apartheid, so I tracked the allegations to see if he was being quoted accurately. One alleged source didn't seem to exist, and another had him commenting on the various different areas (A, B, and C) in the West Bank under the Oslo Accords, asking whether this might be an "apartheid system in creation."[79] That, in my view, was far different than alleging that Israel is an apartheid country. It was late in the day, and under pressure, I resisted the request to produce a draft (Khalidi, I was told by a member of the senior staff, shouldn't be teaching Jewish children, and he certainly shouldn't be training teachers). The agency's credibility was important, and I couldn't yet find enough information about the program he was to run. In the meantime, Klein booted Khalidi from the training, and AJC – feeling it had missed an opportunity to weigh in before the fact – put out a statement (that I didn't write) praising Klein's actions. But the rush to judgment was further flawed. Khalidi wasn't even going to speak about Israel, but on the geography and demography of the region.[80]

Jewish faculty at Columbia told me that Khalidi was a great colleague, and had been reaching out to see if pro-Israel faculty might speak to his classes, and vice versa. Not anymore. As Sam Freedman, a Columbia journalism professor and former *New York Times* reporter, noted,

> instead of being able to play a mediating role between pro-Israel and pro-Palestinian forces on the campus, as I believe he had intended to do, Khalidi was pushed into a corner, from which, predictably, he lashed out. It may serve the interests of politicians, certain advocacy groups, and ideological publications to undermine and polarize Khalidi, but it pollutes the intellectual environment on campus.[81]

In 2013, pro-BDS activists Judith Butler and Omar Barghouti were invited to speak at a Brooklyn College event, which was co-sponsored by the political science department. Members of the New York City Council then wrote the president of Brooklyn College, not only objecting but threatening:

> We are asking you to cancel this event or, if it should proceed, then to remove your school's official support for it ... To give official support and sponsorship to speakers who equate terrorists with progressives and the Israeli people with Nazis – ideas which strike us as either anti-semitic or simply ignorant – is wrong and promotes the worst kind of hate. A significant portion of the funding for CUNY schools comes directly from the tax dollars of the people of the State and City of New York ... We do not believe this program is what the taxpayers of our City – many of whom would feel targeted and demonized by this program – want their tax money to be spent on.[82]

Dov Hikind, a prominent Jewish politician, even called on the president of Brooklyn College to resign.[83]

The event was of course not canceled. Regardless of however else one views Butler's comments during that program, one observation she made was undoubtedly true: but for the calls for censorship by politicians and others, she would have been having "a conversation with a few dozen student activists in the basement of a student center," rather than before a large audience, with press coverage.[84]

In November 2015 four Fordham University students applied for permission to create a Students for Justice in Palestine club at the schools' Lincoln Center campus. For the next thirteen months the students had meetings with administrators and answered questions about what they proposed to do. The students wanted "to build support in the Fordham community among people of all ethnic and religious backgrounds for the promotion of justice, human rights, liberation, and self-determination for the indigenous Palestinian people."[85]

In October 2016 students interested in forming and joining SJP met with school officials, including the director of the Office of Student Leadership and Community Development and Student Orientation, and a dean. The director and the dean asked about the group's support for BDS. According to their lawyers the "[s]tudents responded that they wished to educate the Fordham community on Israel-Palestine, that BDS is a time-honored civil rights tactic that targets Israeli government policy, not the Jewish people."[86]

In November 2016 the student government voted to permit the SJP chapter's creation, but in December the dean wrote:

> I have decided to deny the request to form a club known as Students for Justice in Palestine at Fordham University. While students are encouraged to promote diverse political points of view, and we encourage conversation and debate on all topics, I cannot support an organization whose sole purpose is advocating political goals of a specific group, and against a specific country, when these goals clearly conflict with and run contrary to the mission and values of the University.
>
> There is perhaps no more complex topic than the Israeli-Palestinian conflict, and it is a topic that often leads to polarization rather than dialogue. The purpose of the organization as stated in the proposed club constitution points toward that polarization. Specifically, the call for

Boycott, Divestment and Sanctions of Israel presents a barrier to open dialogue and mutual learning and understanding.[87]

The students' lawyers asked the university to reverse its position, writing, "When Fordham treats a particular viewpoint in a disparate manner based on how much controversy the viewpoint could provoke, it blatantly violates its promise to guarantee freedom of inquiry on campus. When Dean Eldredge decides that BDS is too polarizing to allow students to debate it, he makes a mockery of 'rigorous thinking.'"[88]

When Fordham refused to reconsider, Palestine Legal and the Center for Constitutional Rights sued the university. The school's defense essentially was that as a private institution it was not required to respect the First Amendment, and that courts should generally not second guess the decisions of educators.[89] My suspicion is that if a school wanted to ban a club associated with a group like the Zionist Organization of America, which opposes a Palestinian state, mainstream Jewish organizations would issue press releases and energetically advocate to overturn such a decision, just as in the 1980s they protested when a Jewish group was barred in the UK because it was "Zionist" and the United Nations at the time declared Zionism a form of racism. But sadly, Jewish groups were largely silent when students at Fordham were not allowed to form an SJP chapter.[90] (After years of litigation, a judge ruled in July 2019 that Fordham had violated its own rules in denying the SJP chapter, and ordered that it be allowed.)[91]

Likewise, pro-Palestinian organizations weren't speaking out strongly in the spring of 2019 when Williams College's College Council (made up of students) rejected the application of a pro-Israel campus group called Williams Initiative for Israel (WIFI) to become a "registered student organization." WIFI aimed "to support Israel and the pro-Israel campus community, as well as to educate the College on issues concerning Israel and the Middle East."[92]

A few of WIFI's opponents explained their thinking in an op-ed:

[W]e could not approve of WIFI's mission statement, which explicitly supports the currently existing Israeli state. Given that the Israeli state is engaging in ongoing violent practices and is built on stolen Palestinian land, one cannot "support" the existence of an Israeli state as an abstract concept without ignoring and indirectly endorsing the state's violent practices ... We cannot support groups that, in response to Palestinian students sharing deeply personal accounts of the pain they have suffered during the occupation, trivialize the violence that this campus was supposed to provide them an escape from. We can have a healthy debate around Israel-Palestine on this campus without erasing the voices of Palestinian students, erroneously redefining colonialism or concealing acts of genocide.[93]

Williams's president, Maud Mandel (one of the founding members of the Alliance for Academic Freedom), released a strong statement in support of WIFI's place on campus, noting that "[d]ifferences over such views are legitimate grounds for debate, but not for exercising the power to approve or reject a student group."[94]

Because each side of the campus debate on Israel and Palestine views itself as standing for simple justice, and the other as opposing it, each believing the other side's speech should be silenced, we've seen disruption (Irvine), threats of legal action (Hastings), and refusal to allow students to form clubs to express their political point of view (Fordham and Williams).

But it gets worse.

If the other side is as detestable as if it were made up of Nazis, the logical conclusion is that you should have nothing to do with it. To have a conversation with a student who has a diametrically opposed point of view becomes impossible, because you are conceding, by merely having the conversation, that their point of view might have the slightest bit of merit.

The campus mission to shake up thinking is forgotten, as is the wisdom of John Stuart Mill – that testing your ideas against those who disagree helps you gain clarity. For many on the pro-Palestinian side, the idea of having a conversation with Jewish student groups that are pro-Israel has become impossible. To do so would be to "normalize" the conflict. The morality of purity has to be preserved, and the certainty that there's only one simple single historical narrative underscored.[95] Here's one conversation that illustrates the thinking. In 2010 Malik Ali, who spoke from time to time for Students for Justice for Palestine at the University of California, Irvine, was interviewed by Roz Rothstein from StandWithUs:

ROTHSTEIN: Do you support Hamas?
MALIK ALI: Yes.
ROTHSTEIN: Do you support Hezbollah?
MALIK ALI: Yes.
ROTHSTEIN: Do you support Islamic Jihad?
MALIK ALI: Yes.
ROTHSTEIN: Do you support jihad on this campus?
MALIK ALI: Jihad on this campus …? As long as it's in the form of speaking truth to power, yes. And the reason why I said it's not a good idea to sit down with Zionists, is because when you sit down with Zionists, for cookies and cake, and talk about issues, that kind of thing, right, it gives the impression that Zionism is like, it's okay, that it's okay. Now, you Jews, in all due respect, you wouldn't sit down with Nazis for tea and cake. No you wouldn't![96]

And this refusal to talk isn't only ideological, there are specific rules about it. In October 2011 PACBI defined and endorsed anti-normalization:

… The Palestinian Campaign for the Academic and Cultural Boycott of Israel (PACBI) has defined normalization … "as the participation in any project, initiative or activity, in Palestine or internationally, that aims (implicitly or explicitly) to bring together Palestinians (and/or Arabs) and Israelis (people or institutions) without placing as its goal resistance to and exposure of the Israeli occupation and all forms of discrimination and oppression against the Palestinian people."
… Projects, initiatives and activities that do not begin from a position of shared principles to resist Israel's oppression invariably allow for an approach to dealing with Israel as if its violations can be deferred, and as if coexistence (as opposed to "co-resistance") can precede, or lead to, the end of oppression. In the process, Palestinians, regardless of

intentions, end up serving as a fig-leaf for Israelis who are able to benefit from a "business-as-usual" environment, perhaps even allowing Israelis to feel their conscience is cleared for having engaged Palestinians they are usually accused of oppressing and discriminating against.

... Generally, international supporters of BDS are asked to refrain from participating in any event that morally or politically equates the oppressor and oppressed, and presents the relationship between Palestinians and Israelis as symmetrical. Such an event should be boycotted because it normalizes Israel's colonial domination over Palestinians and ignores the power structures and relations embedded in the oppression.[97]

Campuses are for conversations, and it is hard to have a conversation if you have rules that define merely meeting, speaking, and listening as a form of treachery,[98] the moral equivalent of a union worker crossing a picket line.[99] Tom Pessah, an SJP member and then recent graduate of UC Berkeley, explained why SJP chapters would reject a Hillel student's invitation to dialogue:

In his post on New Voices last week, Tomer Kornfeld recounts how he worked with his campus Hillel to set up "a debate, or 'mock peace talk' with Students for Justice in Palestine." But "instead of reciprocating our goodwill, sitting down with us and working things out, SJP sent out an email to club members announcing that they will host a speaker who will explain to them why 'SJP refuses to cooperate with Zionist groups, like Hillel.'" Tomer feels frustrated about the rejection of his offer, and asks for "suggestions for how to get students on both sides of the divide to work together for peace." As a Jewish Israeli alumnus of SJP at UC Berkeley, I would like to ... explain why SJP's are likely to reject such seemingly benign suggestions, and what people like Tomer can do if they are genuinely interested in peace.

Tomer defines himself as "pro-Palestinian" (as well as "pro-Israel" and "pro-peace"). Our definition is very different. At its first national conference in 2010, SJP endorsed the following three points of unity:

1. Ending Israel's occupation and colonization of all Arab lands and dismantling the Wall;
2. Recognizing the fundamental rights of the Arab-Palestinian citizens of Israel to full equality; and

3. Respecting, protecting and promoting the rights of Palestinian refugees to return to their homes and properties as stipulated in UN resolution 194.

For us, to be pro-Palestinian means actively working to advance those rights ... What is the position of Hillel and its student groups in relation to these three goals? From AIPAC to J Street, they actively oppose them. SJP's across the US try to end their universities' investments in international corporations that violate human rights in the West Bank and Gaza. Whenever this happens, Hillel groups go out of their way to maintain current investments in these corporations, which oppress the communities of Palestinian SJP members – for instance, by profiting from the demolition of Palestinian homes. Instead of joining the international campaigns to stop the displacement of Bedouin citizens of Israel, many Hillel groups spread false propaganda suggesting that Arabs in Israel enjoy full equality. Successive Israeli governments ban Palestinians born in Palestine, as well as their descendants, from returning to where their families lived for generations. Hillel groups work with these governments to organize Birthright trips that offer more opportunities for Jewish-American students to visit or relocate to Israel than to those born there. This policy is causing tremendous anguish to Palestinian-American students.

The current Israeli government wants to have its cake and eat it: to accelerate the construction of illegal Jewish-only settlements on Palestinian lands, while calling for the continuation of endless peace talks. Netanyahu's aim is transparent: peace talks deflect pressure on Israel to change its policies.

Hillel, a member of the Israel on Campus [C]oalition, seems inspired by the same tactic: insist on robbing Palestinians of their rights, then call for campus "peace talks." Probably unintentionally, this tactic is echoed in the suggestion Tomer makes in his post: instead of raising awareness about the systematic segregation and inequality between Jews and Palestinians in Israel, on both sides of the Green Line, SJP's need to stop organizing Israeli Apartheid Weeks and replace them with more vaguely named "peace weeks."

This tactic of presenting complicity with oppression as something natural and normal that we can all agree on, is what we refer to as "normalization." The problem is not with people's identities (SJP chapters are highly diverse, and include many American and Israeli Jews), but with their behavior: if you insist on actively denying Palestinians their basic rights, we see no need to co-produce a feel-good public event with you. Individual SJP members can (and do) engage whomever they want, but public events with Hillel are unlikely to happen until it changes its current policies.[100]

Disagree as one might with Pessah's justification for anti-normalization on campus, he at least laid out his thinking clearly and didn't demonize his political opposition. But not everyone is so thoughtful. There's a Jewish theological idea about keeping clear lines (sometimes expressed as "building a fence around the Torah") – to maintain purity you have to go further and further out. If you can't have discussions with people who are pro-Israel, since that is "normalization," what's the next layer?

Steven Salaita, a pro-Palestinian professor, explained it in a tweet: Zionists are not only to be avoided for purposes of conversations, they must be excluded from everything progressive, like protests. He wrote:

Basic rules for useful protest:

- no cops
- no Zionists
- no corporate sponsors
- no astroturfers
- no snitches

It's okay to demand these exclusions, even at the risk of being called "sectarian" or "anti-Semitic."[101]

He then explained:

I submit that it's both smart and reasonable to exclude Zionists from participating in protest that bills itself as leftist (which can include local organizing, party building, and mass action) for three main reasons:

1. Even in its progressive manifestations, Zionism is in essence reactionary. Nearly all of its variations accept (or promote) structural iniquity mediated by state power. It therefore contravenes the

fundamental aspirations of leftist protestors, who, whatever their disagreements, purport to share a desire for access and equality.
2. Palestine is a central feature of the global left, both imaginatively and materially. Israel can be found in systems of colonization, imperialism, police violence, capitalism, militarization, border control, racialized citizenship, and incarceration.
3. Liberal Zionists have a remarkable ability to dominate conversation. In their presence, we always seem fixated on their needs, their feelings, their anxieties, and their limitations. The Holy Land, if only by implication, ends up being the exclusive concern of American Jews, with Palestine serving as an occasional interruption. We intensely debate what is or isn't anti-Semitism; how various Jewish demographics relate to Israel; why certain outcomes are unacceptable to Israelis; and where Israelis may be willing to compromise. Meanwhile, Palestinian sensibilities disappear into a bottomless void of settler anguish. I know this point will generate indignation and anger. I also know that the pattern I describe is pervasive and can be exhausting for Palestinians.[102]

And then add another layer of exclusion on top of that – Jews, at least those who are not fully in the pro-Palestinian camp, are, as we saw, sometimes dismissed as white and privileged.

Anti-normalization, or its akin exclusions, was likely why the J Street students were told they were not welcome among the progressive groups that opposed giving a platform to Steve Bannon.

You'd think that the largest Jewish campus organization – Hillel International – would be against an anti-normalization rationale, and it is. Except it isn't – it engages in a near-mirror-image policy, refusing to engage those with ideas it defines as detestable.

Having worked in a national Jewish agency, I understand that an organization has to define what it wants to do, and what it refuses to do. I understand that funders are important, and what pro-Israel funder wants to see their donations used to bring speakers to campus who either, in their mind, paint Israel unfairly, or if not unfairly, expose some of Israel's warts, which will be exploited by those who wish Israel harm? People who contribute to Hillel are concerned with Jewish life on campus. They no doubt worry that if the anti-Israel narrative continues to thrive, not only will pro-Israel students feel discomfort but also the next generation's policy makers will be antagonistic to Israel.

So what do you do when a local Hillel chapter wants to co-sponsor a campus event that includes groups that present a Palestinian perspective, or are made up of former IDF soldiers who speak out against the Occupation, or are activists who endorse part or the full menu of BDS? The instinct is to say "this is beyond the pale," and to reassure funders that none of their money is going to help spread messages they abhor.

It is fully understandable why leaders and funders of mainstream Jewish organizations feel this way. What's distressing is that few Jewish leaders have actually *led* on this issue, asking their organizations to think through if this silencing approach is working, and examine why it might not achieve the desired results.

Jewish students, who are eighteen to twenty-two years old for the most part, do not need to be "protected." In my experience, they come to campus frequently having not heard of "the Occupation" in their day school, synagogue, or Jewish summer camp. And when they do hear about it, they wonder why they have this gap in their knowledge. They feel resentment, and don't want to be told anymore what they can hear about Israel, and what they cannot.

Young Jews who take "repairing the world" to heart, and buy the ideology of SJP or Jewish Voice for Peace or IfNotNow (supportive of some of the rationales justifying BDS), are among the groups that Hillel and the mainstream Jewish organizations consider to be anti-Israel.[103]

Hillel's Standards of Partnership states:

Hillel welcomes, partners with, and aids the efforts of organizations, groups, and speakers from diverse perspectives in support of Israel as a Jewish and democratic state. Hillel will not partner with, house, or host organizations, groups, or speakers that as a matter of policy or practice:

- Deny the right of Israel to exist as a Jewish and democratic state with secure and recognized borders;
- Delegitimize, demonize, or apply a double standard to Israel;
- Support boycott of, divestment from, or sanctions against the State of Israel;

- Exhibit a pattern of disruptive behavior towards campus events or guest speakers or foster an atmosphere of incivility.[104]

For those who are not yet ideological soldiers, but want to learn more, and want to do it around their campus Hillel, what sense does it make that adults are telling them they can only bring in certain types of speakers? Yes, the adults define BDS as hateful. But does it make sense to tell students they have to go elsewhere than the Jewish address on campus to hear about it firsthand from those who support it?

Jewish leadership continues to fail these students and their parents. Leaders should be explaining to the adults that what feels good (and self-righteous) doesn't necessarily do good. It's easy to say former IDF soldiers who now speak out against the Occupation are harming Israel's campus image. It's obtuse to say that not bringing in those speakers will somehow shield Jewish students from their message.

Pro-Israel groups correctly note that the campus pro-Palestinian view of Israel is frequently more propagandistic than scholarly. But Hillel's stance is propagandistic too. Shouldn't it be helping students learn the details and complexity of Israeli history? Providing a forum to discuss difficult questions isn't the same as endorsing the views of every speaker. And as Derek Penslar notes, "Not a single one of the founding figures in the history of Zionism and Israel would be allowed to speak on campus today in a Hillel facility. All of them were willing to consider alternatives to pure Jewish sovereignty in Palestine – and that includes Herzl, Ben-Gurion, and Jabotinsky."[105]

Smart students, objecting to this ideological straight-jacketing, have created Open Hillel, an organization that encourages a broader discussion of Israel among Jews on campus. Its mission statement reads (in part):

> Open Hillel promotes pluralism and open discourse on Israel/Palestine in Jewish communities on campus and beyond. We aim to eliminate Hillel International's Standards of Partnership for Israel Activities, which exclude individuals and groups from the Jewish community on campus on the basis of their views on Israel ...

We are Jewish students and recent graduates, supported in our work by rabbis, professors, and Jewish community members. We are united not by a shared perspective on Israel/Palestine, but by a shared commitment to the Jewish values of open discussion and debate. We envision a future in which people of all views on Israel/Palestine can express themselves freely in Hillel and other Jewish communal spaces; learn from each other; and challenge one another. We believe in a Jewish community that is deeply engaged with the most pressing political and social justice issues of our day, and that welcomes rather than silences divergent perspectives ...

We believe that free discourse, even on difficult subjects, is essential in the context of an educational institution and a democratic society; and that open discussion and debate are core Jewish values. We are proud of our culture's long tradition of encouraging the expression of multiple, and sometimes contradictory, views and arguments.[106]

There's another reason to agree with the Open Hillel students. As we've seen in this chapter, and elsewhere in this book, the binary nature of the Israel/Palestine debate is having a toxic impact on the campus. There are strong senses of identity and perceptions of justice on each side. Each side tends to define the other as not only misinformed, but hateful and dangerous. My group or your group (and your group undercuts my right to an identity)? Who will win and who will lose? That's the binary. That's what SJP's anti-normalization relies on. So, you'd think, Jewish groups would be smart enough to know they shouldn't jump in this game and play by these rules. They'll lose.

One of the smartest parts of AJC when I was on staff was its Project Interchange program. It took leaders (from government, from campus, from religious and ethnic groups, and others) to Israel and the West Bank, and exposed them to a wide range of voices, from right-wing settlers to left-wing and Palestinian groups that would now likely fail Hillel's guideline test.

People returned, not necessarily changing their view of the equities of the conflict. That wasn't the goal. They came back understanding that the conflict is complicated, that there are competing narratives and interests and perspectives. They see that while one may have good reasons to allocate more justice to one side or the other, it's not 100 per cent black/white or good/bad, and certainly not easy.

Hillel should have enough respect for its students to explain to its funders why voices considered hateful of Israel shouldn't be excluded but rather sought out. Some might not come if invited – again, SJP's rules on "normalization." But some will, and it is best to help students explore the complexities of Jewish life and issues of Israel on campus.

Or Hillel can say it is no longer a big tent for Jewish students who want to wrestle with all things Jewish as they are becoming young adults, and it instead is yet another pro-Israel advocacy organization. But it can't have it both ways. Its funders might prefer the latter, but if the goal is to keep Jewish students connected with their Jewishness, this is a fool's path. In fact, Hillel's guidelines are helping the Jewish community alienate the next generation of Jewish students *from* the Jewish community. A Stanford University study of five California universities concluded that Jewish students felt pressured to declare a stand – pro-Israel activist or pro-Palestinian activist. Many concluded it would be better, if that's the choice, to avoid the campus Jewish community altogether.[107]

One of the great connectors of Jewish identity is Jewish summer camp. But the question of support for Israel now threatens that too. You'd think Camp Ramah – a Jewish summer camp affiliated with the Conservative movement – would encourage its campers who are associated with IfNotNow, a Jewish student group highly critical of Israel's policies, to participate in camp discussions about Israel, as they requested. After all, campers are going to go to college and hear things about Israel that they might find disturbing. What better way to talk about that than with young Jews who obviously care about Israel and Ramah? The camp leadership refused: "Ramah will not partner with any organization that is not unequivocally pro-Israel," its director wrote.[108]

I grew up in the era when the famed Israeli diplomat Abba Eban quipped, "The Arabs never miss an opportunity to miss an opportunity" (often misquoted as "The Palestinians never miss an opportunity to miss an opportunity").[109] You can say the same today about many mainstream Jewish groups, and the campus.

chapter seven

The Antisemitism Awareness Act

There is no doubt that many would find the expression outlined in the examples [in the definition of antisemitism] to be gravely offensive. But one foundational principle of First Amendment jurisprudence, reinforced in decisions dating back decades, is that speech does not lose protection simply because some, many, or even all find it offensive.

Foundation for Individual Rights in Education, 22 May 2015[1]

In the prologue, I mentioned a 2011 op-ed I co-authored with Cary Nelson, then president of the American Association of University Professors, cautioning about the abuse of a definition of antisemitism to chill pro-Palestinian campus expression. The Jewish communal promotion of this definition for campus application continues as of this writing. It poses one of the most significant threats to the campus today, and to Jewish students and faculty.

Here's how the definition came about.

After the collapse of the Israeli-Palestinian peace process in the summer of 2000, attacks against Jews in Western Europe escalated. Synagogues were torched. Jews were assaulted. Cemeteries were desecrated. The hate crimes and terroristic acts continued, and while Jewish communities felt increasingly vulnerable, the political leaders in many European countries prevaricated. I recall a meeting with one European official who said that the problem would be solved when peace comes to the Middle East. Was he willing for Jews to be attacked until then? Why did he not see protecting citizens from violence as a basic police function?

The attacks persisted, and in 2003 the European Monitoring Centre on Racism and Xenophobia (EUMC) refused to release a report
on antisemitism it had commissioned from two German scholars,
allegedly because it showed that Jews were not only being attacked
by the traditional culprits–neo-Nazis and other white supremacists–
but also by Arab and Muslim youth. Ultimately the report was
leaked,[2] then released, and the following year, the EUMC issued a
new report,[3] documenting what we all knew was true, that some
of the attacks were by young Muslims and Arabs.

This EUMC 2004 report had other problems. Its authors noted the
challenge of gathering data on antisemitism. How did the people
tasked with collecting information in each of these European countries
know what to include and to exclude? Most countries didn't have a
definition of antisemitism, and those that did had differing ones.

Working around this challenge, the EUMC report concluded that
antisemitism was a collection of stereotypes about Jews. While there
is some justification for this approach (attitudinal surveys historically have inquired about such views), it is intellectually backwards –
the stereotypes are derived from what antisemitism is rather than
its defining characteristics.

I sensed the report had gone out of its way to talk about stereotypes because of a political problem: What should a monitor do if
a Jew on the streets of a European city was attacked as a stand-in
for an Israeli? The report concluded that if the actor believed those
stereotypes about Jews, applied them to Israelis, and then attacked
the Jew in front of him as a stand-in, then that could be counted as
antisemitism. But if he was upset about an Israeli action, and took
it out on the Jew in front of him, while lamentable, that could not
be counted as an act of antisemitism.

That made no more sense than saying if a black person was
lynched in the Deep South in the 1960s and the mob with the rope
thought blacks shiftless and lazy, then that could be a racist crime,
but if the mob's act of terror was in reaction to the passage of civil
rights legislation, then that would not be a racist crime.

Later that spring, Beate Winkler, the head of the EUMC, spoke
at the annual meeting of the American Jewish Committee. Just
weeks before, a Montreal Jewish school had been firebombed, on

the eve of Passover. The assailant attacked the building because he was upset that Israel had assassinated a leader of Hamas.[4] I politely but firmly confronted Winkler. Are you saying, based on your definition, that the firebombing of synagogues as revenge for Israel's actions shouldn't be counted among acts of antisemitism? She agreed to work with me and my AJC colleagues, particularly Rabbi Andrew Baker, to figure out if there was a better approach. Andy did the follow-up political work with Winkler. I set out to draft a definition and to get leaders in the field on board.

Over the next months, I drafted, redrafted, and coordinated with antisemitism scholars and experts from around the world, including Dina Porat of Tel Aviv University (who at a conference in Berlin earlier that year had been the first to suggest we come up with a definition); Mike Whine of the Community Security Trust in the UK; Jeremy Jones from the Australian Jewish community; Yehuda Bauer of Hebrew University; Michael Berenbaum (formerly of the US Holocaust Memorial Museum); AJC colleagues Deidre Berger and Felice Gaer; Ronnie Stauber of Tel Aviv University; and a few others.

The definition was not perfect; no definition could be. But it captured the essence of antisemitism: charging Jews with "conspiring to harm humanity [and blaming] Jews for 'why things go wrong.'"[5] The purpose of the definition, of course, was not to label anyone an antisemite but rather to guide data collectors, so they'd have a better sense of what to include and exclude. For example, what should be counted as an antisemitic hate crime? The definition wanted to avoid asking the data collector to look into the actor's mind, to see if he/she really hated Jews. After all, from time to time Jews were kidnapped or robbed because people thought all Jews were rich. Borrowing from the United States Supreme Court's hate crime case of *Wisconsin v. Mitchell*, the pertinent question was whether the victim was selected to be the target of a crime because he/she was, or was perceived to be, a Jew or linked to Jews. Thus, the firebombing of the Montreal Jewish school would be included. It was not required to look into the arsonist's heart to see what he really thought about Jews. It was enough that he intentionally selected a Jewish-linked property to be a victim of his criminal act, because it was Jewish.

Most difficult was the question of Israel. The main purpose of the definition was data collection. We wanted to have relevant data to compare over time. Events in the Middle East were clearly related to rises in antisemitic hate crime. I recall my UK colleague Mike Whine telling me he used to show two charts: one of the number of mentions of Israel in the UK press (frequently around a confrontation with Palestinians), and one of the number of antisemitic hate crimes in the UK. Superimposed, one over the other, they were nearly identical.

All of us involved in the drafting and negotiation realized that the definition had to be politically palatable for the EUMC to use it. In Berlin in 2004, the Organization for Security and Cooperation in Europe (OSCE) had declared that "international developments or political issues, including those in Israel or elsewhere in the Middle East, never justify Anti-Semitism."[6] We wanted the EUMC's definition to build on that observation.

The definition, noting that "criticism of Israel similar to that leveled against any other country cannot be regarded as antisemitic," states, in this section:

> Examples of the ways in which antisemitism manifests itself with regard to the State of Israel taking into account the overall context could include:
>
> - Denying the Jewish people their right to self-determination, e.g., by claiming that the existence of a State of Israel is a racist endeavor.
> - Applying double standards by requiring of it a behavior not expected or demanded of any other democratic nation.
> - Using the symbols and images associated with classic antisemitism (e.g., claims of Jews killing Jesus) to characterize Israel or Israelis.
> - Drawing comparisons of contemporary Israeli policy to that of the Nazis.
> - Holding Jews collectively responsible for actions of the State of Israel.[7]

Under the First Amendment to the United States Constitution, each of these statements is fully protected. But if the task at hand was to gauge relative levels of antisemitism from year to year, and from place to place, these examples were important. Certainly holding all Jews somehow responsible for the acts of Israel was germane to the targeting of Jews and Jewish institutions, like the Jewish school in Montreal.

The claim that Israel was doing to the Palestinians what the Nazis did to European Jews needed to be counted for two reasons: it diminished the significance of the Holocaust, and it demonized Israelis unfairly. However deplorable the Israeli treatment of Palestinians may be, the state's mission is not to track down Palestinians wherever they are and kill them or create factories to gas them.

Historically, antisemitism meant that a different standard was applied to Jews than to other peoples. It was not antisemitism to expect that Israel behave better than a totalitarian state, but it was relevant to the level of popular antisemitism if Israel was being asked to behave in ways not expected of any other democracy.*

---

* In reality, no two countries are the same, and there are legitimate reasons to take those variations into consideration. Israel is different from many other democracies in significant ways, including the facts that two peoples claim indigenous ties to the same land, that the country is located in the Middle East, and so on. It is not antisemitism to put Israel into a comparative context recognizing these and other complexities. Nor is it necessarily antisemitism if someone cares about this issue more than another. Perhaps someone is deeply concerned with Palestinians; perhaps they are Jewish and want the Jewish state to behave in ways they believe are more aligned with their understanding of "Jewish values." It is not antisemitism to focus on Israel's actions without first proclaiming they are equally concerned with similar issues in a list of other countries. What was of interest for data collection was, for example, the idea that Israel should allow its citizens to be attacked when no other democracy would tolerate such violence.

Double standards are not unusual in college or in political advocacy, and need not reflect bigotry. Vietnam-era protestors, horrified at the actions of the US government, weren't required to complain about other countries too. Most people advocating freedom for Soviet Jewry in the 1980s weren't also organizing rallies for Tibetan or Chinese dissidents. The 1950s civil rights activists, working to end segregation, usually weren't calling out human rights violations in the Soviet Union (the failure to do so was precisely the complaint of some anti-communists, including some segregationists). Is it possible that antisemitism is in play when people who say they care about Palestinians are vocal when Israel is seen as their victimizer, but ignore Palestinian deaths by others (such as in Jordan or Syria)? Yes. (We certainly saw examples of that in Durban, where discussion of racism worldwide was derailed by hatred of Israel and of Jews.) But it is also possible that people care more about perceived attacks from an "outgroup" than from within an "ingroup."

The trope seemed to be transferred from the Jew as an individual to the Jewish state.

Most challenging was the equation of anti-Zionism with anti-semitism. Recall that in 1975 the United Nations had called Zion-ism racism, and Jews were discriminated against because of that. In 1991, the United Nations rescinded that definition, but as we saw in chapter 4, at the UN's World Conference against Racism in 2001, the equation was functionally reasserted. If the Jewish quest for self-determination, alone among those of the peoples of the world, is defined as racist, then a "logical" conclusion is that the Jewish state has no right to exist; in fact, people then have justifica-tion to call for the destruction of Israel, and the Jews in it.

It was the attempt to rekindle the Zionism = racism charge, and the antisemitism at Durban and its aftermath, that made the inclu-sion of anti-Zionism in the definition appropriate. There was, and is, a clear correlation between the normalization of the view that Jews alone don't have a right to self-determination with the level of antisemitism in Europe.

After a series of negotiations, the EUMC adopted the definition as a "working definition." It would have been difficult to have the EUMC officially adopt it, but to try it out, use it as a working defi-nition made sense.

It also had other applications. Around the same time, I worked with law enforcement expert Paul Goldenberg as we created a police train-ing program for the OSCE on hate crimes. The idea of illegal selec-tion (rather than bias motive) was at the core of our training, which included a cadre of police officials from Europe, the United States, and Canada. The "working definition" was part of the police training.

I also encouraged members of parliaments who attended con-ferences on antisemitism in London and in Ottawa to try and insti-tutionalize the definition in their own countries. And in the United States, I suggested to Gregg Rickman, the first special envoy of the Department of State on Antisemitism (under President George W. Bush) and Hannah Rosenthal (his successor under President Barack Obama) that they utilize the definition in the US's bilateral and multilateral relations. Rickman used the definition as a frame-work for one of his office's reports on antisemitism, and Rosenthal trained US diplomats on it. So rather than just bemoan antisemitism in a particular country, now diplomats could point to a text and explain it.

In 2010 the United States Department of State adopted a slightly altered, somewhat broader version of the "working definition."[8] That same year (30 August to 2 September 2010), Dina Porat – who first suggested a definition – convened a conference in Paris to evaluate the "working definition," five years after its implementation. The conference, which I attended, hosted several speakers on the subject.

In my remarks, I found much to praise, but one deeply troubling abuse. Some pro-Israel activists were trying to use it to counter speech they didn't like about Israel on college campuses, bastardizing what it was intended to do. My concern, at the time, was more that the abuses would give ammunition to those who didn't like the definition and were trying to undermine its proper uses, rather than the destructive impact on campus. I said:

> Two months ago a group of American Jewish organizations from the right side of the political spectrum wrote a letter to the president of the major university system. They complained about a series of antisemitic incidents on his campuses, prejudged a system the president had set up to tackle the problem as inadequate, and asked that he "issue a written statement to the entire University … community which: unequivocally condemns all forms of antisemitism … including language or behavior that demonizes or delegitimizes Israel, as per the 'Working Definition of Antisemitism,'" which they then quoted. They additionally demanded that campus policy language be changed to define antisemitism according to the Working Definition, and that such policy language "singles out antisemitism from other forms of bigotry and discrimination and provides clear guidelines for the prosecution of antisemitic behavior."
>
> The problems with this approach, using the definition in a way it was never intended, and with the subtlety of a mallet, are real. First, on a campus – at least in the US – hateful statements of opinion (as distinguished from harassment or acts of physical destruction or violence) are allowed. I can say I think Israel is Nazi-like, and shouldn't have to

worry about being prosecuted. If the campus is working well, promoting critical thinking, there should be voices pushing back showing why this is an inappropriate comparison, and of course using the definition in making that case is a fine thing to do. But people, be they students, faculty, or outside speakers, should not get into trouble with the campus "criminal law" for saying such things.[9]

It didn't take long for the problem that was troubling me to get worse. These right-of-center pro-Israel groups found a way to weaponize the definition.

Title VI of the Civil Rights Act of 1964 protects people from severe harassment and discrimination in educational institutions. It, however, does not include religion as a protected category. In October 2010 the Department of Education issued a "Dear Colleague" letter,[10] noting that Title VI protections would be available to groups such as Jews, Sikhs, and Muslims when "harassment is based on the group's actual or perceived shared ancestry or ethnic characteristics, rather than solely on its members' religious practices." The Department of Education or the Department of Justice can enforce Title VI. In theory, a violation can lead to a school losing all federal funding. If that happened to a college or university, even a private one, it would likely have to close.

I supported this clarification by the Department of Education, and used it to help Jewish high school students in the Binghamton, New York, area. I filed a complaint on their behalf after they had been harassed and assaulted. They had been kicked (there was a "Kick a Jew Day") and bullied with "anti-Semitic remarks and gestures." The Department of Education sustained the complaint, and entered an agreement with the school district to remedy the problem.[11]

But these right-of-center Jewish groups had another idea. Why not marry the "working definition" with the new authority under Title VI and take legal action against universities? The cases they brought were not purely about expression. Some did include allegations of actions, such as spitting or shoving. And some speech that they objected to could be potentially problematic as threats. But the complaints, again and again, included allegations of political expression they believed should form the basis of a civil rights violation.

For example, it was alleged that a pro-Palestinian student group promoted Boycott, Divestment, and Sanctions against Israel, and that doing so was "an infringement of academic freedom as described by the [AAUP]. Said campaign is anti-Semitic according to the Working Definition."[12] That "professors, academic departments and residential colleges ... promote and encourage anti-Israel, anti-Zionist and anti-Jewish views and behavior, much of which is based on either misleading information or outright falsehoods [and] rhetoric heard in [classrooms] and at ... events sponsored and funded by academic units on campus [that go] beyond legitimate criticism of Israel."[13] That a program about the Occupation was "a platform for anti-Israel propaganda."[14] That a program "Understanding Gaza," caused Jewish students to feel "emotionally and intellectually threatened."[15] That readings for a class included "false statements designed to provoke hatred for the Jewish State."[16] That "three of the articles in [a class's] recommended texts were not only unambiguously one-sided and anti-Israel, but contained material defined as anti-Semitic by the US State Department."[17] That an invited speaker "inflame[d] the audience against Israel."[18] That a program on "Arabs and the Holocaust: A History of Competing Narratives" alleged that Israel's founding was a "tragedy" for Palestinian Arabs.[19] That a film on the Occupation was shown, and "the term 'occupation' is itself a propaganda tool used to promote hatred of Jews."[20] That a campus group co-sponsored a "Palestinian Culture Festival" that celebrated a "legacy of resistance," which is "code for the endorsement of ... murder of Israeli Jews."[21] That an "apartheid wall" was erected, "falsely representing the security fence that Israel has been forced to construct to protect innocent Israeli civilians from terrorists entering Israel."[22] That a "Never Again for Anyone" event was intentionally scheduled to coincide with Holocaust Remembrance Day.[23]

If I were a pro-Israel student on one of these campuses, I might be disturbed by some of the anti-Israel ideas, and the forceful manner by which they were communicated. But the intent of the Title VI cases was clear. Tammi Rossman-Benjamin, a lecturer who filed a Title VI case, admitted that her argument was that "Jewish students ... deserve to be protected from antisemitic hate speech."[24] No one likes hateful speech. But Rossman-Benjamin's definition of what was hateful was overly broad, and in any event, campus speech that is antisemitic (or racist or homophobic) is expression, and thus allowed. What are prohibited are intimidation and discrimination.

After Marc Stern's letter to the Hastings Law School wasn't sent (see above, on pages 117–18), and while the Title VI cases were pending, the abuse of the definition was discussed by AJC's Legal Committee. It insisted that the ZOA and Rossman-Benjamin and others on the Jewish Right shouldn't have a clear field in their attempt to misuse the "working definition" as a de facto hate speech code. The Legal Committee decided that AJC should speak out, and I volunteered to craft a statement, which was envisioned as an opinion piece, so it could have a wide impact.

I shared drafts internally, and externally – in particular with Cary Nelson, then president of the AAUP. Cary said he'd be happy to sign on to this statement, with some minor changes, and he volunteered to send it via email to thousands of academics through the AAUP. Professors were precisely our target audience. And having the statement come from both AJC and the president of AAUP gave it more credibility and gravitas.

The text was approved internally, and then released. Because it became so contentious, I present the entire op-ed here:

Antisemitism on Campus

Recently, there have been allegations of antisemitism at three universities – the University of California at Berkeley, the University of California at Santa Cruz, and Rutgers. Any claim of bigotry must be treated with the utmost seriousness, not only because hatred harms its victims, but also because it can undermine academic freedom: students become afraid to be who they are and thus say what they think. Conversely, a climate which values academic freedom can unleash the best responses to bigotry, by promoting critical thinking and clear ideas.

Yet some, in reaction to these recent incidents, are making the situation worse by distorting the provisions of Title VI of the Civil Rights Act of

1964, and what has been called the "working definition of antisemitism." Opposing anti-Israel events, statements, and speakers, they believe the only way to "protect" Jewish students is by imposing censorship.

There has been a debate in recent years about whether Title VI, which prohibits discrimination on the basis of race, color or national origin in federally-funded programs, extends to Jewish students when antisemitic intimidation or harassment is directed at them based on the perception of ethnic, as opposed to religious, identity. In October 2010, the Office for Civil Rights of the Department of Education issued a letter clarifying that in certain limited contexts, antisemitic behavior or intimidation (the letter gave examples of swastika daubings and Jew-baiting bullying) is clearly based on a perception of ethnicity or national origin and is therefore covered by Title VI. "Harassment" encompasses both "different treatment" and the "existence of a racially hostile environment," meaning that the offending conduct is so severe or pervasive that, in order to continue their education, a student has to suffer an educational environment that a reasonable person would consider intimidating, hostile, or abusive.

While some of the recent allegations (such as charging pro-Israel Jewish students admission to a university event while allowing others to attend for free) might well raise a claim under Title VI, many others seek to silence anti-Israel discourse and speakers. This approach is not only unwarranted under Title VI, it is dangerous.

Six years ago the European Monitoring Centre on Racism and Xenophobia (EUMC) created a "working definition" of antisemitism. Some European countries had no definition of antisemitism, and the few which did had different ones, so it was very difficult for monitors and data collectors to know what to include or exclude. The "working definition," while clearly stating that criticism of Israel in the main is not antisemitic, gives some examples of when antisemitism may be in play, such as holding Jews collectively responsible for acts of the Israeli state, comparing Israeli policy to that of the Nazis, or denying to Jews the right of self-determination (such as by claiming that Zionism is racism). In recent years the US Department of State and the US Commission on Civil Rights have embraced this definition too.

It is entirely proper for university administrators, scholars and students to reference the "working definition" in identifying definite or possible instances of antisemitism on campus. It is a perversion of the definition to use it, as some are doing, in an attempt to censor what a professor, student, or speaker can say. Because a statement might be "countable" by data collectors under the "working definition" does not therefore mean that Title VI is violated. To assert this not only contravenes the definition's purpose (it was not drafted to label anyone an antisemite or to limit campus speech), it also harms the battle against antisemitism.

The purpose of a university is to have students wrestle with ideas with which they may disagree, or even better, may make them uncomfortable. To censor ideas is to diminish education, and to treat students as fragile recipients of "knowledge," rather than young critical thinkers. When the disquieting ideas are bigoted, it is incumbent on others on campus to speak out. University leadership should say something when appropriate too (not in every instance, because its role is not to be a quality control on campus debate).

Universities can do many other things to combat bigotry, from surveying students to see if and how they are experiencing bigotry, to offering courses on why and how people hate, to bringing in outside scholars and others to speak on relevant topics. Title VI is a remedy when university leadership neglects its job to stop bigoted harassment of students; it is not a tool to define "politically correct" campus speech.

Antisemitism should be treated with the same seriousness as other forms of bigotry. But one should not, for instance, suggest that a professor cannot make an argument about immigration simply because some might see any such argument as biased against Latino students. Nor was Title VI crafted with the notion that only speakers who are "safe" should be allowed on campus.

By trying to censor anti-Israel remarks, it becomes more, not less, difficult to tackle both antisemitism and anti-Israel dogma. The campus debate is changed from one of exposing bigotry to one of protecting free speech, and the last thing pro-Israel advocates need is a reputation for censoring, rather than refuting, their opponents.

The "working definition" is a useful tool to identify statements that merit attention on campus, but deciding whether a given remark is antisemitic can require careful attention to rhetoric, context, and even intent. As the AAUP has suggested, even objectionable statements can have content worthy of debate. Most individual remarks, moreover, do not rise to the level of creating hostile environments.[25]

The pushback against this op-ed was swift and vociferous. Publicly and privately, right-wing activists saw the piece as treachery. Why, they asked, should we advocate taking away what they claimed was a tool to protect Jewish students? I explained privately (I wasn't allowed to speak publicly) that the definition was put in danger by this abuse, but more importantly using it this way harmed Jewish students. Pro-Israel students can answer or expose anti-Israel speech. But if Jewish organizations are suppressing it, it says that they can't answer it.

One person asked if I was religious and said that if I were, I should atone for the op-ed on Yom Kippur.

AJC, under pressure from at least one major funder and from a relentless email campaign from the Jewish Right, eventually withdrew from the joint letter.

I left AJC a few years later, and in the interim, all these Title VI cases lost. While upset with this result, Kenneth Marcus of the Brandeis Center, one of the key proponents of using Title VI in this way, was honest enough to say that even when the cases failed, they had what he believed was a positive result, forcing administrators to deal with "bad publicity," and by making it more difficult for those he called "Israel-haters" to "recruit new adherents ... Needless to say," he wrote, "getting caught up in a civil rights complaint is not a good way to build a resume or impress a future employer."[26]

In March 2015, twenty-three Jewish groups wrote to the University of California president Janet Napolitano, urging that the UC system adopt and apply the State Department definition to its campuses.[27] They said that antisemitic incidents such as "swastikas drawn on a Jewish fraternity house at UC Davis and the inappropriate questioning of a candidate for [the] student judiciary board about her Jewishness and Jewish affiliations at UCLA" were "an inevitable consequence of pervasive anti-Israel activity, particularly Boycott, Divestment, Sanctions (BDS) campaigns, being promoted on UC campuses."[28] The letter, of course, didn't explain why anyone would need a definition to recognize the problems with a swastika on a building or discriminatory questions to a Jewish student.

Napolitano said she agreed with the definition, and that the Regents would vote in July whether to apply it to the UC system.[29] I presumed that Napolitano had no idea of the reason behind this push for formal adoption (the lost Title VI cases that complained about pro-Palestinian speech), and I felt reasonably confident that colleagues in the Jewish communal world who believed, as I did, that the application of the definition would be harmful to the campus and interests of Jewish students would likely not speak out. So I did. By this time I had become the executive director of the Justus & Karin Rosenberg Foundation.

I wrote an op-ed for the Los Angeles *Jewish Journal*, outlining the history of the definition, and underscoring that while antisemitism was of course a concern, institutionalizing the definition would be harmful and invite violations of academic freedom and free speech.[30] I pointed out that one of the organizers of the letter to Napolitano (Tammi Rossman-Benjamin) had stated that BDS violated the definition, so administrators would be pressured to act against political speech that she found offensive, including the erection of mock walls replicating Israel's separation barrier.[31]

The question wasn't whether some of the pro-Palestinian speech was disturbing to Jewish students, or that I might tend to agree with those Jewish students and be disturbed too. The question was whether the university should adopt a definition knowing it would be used to identify and chill, and likely to suppress and censor, political expressions. The whole point of the hundreds of presidents who signed on to the statement AJC organized about the campus in 2002 was that the problem to be addressed was harassment and intimidation, not expression. But now the agenda seemed to be creating a weapon to empower the hunting of "wrong" political speech.

Additionally, I wrote to Napolitano[32] and co-authored an op-ed in the *San Francisco Chronicle*, urging that the definition not be adopted as official policy. I also pointed to other things the university system could and should do against antisemitism and all forms of hatred, things that were consistent with academic freedom, many of which were based on the Bigotry on Campus training program.[33]

In March 2016 the UC System adopted a set of principles on intolerance. While mentioning antisemitism and "anti-semitic forms of anti-zionism," it did not adopt the definition.[34] If it had, other systems would likely have been pressured to do so too.

Now the groups – particularly Kenneth Marcus's Brandeis Center – tried another, bolder approach: asking Congress to adopt the definition and apply it to the campus.

In December 2016, the United States Senate unanimously passed the Antisemitism Awareness Act. It would have required reference to the definition when either the Department of Justice or the Department of Education was investigating Title VI cases claiming discrimination against or harassment of Jews. There was speculation that it would sail through the House of Representatives too.

I was concerned. For this bill to pass unanimously suggested it was seen as uncomplicated and uncontroversial. Who would be against opposing antisemitism? I immediately wrote to members of the House, to give them the background to this bill, and to argue that it was neither consistent with academic freedom and free speech nor something that would be effective in countering campus antisemitism – in fact, quite the opposite.[35]

An editor from the *New York Times* asked me to write about the legislation and why it was a bad idea.[36] The day before it was to appear in print (it was posted online), the House said it would not take up the legislation before the session ended, and it would have to be reintroduced during the next Congress.

In 2017 I was invited to two meetings hosted by House Judiciary Chairman Bob Goodlatte, a Republican from Virginia. He wanted to hear from a few proponents and opponents of the legislation. We all agreed that the "Dear Colleague" letter should be institutionalized in legislation, so Jewish and Muslim and Sikh students would be protected in the future. Right after the meeting I suggested to Kenneth Marcus, who also participated, that he and I and others could write a guide on antisemitism that could be used for Title VI purposes. That wasn't satisfactory for him. He and his colleagues were insistent upon formal adoption of the definition.

Chairman Goodlatte held a hearing on campus antisemitism before the full Judiciary Committee in November of 2017. I was asked to testify. I said that antisemitism was, of course, a concern, and I had seen such a campus. I recounted how a Jewish student at the Evergreen State College in Washington state had been harassed and bullied, his pro-Israel flyers defaced or destroyed, how other students intentionally bumped into him and made his life miserable. I had offered to meet him on campus, but he wouldn't for fear that being seen with an official of a Jewish organization would make his life worse. He wouldn't meet in a restaurant either – too risky. We met in a local synagogue.

But the law, as it stood, already protected students from such harassment. The legislation's backers were clear that their intention was broader – to restrict speech.

I told the story of the proponents' efforts to enact similar legislation in a few states, in particular South Carolina. A rabbi supporting the definition's formal adoption into that state's law had written:

> Genocide begins with words. It starts, almost imperceptibly, with careful characterization of a people as less than the rest of us. I remind everyone I meet that Adolf Hitler, as far as I know, never murdered anyone. All he did was speak. And through his carefully crafted words, he caused mass murder, unfathomable brutality and millions of deaths across the globe ... Is it really necessary to debate whether to decry anti-Semitism? I thought it would seem self-evident that inciting hatred has no place in America.[37]

A state lawmaker had tweeted the rabbi's piece, and Kenneth Marcus of the Brandeis Center had retweeted it, calling it "very important."[38]

I cited an article I had co-authored with former AAUP general secretary Ernst Benjamin against the South Carolina bill, in which we had answered the rabbi:

> The Holocaust was certainly driven by hateful ideas about Jews and others. But perhaps the rabbi should have considered that it was also made possible by the silencing of dissent, and official pronouncements of what thoughts were disapproved.

We are not drawing a parallel between this bill and Nazism. Some well-intentioned people, including the rabbi, are concerned – as we are – of the level of hate and antisemitism in the world today, and unfortunately on some campuses too.

But this legislation, like the proposed Anti-Semitism Awareness Act in Congress, is a hate speech code which, if enacted, will do much damage to the university and to the Jewish students proponents seek to protect.[39]

There was of course other evidence that the proponents desired to suppress speech. When the US Senate version had been introduced in 2016, they had argued that Jews don't receive the same protection as other groups. Two examples were cited: that a Marquette professor was suspended because of a blog post that was considered anti-gay, and that students at the University of Michigan stopped the showing of the movie *American Sniper* because it was alleged to be anti-Muslim.[40] Rather than see these instances as troubling violations of free speech and academic freedom, the bill's proponents said, protect us too.

It was telling that the people testifying for the legislation were representing off-campus interests, particularly pro-Israel groups, some of which had a track record of trying to censor campus speech they perceived as anti-Israel.[41] Jewish faculty, including the head of the Association for Jewish Studies, testified in opposition.*

If the legislation passed, I warned, Jewish studies professors would be worried that they could not teach effectively. They knew that outside groups, including the ones that had brought the failed Title VI cases, would be looking over their shoulders, hunting for statements and assignments and programs and classroom texts and invited speakers that they believed transgressed the definition. If your PhD is in nineteenth-century Jewish shtetl life, and you're going to get beat up for teaching about modern Israel, you'll

---

* While, as noted above, hundreds of college presidents signed statements in 2002 and 2007 against intimidation on campus and against academic boycotts. I'm aware of no college president, Jewish or not, signing statements saying the antisemitism definition should be applied to college campuses. This should give Jewish organizations pause.

likely choose to teach about older, less controversial, Jewish history instead.

Administrators would be influenced too. Imagine you know that off-campus groups would threaten to sue if you failed to suppress, or at least condemn, language allegedly contravening the definition. If that's how you were going to be evaluated – did you do things to diminish the chance that the university would be sued – you'd want to denounce pro-Palestinian speech that outside groups might find troubling. You wouldn't do the things that would actually help Jewish students like conducting campus surveys, encouraging curriculum expansion about antisemitism, and so forth, if condemnation of political speech was the only metric that mattered. This isn't just a theoretical concern. AMCHA's leader, for instance, referenced the definition, said that pro-Palestinian advocates, such as Omar Barghouti, had track records of violating that definition, and that administrators must "put a stop to this anti-Jewish bigotry and discrimination immediately. Jewish students' safety is at stake."[42] The Simon Wiesenthal Center applauded the use of the definition to stop an Israel Apartheid Week event at a university in the United Kingdom, and advocated that other universities[43] should do the same.*

In our small meetings, Chairman Goodlatte seemed particularly concerned with what I called the "Pandora's box" problem. In my written testimony I explained in great detail what might happen if the bill passed. I started with a statement from Cheryl Glantz Nail, community relations director for the Columbia Jewish Federation, who said, "Anti-Semitism is on the rise, [Jewish students] need to

---

* And such efforts continue. Three Jewish students sued the University of Massachusetts, Amherst, asking a state court to stop a campus program called "Not Backing Down: Israel, Free Speech, & the Battle for Palestinian Rights," scheduled to be held on 4 May 2019. The complaint included past statements attributed to the announced panelists (among them Linda Sarsour and Roger Waters) and asserted that "[m]uch of the ... speech engaged in by these panelists is in direct violation of the definition of anti-Semitism" (Hurvitz, "Verified Complaint for Declaratory and Injunctive Relief"). The request for an injunction was denied, with the judge saying, "I can't enjoin a forum just because someone may say something at that forum that fits someone's definition of antisemitism" (JNS.org, "Judge Dismisses Lawsuit to Stop Anti-Israel Event at U Mass Amherst").

be protected as do other students ... If this is passed, this could also be the gateway to other laws being put in place for other minority students."[44] I wrote:

> Let's imagine what that might look like. Imagine African American groups asking for a specific definition of racism for consideration under Title VI. Would it include opposition to affirmative action? Opposition to removing statues of Confederate leaders? Opposition to the agenda of Black Lives Matters? Saying something favorable about the scholarship of "Bell Curve" author Charles Murray? Imagine a definition designed for Palestinians. If "Denying the Jewish people their right to self-determination, and denying Israel the right to exist" is antisemitism, then shouldn't "Denying the Palestinian people their right to self-determination, and denying Palestine the right to exist" be anti-Palestinianism? Would they then ask administrators to police and possibly punish campus events by pro-Israel groups who oppose the two-state solution, or claim the Palestinian people are a myth? How about a definition for Hispanic students? Would calling for a border wall and stepped up deportations be included? Or a definition to "protect" Muslim students. Would support for a travel ban be a listed item? Or let's consider definitions to protect Armenian students and Turkish students. The former might include being supportive of the Turkish government, or denying the Armenian genocide, as items to consider. The latter would certainly say that if one says there was an Armenian genocide, that is an example of being anti-Turk. One can but imagine the debates between communities, let alone between differing groups inside a particular community, about what a definition should include and exclude. Add to that the fact that indicia of bigotry change over time.[45]

Chairman Goodlatte picked up on this last point, when he questioned my former AJC colleague Andy Baker, who had said antisemitism changes over time, and thus a definition was needed. Chairman Goodlatte pointed out that if it changes over time, then that's a reason not to enshrine a definition into law. Imagine the continual fights between and among different groups about what the formal definitions should be. Congress should, I argued, not be in this business.[46]

But there was another reason to avoid the formal adoption of the definition. The Jewish groups pushing the legislation were concerned, as I was, about instances of harassment of pro-Israel Jewish students and faculty. But in preparing to testify I discovered that there were instances of Jews being harassed for what was perceived as their anti-Israel view. I wrote:

> [A] Columbia University professor who teaches about Israel … received an email on September 7, 2016, referring to him as a "KAPO piece of s**t." Likewise a Jewish Barnard student informed me … that "during a Simchat Torah celebration hosted by Barnard/Columbia Hillel this year, students began singing Hatikvah. Several students stepped outside of the circle (not wanting to participate in singing the Israeli national anthem) and another student yelled "F**k you kapos!" The Jewish Virtual Library defines "Kapo" as concentration camp "trustees [who] carried out the will of the Nazi camp commandants and guards … Some of these Kapos were Jewish …"
>
> Further, we have seen instances where students seen by others as "progressive" … have been harassed and threatened, by other Jews. Last May, at the University of California – Irvine, former Israeli Defense Forces soldiers visited the campus and a Jewish student told me he was "repeatedly told as a Jewish student that I am not a real Jew, that I don't deserve to be Jewish given my support for Palestinian rights, and that I should take off my kippah." Also last year, at the University of California – Santa Barbara, a Jewish student, who supported a divestment resolution, was called a "token Jew," and said he was "harassed … multiple times throughout the year for not wearing a kippah [because I wore a kippah during the hearing] and called … a fake Jew for not wearing one … [A]t the hearing [an official with a campus Jewish organization] explicitly said that Jews in favor of divestment could not call themselves Jews doing what we were doing."[47]

The question of whether Jewish identity today requires (or perhaps is most informed by) support for Israel is a difficult question. It has much to do with the parameters of the ingroup and outgroup, who is a traitor, and so forth.[48] This internal debate is complicated. Most Jews would say Satmar Jews, who have a theological objection to Zionism, are part of the Jewish family. But Jews who might have other theological objections to Zionism (because they can't square Zionism with their interpretation of what it means to be a Jew and how the stranger should be treated, for instance), or ideological objections, are called traitors, antisemites, self-hating, even "kapos."

I am a Zionist, I told the committee. I don't know how this internal debate should be decided, or even if it can. But one thing I knew – Congress shouldn't be deciding this issue, and if it adopted the definition, it would. Jewish students who were pro-Israel would be protected more than they should be under the law from expressions that were anti-Israel, while harassment of pro-Palestinian Jewish students would be harder to prove.

I asked the Committee to think about the impact of the legislation on professors. We should want them to explore new ways to teach the complexities of the Israel/Palestine conflict. But the legislation would have the opposite incentive.

I testified that

some outside groups have filed online dossiers of professors they assert are anti-Israel, frequently based on such things as signing political statements against Israel. Through a shadowy website called Canary Mission, they are trying to impact the employment of faculty and students whom they target ... [C]lassroom texts and academic papers have been complained about in Title VI litigation. Armed with a congressional determination that effectively says campus anti-Zionism is antisemitism, these professors will correctly see themselves at risk when they ask their students to read and digest materials deemed anti-Zionist, whether the writings of leading 20th century Jewish thinkers who were skeptical of Zionism, such as Hannah Arendt and Martin Buber, or of contemporary Palestinians.

I stressed that

passage of this legislation might make some pro-Israel students feel better, that Congress agrees with them, but it will give ammunition to anti-Israel students saying that Congress has enshrined a definition that can only help to chill, if not suppress, their political speech. And they will be right. The EUMC's "working definition" was recently adopted in the

United Kingdom and applied to campus. An "Israel Apartheid Week" event was cancelled as violating the definition.[49] A Holocaust survivor was required to change the title of a campus talk, and the university mandated it be recorded, after an Israeli diplomat complained that the title violated the definition. Perhaps most egregious, an off-campus group citing the definition called on a university to conduct an inquiry of a professor (who received her PhD from Columbia) for antisemitism, based on an article she had written years before. The university then conducted the inquiry. And while it ultimately found no basis to discipline the professor, the exercise itself was chilling and McCarthy-like.[50]

I emphasized that all Jewish students should be protected from discrimination and pervasive harassment and intimidation. None should be protected from having to wrestle with ideas. That, after all, is what a college education is supposed to be about.

Despite the fact that some of the contemporary anti-Israel rhetoric is antisemitic, adoption of this definition would paint with much too broad a brush. Michael Oren's University of California, Irvine speech should not have been disrupted. But was this antisemitism? On many of today's campuses, allowing a Charles Murray or an Ann Coulter to speak is seen as being complicit in "verbal violence," and therefore such conservatives, it is argued, cannot be given a platform. Support for Israel is seen by many as a conservative position too. Was Oren shouted down because he was Jewish, or because he was seen as representing a conservative position?

Title VI does not, and should not, prohibit antisemitic expressions. Campuses should make sure that none of their students – Jews and non-Jews, pro-Israel and anti-Israel – is the victim of pervasive intimidation or harassment. That's quite different from protecting them from hearing unpleasant, and even bigoted, ideas.

I was indexing the pages of this chapter when President Trump signed an executive order[51] at the 2019 White House Chanukah party, adopting the definition for Title VI purposes. Compared to an act passed by Congress and signed into law by the president, an executive order can be more easily amended or undone by a president in the future. But it still has the force of law.

Why this route? Perhaps because the legislation seemed stalled in Congress. Yet Kenneth Marcus, now an official at the Department of Education, had already made clear he was going to use the definition,[52] so why the rush? Some speculated President Trump was trying to court Jewish voters. Perhaps. But the more fundamental reason might be that the antisemitism definition in whatever form – the original EUMC "working definition," the Department of State version, or the almost identical International Holocaust Remembrance Alliance's iteration – has become a sacred symbol for much of the Jewish community. As we saw earlier in this book, it is difficult to have a rational policy discussion when a sacred symbol tied to your identity and well-being is seen as under attack.

The president's son-in-law and senior advisor, Jared Kushner, writing in the *New York Times*, said the order was "meaningful action to crush th[e] evil [of antisemitism],"* doing so by "adopt[ing a] definition of anti-Semitism ... [that] makes clear what our administration has stated publicly and on the record: Anti-Zionism is anti-Semitism."[53]

Decrying anti-Zionism at the UN or in bilateral relations or recognizing it for data collection is one thing; declaring anti-Zionism

---

* I found the imagery at the party where the executive order was signed deeply disturbing. If the celebration was to highlight an effort to combat antisemitism, why were the Jewish leaders there silent about the president's repeated use of antisemitic tropes? Recall that his campaign ads were tinged with antisemitic images and that he continues to use stereotypes about Jews and money. Recall that he had kind words for participants at the Charlottesville rally despite their Nazi flags. Even more troubling than what the president has said about Jews, he and his administration are dividing Americans by race, ethnicity, and religion. Historically, when leaders gain support by pointing to enemies within, antisemitism is likely to increase, even flourish. Jewish groups instinctively know this. But when the person creating the danger is seen as the most pro-Israel president in recent memory, he seemingly gets a pass on antisemitism at the exact moment leaders have his ear. The Jewish leaders in the room praised President Trump for an order that will chill Israel-related campus speech they find offensive. But at that same moment their silence spoke louder. They were conveniently forgetting that the year before, as Trump was repeatedly and energetically denouncing brown-skinned people as "invaders" coming over our southern border, Robert Bowers decided he had to act. Seeing Jews as behind a conspiracy to harm white people, he walked into the Tree of Life synagogue in Pittsburgh and murdered eleven of us. Why didn't the Jewish leaders plead with Trump to stop demonizing and dehumanizing other human beings?

as antisemitic for campus application can only chill speech. As I wrote in *The Guardian* after the order was issued, "I'm a Zionist. But on a college campus, where the purpose is to explore ideas, anti-Zionists have a right to free expression. I suspect that if Kushner or I had been born into a Palestinian family displaced in 1948, we might have a different view of Zionism, and that need not be because we vilify Jews or think they conspire to harm humanity."[54]

Inevitably, there will be litigation over the definition, either in reaction to a Department of Education case that references it, or against a state law that enshrines it (such legislation has been enacted in South Carolina and Florida and is being promoted in New Jersey).[55] In the appropriate case, FIRE or the ACLU or Palestine Legal or the Center for Constitutional Rights or a campus administration or someone else will argue that the right of free expression has been abridged. Regardless of the legal outcome, the real damage will have been done. Newly empowered by the executive order, right-wing Jewish groups will step up their efforts, scouring campuses for expressions they believe violate the definition, and asking university administrators to stop the speech, or at least condemn it publicly. The toxicity of the Israel/Palestine debate will increase, pro-Israel Jews will get a reputation for shutting down speech they don't like, professors – especially those without tenure – will avoid teaching about contemporary Israel, and the academy as a whole will suffer.

chapter eight

Blueprint for Rational Campus Discussion on Israel and Palestine

The invitation by an academic center on a college campus ... does not constitute either legitimation or endorsement. [Extremists] are a reality of modern political life. We cannot pretend they do not exist. We need to hear what their representatives claim directly so that they can be properly challenged.

Bard College president Leon Botstein[1]

[R]ationality is generally served by broader and more comprehensive frames, and joint evaluation is obviously broader than single evaluation ... [C]omparative judgment, which necessarily involves system 2, is more likely to be stable than single evaluations, which often reflect the intensity of emotional responses of system 1.

Daniel Kahneman[2]

How can the campus dynamic around Israel/Palestine be changed? After all this is an issue that should be ideal for teaching critical thinking, the value of justice, the role of hate, and so many other important ideas. As we've seen, outside actors on both sides of the conflict are having a destructive impact on the campus and its mission, frequently doing things out of zealotry and self-righteousness that also undermine their stated goals. Let's start there, with the pro-Israel side. Below are some suggested rules and examples.

Don't confuse feeling good with being smart.

There is no question, as we saw in the last chapter, that there has been a toxic environment for pro-Israel students at the Evergreen State College in Olympia, Washington. I understand why some in the Seattle/Tacoma/Olympia Jewish community were upset with the level of anti-Israel organizing. The local food co-op had even voted to remove the few Israeli products from its shelves. But when an anti-Israel group was about to run advertisements on Seattle buses that read "Israeli War Crimes: Your Tax Dollars at Work,"[3] my AJC colleagues and I suggested the community ignore them. Seattle was a large city, the advertisement was to run on a handful of buses, for a very short time. Few people would see them.

But there's a sense in the Jewish community – as reflected in the comments of the South Carolina rabbi who is quoted in the previous chapter – that words of course have consequences, and ignoring them is dangerous. That's true. It's also true that a useful barometer of any hateful ideology is whether it is on the margins or in the mainstream. The temptation to suppress speech derives in part from this observation. It is a desire to force speech that was formerly considered taboo back to that status.

But efforts to suppress are no more than treating the symptoms. They don't address the dynamics that make the expression more acceptable in the first place. And even in the few instances where suppression might have the desired impact (such as the Battle of Cable Street in the UK in 1936, when Jews and communists and anarchists and socialists violently confronted British fascists in order to stop a planned march and demonstrate a mass rejection of the fascists and their ideology), there were reasons to think that strategy might work.

In Seattle, to the best of my knowledge, there was no such analysis. Anti-Israel speech was not to be ignored, period, and thus pressure was put on the city to reject the ads. The rhetoric became so heated that the city was concerned its bus drivers and passengers could be endangered. It rescinded approval for the ads.

Litigation followed. The Jewish community was seen as trying to suppress speech, and as somewhat thuggish. The stated goal of those who organized against the ads – that people shouldn't see them for fear of being influenced (recall the media bias discussion in chapter 1) – not only wasn't achieved, the opposite result was. Few people would have read the ads if they had been allowed to appear on the buses. Instead, the ads were shown on the evening news and on the front pages of the newspapers. While the city's refusal to allow the ads was ultimately sustained because of the rules pertaining to speech and ads on buses,[4] I'm reasonably confident that the small group that wanted to place the ads was pleased with the outcome. They received hundreds of thousands of dollars of free publicity for their message, and they were able to paint themselves as having their rights to political speech suppressed by activists for Israel.

But I could be wrong. The pro-Israel groups, despite the free publicity they gave to their anti-Israel adversaries, might feel they were ultimately vindicated by the courts, which refused to force the city to run the ads, and the anti-Israel groups might feel they were let down by the judicial system.

There's an almost childlike reverence of authority taking place, as if two siblings are arguing and each wants the parent to approve their actions and disapprove the other's. These instincts – to have the authority figure ratify your strongly held views, and to chill speech you find offensive – are on full display on the college campus, particularly over Israel and Palestine. Along with these strong emotions comes a lack of clear thinking.

Recall in chapter 5, that the ADL's initial response to the proposed UK boycott of Israel academics was to say if you're going to boycott Israel, we might ask American academics to boycott you. That instinct – tit for tat – is understandable, until you stop, think, and realize you're giving away your own argument: that academic boycotts are anathema.

One day at AJC, I received a call from the director of a Jewish Federation in New England. He phoned because he knew I had organized hundreds of university presidents to endorse Columbia University president Lee Bollinger's 2007 statement opposing the academic boycott of Israel. The president of a university in the Federation director's state had signed the statement. There was to be a new program, to bring professors from around the world to this campus to meet with its faculty. One of the newly appointed co-directors was on the board of the US Campaign for the Academic and Cultural Boycott of Israel.

The Federation director told me that a group of Jewish alumni was about to go public with a demand: the university must rescind the appointment. If it didn't, these alums would stop supporting their alma mater, and encourage others to refuse to donate too. The Federation director wanted to double-check that the president of this university was indeed a signer of the Bollinger statement, because his group wanted to accuse the president of going back on his word. I asked the Federation director to hold off, and give me a few days to see what I could do.

I reached out to the leadership of the university, and explained the situation. I told them, in no uncertain terms, they should *not* rescind the appointment. To do so would violate academic freedom. The person was appointed because the leadership of the university thought he had the qualifications for the job. His personal political position on Israel should not matter.

However, I stressed that the university – even without the president's agreement with the Bollinger statement – had an obligation not to discriminate, and that in this new administrative role, the co-director would have to agree with that policy.

The university leadership spoke with the co-director, who both maintained his personal position for the academic boycott of Israel, but also made clear – in a statement that would be issued by the university – that he would abide by its no discrimination, anti-boycott policy.

Imagine the damage if the alums, helped by a major Jewish Federation, were trying to get a professor fired from a position in the university because of his political views. The backlash would have been intense, and the Jewish groups would be seen as attacking academic freedom and free speech. Professors and others who had no concern about Israel, and even those who were pro-Israel, would have made this professor their cause. He would have been protecting *their* academic freedom and free speech rights.

Instead, by insisting that his personal views about Israel had no bearing on his fitness to hold this position at the university, a crisis was averted. He had to make the choice – did he want to advance his career by taking the position and promising to follow the university's anti-boycott position (thus embarrassing himself before his pro-boycott colleagues), or turn the job down? He chose the former.

When I told the Federation director what was about to happen (the university would soon release its statement with the co-director's promise to abide by the no-discrimination rules), I suggested he tell the alumni that rather than withhold contributions, they should increase them, and put the co-director to the test. Further, they should fund participation by Israeli academic experts, including those who had right-wing politics, in the program.

Jewish communal groups will continue to care about the campus, and try to impact how it approaches Israel. But as we saw in chapter 4, many think they know best yet make things worse. When the Alliance for Academic Freedom issues a statement about a campus-specific issue, it does its due diligence first – reaching out to faculty and others at the institution, to gain a better understanding of the situation, and whether a statement by AAF would be helpful. It's called being responsible.

Likewise, the group of Jewish professionals from different organizations who cooperated in the APHA, ASA, and MLA fights, saw their role as supportive. Our agenda was to help bring together the members of the groups who opposed the anti-Israel resolutions. Then THEY said what they needed from us. Someone once quipped that organizing faculty was like herding cats. Faculty members teach, write books, have administrative responsibilities, and have lives beyond the campus. If they wanted to work together to oppose an academic boycott, they needed help with call-in numbers for conference calls, research, advice from colleagues in other organizations who had gone through similar experiences, and so forth. The Jewish communal professionals with whom I worked in 2013 and 2014 wanted no credit for what they did, and none of us was dictating or defining what to do (other than stressing what faculty already understood – that to be successful, strategies had to be consistent with academic freedom). Our job was to help the members of the associations have capacity to do what THEY thought was important.

If more Jewish organizations saw their job as helping faculty who opposed boycotts and antisemitism, working quietly in the background and at the faculty's direction, taking no credit and asking "What do you need us to do to help you?" – much more could be accomplished.

Partisans on both sides of the Israel/Palestine conflict frequently profess they care about academic freedom. But it's academic freedom – but. Yes, pro-Israel groups will say, we support academic freedom – but opposing antisemitism (and/or anti-Israel animus) is more important. Yes, pro-Palestinian groups will say, we support academic freedom – but fighting for the rights of Palestinians is more important.

If a strategy explains academic freedom away, or diminishes it, the approach will not only fail but also it will harm the university's mission of teaching young adults how to think critically. And it will harm Jewish students.

N. Bruce Duthu is an associate dean and faculty member at Dartmouth College. He is an admired scholar in Native American studies, and widely respected by his faculty colleagues, among them Susannah Heschel, head of the Jewish studies program there. She wrote:

> Bruce helped me … with our student exchange program with Israeli universities, set up two courses per year on Israel [and brought] visiting faculty to teach at Dartmouth, including Hillel Cohen, director of the center for the study of Zionism at Hebrew University; Israel Yuval, a professor of medieval Jewish history at Hebrew University and director of Scholion and of the Hebrew U's humanities center; and Jeremy Cohen, a professor of medieval Jewish history at Tel Aviv University – all teaching at Dartmouth within the space of two years. In each case, Bruce arranged everything quickly and enthusiastically – and believe me, no dean has ever been as efficient and supportive. Plus, Bruce has been invited to lecture at Hebrew University and accepted with enthusiasm.[5]

In 2017 Dartmouth announced that Duthu would become the new dean of the faculty. Heschel was pleased, both because she liked and respected him and because of his tangible track record in support of Jewish studies. But it turns out that in 2013, when Duthu was on the executive committee of the small Native American and Indigenous Studies Association, he helped draft its statement in support of a boycott of Israel. When this became known, a huge controversy erupted. BDS has become a sacred symbol for pro-Israel Jews; context and nuance, let alone facts, become irrelevant. Despite Duthu's strong support from the Jewish studies faculty, his track record of bringing Israeli scholars to Dartmouth, his acceptance of an invitation to speak in Israel, a statement of support from the Alliance for Academic Freedom,[6] and that, in Heschel's words, "Truth: he is no boycotter"[7] – the pressure on him was so intense that he withdrew his acceptance of the deanship.

For some pro-Israel activists, on and off campus, any support of BDS is seen as blasphemy. Even an examination into the context of a BDS statement, or evidence that demonstrates its unimportance to the issue at hand, do not matter. Being strong in denouncing BDS is what's valued, it feels good. But viewing any entanglement with BDS as the equivalent of being a Nazi does no good; in fact, it can cause great damage.

Take risks, show leadership, demonstrate what debate looks like.

I was asked to speak at the Academic Engagement Network's 2017 conference in Chicago. AEN is an anti-BDS group of academics. A week later, I was debriefing with Kenneth Waltzer, AEN's executive director at the time. I told him, while I found the conference useful, there was a sense of unreality. Most of, if not all, the participants opposed BDS. But BDS was a straw man, a cartoon. Speaker after speaker were dismissing it, calling it hateful, disingenuous, ill-informed.

This was a group of academics. Wouldn't it have been useful, I asked Ken, if a BDS advocate had been invited? The AEN members could then react to what a BDS supporter says and to his/her arguments, rather than the illusion of what BDS opponents envision. I doubt AEN will ever do something like this, for the same reasons Hillel has its guidelines and SJP has its anti-normalization approach. To hear the other side, even just as firsthand evidence so you know more clearly what you are opposing, would both upset funders and make your opponents seem less detestable.

After I wrote the 2015 *Jewish Journal* op-ed saying the University of California system shouldn't adopt the antisemitism definition, Elizabeth Jackson called me. She is one of the top lawyers at Palestine Legal. We have communicated regularly since. She and I disagree a lot, as you might imagine. She supports BDS. I oppose it. But I value hearing her thoughts and analyses, and there are places where we agree. I am enriched by my conversations with her, and I hope she feels the same.

During my years at AJC, I would never have been able to develop such a relationship. There was a time when staff was told it couldn't even have contact with people from J Street. Of course there were Palestinian organizations with which we met from time to time, but they did not have stark differences with AJC's positions on Israel.

The Jewish community correctly criticizes various Christian groups for relying on Jewish Voice for Peace (JVP) to get a Jewish point of view, as if JVP is representative of the mainstream Jewish community. JVP is invited because it agrees with those Christian groups that lean towards or have endorsed BDS. But mainstream Jewish groups are only connecting with and hearing directly from Palestinian groups with which they largely agree too.

During the controversy over the John Mearsheimer and Stephen Walt essay and book *The Israel Lobby and US Foreign Policy*, when they essentially blamed pro-Israel groups for the war in Iraq, I suggested that AJC leadership invite them to speak to the AJC board. I argued that it would be good to hear these academics firsthand (and question them forcefully). Inviting them would accomplish something else. Walt and Mearsheimer were alleging that the pro-Israel forces were silencing people with their point of view. What better way to demolish that argument than to invite them to speak at a national Jewish agency?

That invitation was never extended. But imagine if, rather than a risk too difficult to take, advocacy groups had a culture of inviting real representatives of their opposition to speak to them firsthand? Yes, blood pressure would increase and decorum would have to be enforced. These would be difficult discussions. But some increased clarity would result. Imagine Dima Khalidi of Palestine Legal or her father, Rashid Khalidi, being given a half hour to explain their views in front of AJC or ADL? Imagine Jonathan Greenblatt of ADL or David Harris of AJC speaking to a pro-BDS pro-Palestinian group?

If these outside advocacy groups on either side of the conflict really cared about promoting thoughtful, difficult, nuanced discussions on campus, rather than rallying troops to paint the other side as demonic, it would help if they modeled such an approach.

Instead of trying to curtail speech on campus, invest in promoting critical thinking about Israel/Palestine, and the subjects (hatred, identities, free speech, etc.) that inform our ability to discuss this difficult issue.

One of the side-benefits of the creation of the Alliance for Academic Freedom, beyond its capacity to push back against the academic boycott of Israel and the threats to academic freedom from the Jewish right-wing, is its listserv. Every day smart academics share their thoughts about these issues, and related ones.

In 2015 Amna Farooqi, a Pakistani-Muslim student at the University of Maryland, was elected president of J Street U, J Street's campus organization.[8] This was, to say the least, an unusual fact, and it precipitated discussion on the listserv. Paul Scham, who is managing editor of the *Israel Studies Review* and teaches at the University of Maryland, is a member of AAF and an active listserv participant. Amna, he wrote, was a student of his, talented and bright.

What was the course, I asked? It was an examination of the Israeli/Palestinian conflict from the 1880s through the 1930s. In other words, the guts of the conflict. It stopped before the Holocaust, before the Declaration of the Establishment of the State of Israel and/or the Nakba in 1948, the 1967 War, current events. Half the course was an historical simulation game – an educational module that allowed students to experience the issues from the perspective of various historical figures. Scham's simulation game looked closely at the events surrounding the Royal Peel Commission of 1936–7. At the time the British had the responsibility of administering Palestine. Given the hostility between Jews and Arabs, the government sent

Lord Peel and other commissioners to talk to representatives of the competing groups, and come up with recommendations for how to address the conflict.

Each student in Scham's course had to do primary research, get into the head of the historical figure they were assigned to represent, and loyally speak for them and their perspectives in a series of debates, remaining in character throughout the module. Those representing Jews or Arabs had to testify to the British, and those representing the British had to listen and analyze testimony and other evidence. In the 1930s there were also deep divisions within the Jewish and Palestinian Arab communities, so the students had to confront classmates on "their" side too. Where possible, students took on the role of someone whose background and beliefs were different, or even in strong opposition, to their own. For half the semester, Amna Farooqi represented David Ben-Gurion, Israel's founding prime minister.

When I spoke to Amna, she laughed, saying you think *that* was weird? An Israeli classmate had to spend weeks inside the skin of the Mufti of Jerusalem. And as much of a pain in the butt as he was, her classmate who portrayed the far-right Israeli Ze'ev Jabotinsky was more difficult.

Scham told me that professors Natasha Gill and Neil Caplan had co-authored "The Struggle for Palestine 1936" module as part of a program of historical "games" called "Reacting to the Past," an innovative and widely disseminated series of historical "games" created by Barnard historian Mark Carnes.[9] I tracked Natasha down in London, and she explained the course to me. By thrusting students into an historical event and having them study primary sources, rather than merely asking them to use secondary sources or look at issues through an historical lens, the students observed the realities on the ground through the eyes of the various players, and engaged in a realistic and challenging series of exchanges. The experience was almost like putting students in a time machine.

The goal of the game, she said, was not to be confused with traditional dialogue groups or peace projects that ask participants to humanize or gain empathy for "the other." Instead, students were encouraged to adopt what she called "functional empathy" –

understanding a variety of perspectives (including those that are offensive to them) in great detail, firsthand, in order to be able to have a truer sense of what the real issues and impasses were (and are). Students would, Natasha said, frequently start the class saying something like: "This is wonderful – now we have a chance to figure out how the Israeli/Palestinian conflict could have been solved!" By the end of the class, they are likely to say, "We now know why the conflict hasn't been solved, eighty years after the Peel Commission." That understanding – albeit disheartening – is the point. Education is about teaching students to wrestle with history and ideas, in this case about understanding what seems to be an intractable conflict.

Further, taking on the role of an historical figure allows students to realize that many of the fundamental beliefs, articles of faith, and sacred symbols of the other side can't simply be wished away. This gives students a mature sense of how to approach the other side, recognizing that regardless of which side they believe holds the higher moral ground, neither will be able to get all it wants. The goal, she stressed, is not to convert students to a different perspective, soften their views, weaken their loyalties, or seek some sort of artificial "middle ground." If played well, the game exposes the experiences, beliefs, grievances, and, yes, anger on all sides, without any expectation that they be "balanced."[10] Thus if they are, and remain, passionate advocates for one side or the other, they also become equipped to support their cause more effectively (much like when I was a criminal defense attorney, I'd always ponder how I'd approach the case if I were the prosecutor).

Natasha also said that while Amna might have found the role reversal to be an exciting learning tool, for many participants the process, while instructive and even enlightening, can be very challenging and even disturbing. In fact, when I asked Natasha to look over a draft of this section, she wrote back that she "did not think it was appropriate to mention Amna as a representative example of the goals or impact of this game." She said "that the kind of experience Amna had, where a Muslim student later becomes an advocate for a pro-Zionist organization, was highly atypical and sounds – disturbingly – as though the process was meant to produce a conversion of sorts, an experience that is contrary to the entire spirit and pedagogy of the module."[11] No one should read about this class and think it was designed to turn Muslims into Zionists or Zionists into pro-Palestinian activists. It was designed to get students to focus on a difficult historical conflict in new and more creative ways. Indeed, thinking like one of these historical figures also had another benefit, something touched on in chapter 1, "Thinking about Thinking": strong passions, informed by one's core beliefs but lacking insight into the other side's sacred values may lead to intuitive reactions that are counterproductive to one's goals.

Natasha and I talked about how this novel class might be taught in more colleges. Part of the success and broad appeal of Mark Carnes's model is that professors are able to teach games that lie outside their own field of expertise: each module is so tightly structured and well-designed that non-specialists are able to guide students through any game. However, Natasha felt that this particular game would increase tensions between students if it weren't taught by professors who were specialists in the history of the Middle East or the Israel/Palestine conflict. So, with help from Paul Scham and scholar Neil Caplan, Natasha and I spent about two years planning a project: a three-and-a-half-day workshop for twenty-five professors, knowledgeable in the subject, who were willing to learn how to teach the Struggle for Palestine course. Their views on the conflict were not relevant, we asked simply that they be committed teachers who could attract students, agree to follow this model, and provide a letter from a dean or provost that they'd be allowed to offer it. We wanted to have many of these classes taught the same semester at different colleges, so that the professors could support each other, and there might be opportunities for the students to do so too. We also hoped that the workshop might be repeated, and a community of scholars using this method – and improving it – would result.

Unfortunately, we could not raise enough money (about $70,000) to run the workshop. Part of the challenge was that I am not a great fundraiser. But there was more to it. First, there was the difficult question of where to go for the money. Natasha and I recognized that some academics who had strong views about the conflict would have problems attending a program funded, in part, by the "other side." Second, many Jewish groups and individuals

I approached, while fascinated with the idea, passed. My strong suspicion is that they either thought "Why should I be spending half my contribution to teach the Palestinian narrative?" or were worried that others would criticize them for that sin.

There was a similar and even stronger sentiment present on the pro-Palestinian side: Palestinians feeling that for decades the Jewish narrative – both the history of Jewish suffering and the narrative about Israel – had been put forward and unconditionally accepted; that attempts to create "balanced" narratives in the end had created even more imbalance; and that their efforts should, therefore, be put to getting their own version of history clearly in the public domain. This last issue was not only a point made by activists but it was also echoed when I approached one college I thought would want to collaborate. While some faculty members liked the idea, others said no – the course suggested that the two narratives were on the same moral plain, when in their view the Palestinian narrative was the more legitimate.

Since we could not raise the funds, we failed in our effort to offer a creative way to understand the root causes of the Israel/Palestine conflict, wrestling with and inviting examination of issues too often avoided because they were considered offensive, taboo, or treacherous, all the while developing analytical skills to examine why this conflict remains so difficult to discuss, let alone resolve. I hope someone else can succeed where I didn't.* I would have loved to have taken such a course. Wouldn't you, scary as it might have been? But the difficulty we faced in trying to fund this project was a direct result of the toxic environment which, we hoped, such a training might help offset.

In 2011, when I had a summer sabbatical at AJC, I had a question – how many full-semester courses on antisemitism existed? I emailed most of the professors and college presidents I knew, as well as Jewish communal institutions around the world. There were literally

---

* This description only gives a few highlights of how Natasha Gill's game module is constructed and how powerful it can be as an educational exercise. She has more information on her website, and I encourage academics interested in learning more about it to visit http://www.track-4.com/about/our-approach.

only a handful of classes, some were no longer taught and some were neither interdisciplinary nor historical (for example, one course focused on antisemitism and literature).

I spent the summer creating a model syllabus on antisemitism, and then taught it as a visiting assistant professor of Jewish studies at Bard College in 2012, and again as a visiting assistant professor of human rights at Bard in 2016. I didn't start the class with readings about Jews, but about hatred, reviewing some of the material in chapter 1 of this book, about the human capacity to define an "other," and the implications of that part of our makeup. With that foundation, we studied the history of antisemitism, particularly in Europe, with emphasis on the different types of antisemitism (anti-Judaism, racial antisemitism, and political antisemitism), and short but deep dives into particular antisemitic manifestations, such as Holocaust denial.

Towards the end of the class I asked the students to compare and contrast antisemitism with another form of hatred or prejudice. (Among the topics the students chose were the Moscovites' hatred for Chechens; how Egyptians would have viewed Jews if European antisemitism hadn't been imported into the Middle East; and discrimination against Dominicans related to the darkness of their skin.) Placing antisemitism into the families of hatreds and examining where it was the same and where it was different, and why, rounded out the students' understanding.

Some students were pro-Israel, including one who had family in the IDF. Others were pro-Palestinian. By the time we got to issues of Israel and Zionism in the second half of the class, everyone had coalesced as a group, they had a common understanding of the history of antisemitism (and of Jews), and were able to have a rational, thoughtful discussion of contemporary issues. And yes, I assigned staunch anti-Zionist writers. How else do you have a discussion of ideas if you don't assign them?

I had students create an attitudinal survey about antisemitism and then interview their schoolmates. This wasn't done so much to find the results (the samples were small, questions few), but to have them think of what questions to ask, and hear what other students on campus had to say. I insisted one question deal with Israel or Zionism. We all chuckled that most of their interviewee schoolmates had no idea what the word "Zionism" meant – they'd pull out their smartphones and look it up.

My expectation was that the students who participated in the antisemitism class, even if they were or became extreme partisans around the Israel/Palestinian conflict, would do so with the ability to think rather than merely react in the fashion of what was expected of their side.

Antisemitism is one of the oldest and least understood forms of hatred. To the extent it is studied in college, it is either focused on one event – the Holocaust – or subsumed and mentioned briefly, if at all, in classes about racism. There should be at least one full-semester interdisciplinary antisemitism class in every school of higher education. This isn't only to enable reasoned discussion about Israel/Palestine but also, more fundamentally, to have a better understanding of the role antisemitism plays in democracy.

Why, for instance, were white supremacists marching for the preservation of Confederate statues in Charlottesville, Virginia, chanting "Jews Will Not Replace Us"? Study antisemitism, and it's easy to understand. White supremacists in the United States fear they are losing a battle to people of color, whom they define as inferior. How can it be, they ask, that they are losing to inferiors? Someone has to have their thumb on the scales. It's of course the Jews, who conspire against whites, promoting affirmative action, immigration, multiculturalism, and so forth. They even have a name for how they believe Jews are pulling this off: the Zionist Occupied Government. A knowledge of antisemitism will help students understand extremism of all types – including among proponents and opponents of Israel and Palestine.

If Jewish organizations want to reduce antisemitism on campus, rather than try to suppress pro-Palestinian speech, they should instead invest in education – teaching about antisemitism, about hatred, and about how to have difficult discussions.*

---

* The Bard Center for the Study of Hate maintains a database of syllabi about hate, including ones on antisemitism, as well as a model syllabus about how to think about and discuss difficult issues. See https://bcsh.bard.edu/hate-studies-syllabi/.

I don't expect advocates for the pro-Palestinian position to pull their punches or show introspection any more than I expect that from pro-Israel advocates. Despite my disagreements with BDS (among them it plays into the binary, empowers the extremes) and anti-Zionism (Jews are never going to give up their right to self-determination any more than the Palestinians are, and choosing one side or the other to win means support for endless conflict),[12] it pains me to see people so blinded by the perceived justice of their position that they, too, lose perspective, thereby sacrificing their ability to be taken seriously when they have an important point to make (such as about the chilling impact on their speech through laws proposed or promoted by pro-Israel advocates).

Israel passed its unnecessary, anti-democratic, anti-Arab, and ill-advised "Nation-State" law in the summer of 2018. As I briefly mentioned in the prologue, a Palestinian Stanford student named Hamzeh Daoud, obviously angered, posted he would "physically fight" Zionists.[13] He wrote: "I'm gonna physically fight Zionists on campus next year if someone comes at me with their 'Israel is a democracy' bullshit. And after I abolish your ass I'll go ahead and work every day for the rest of my life to abolish your petty ass ethno-supremacist, settler-colonial state."[14] Four hours later, he amended the post to say "intellectually," not physically. The College Republicans called for Daoud to be removed from his position as a residential assistant (RA). "Threatening to assault other students who hold a different point of view is anathema to a free society and any kind of education, let alone the operation of the premier research university in the world," they wrote.[15]

Jewish Voice for Peace at Stanford then started a petition online in support of Daoud. In part it read:

> No mention was made [by the College Republicans] to the edited post or Daoud's clarification of intent. In other words, the Stanford College Republicans intentionally misinterpreted the post. This intentional misinterpretation comes as no surprise as the Stanford College Republicans have demonstrated on multiple occasions that they support racists and Islamophobes and have previously run smear campaigns against professors and students who express strong support for the Left.[16]

Black/white. Good/bad. JVP apparently saw a Palestinian student targeted by the Right and leapt to his defense, just as a defense lawyer would (when I was in practice, this is how a colleague defined the job: "Contest everything, concede nothing, and when defeated allege fraud").

What if this had been a threat against JVP members by a College Republican RA, first saying they would be "physically assaulted," four hours later changed to "intellectually assaulted," with the explanation that "I edited this post because I realize intellectually beating [JVP] is the only way to go. Physical fighting is never an answer ... when trying to prove people wrong." Would that have been accepted as a sufficient apology?[17] I think not, especially in the case of someone who is an RA. To leap to his defense in this unqualified way, to suggest there is no valid reason for concern when someone's reaction is to post that he's going to criminally assault people with whom he disagrees, is simply blind partisanship (what if he had said this about "feminists," and was an RA?). JVP's position reminded me of President Donald Trump's assessment that his supporters were so dedicated that he could shoot someone on Fifth Avenue and not lose their votes. That's one instance when Trump clearly told the truth, but when advocates about Israel/Palestine operate with the same standards as the most ardent of Trump's promoters, that's a reason for concern on a campus. (A few days later, Daoud resigned from his RA position.)[18]

Kenneth Marcus was wrong to call Dima Khalidi of Palestine Legal the equivalent of a Holocaust denier – he had blinders on when he said this, seeing nothing in the realm of reasonable debate about her positions. But just as pro-Israel advocates frequently neglect to mention relevant facts (like ones they might notice if they had happened to be born Palestinian), JVP, SJP, and other pro-Palestinian groups frequently leave out things, or distort facts, too.

They argue that the academic boycott of Israel is simply of academic institutions, not of individuals. But as we saw in chapter 5, it is impossible to boycott a country's universities without blacklisting its academics. Strident pro-Palestinian ideology leads to defining the Jewish state as Nazi-like, and once a state is a Nazi equivalent, anything associated with it is either Nazi or complicit. In this viewpoint, how are scholars who work in that institution, and are paid by it, somehow exempt from the Nazi charge? They can't be, and the academic boycott which is thereby "justified" remains a horrid violation of academic freedom, and an assault on the basic principles on which higher education rests. I suspect that some of the boycott proponents know the academic boycott is beyond the pale, and that it harms Israeli academics and those who work with them. But it would be unfashionable or seen as traitorous to say, yes, we'll boycott Golan wines or products made in the West Bank but, no, we won't target Israeli scholars or put them at a disadvantage.

In 2005 there was broad concern in the Jewish community that many, if not most, college courses about the Middle East that mentioned Israel were hostile to it. AJC convened a meeting with key staff and lay people, and various thinkers about the problem, including some college presidents, most particularly Jehuda Reinharz of Brandeis.

Some of the participants wanted to figure out how to attack professors who, it was alleged, were teaching about Israel in an unfair way. The presidents and leading academics around the table made clear that such a strategy wouldn't work. These anti-Israel professors had a right to teach, even in a manner that pro-Israel folk considered propagandistic. More importantly, why, people were asking, was money continuing to flow from Jewish contributors to set up more and more Holocaust-related programs when there were so many already, but too few courses that looked at Israel in a non-propagandistic way?

Brandeis University's Summer Institute for Israel Studies was born at that meeting. The idea was to identify academics who were serious scholars and wanted to teach this subject. About twenty of them would spend a part of their summer learning the scholarship about modern Israel, and visit Israel too. Over time, a few hundred academics have gone through this program, and so every year there are more and more courses about modern Israel taught in American colleges and universities.

This is a long-term approach, not towards promoting a pro-Israel counterpropagandistic view of Israel on campus, but rather towards increasing teaching by faculty who are committed to addressing the complexities. While I suspect that pro-Israel professors are the most likely to participate in this program that is funded by pro-Israel philanthropists, the important consideration is that faculty are committed to teaching rather than to persuading. The Jewish community would do well to emulate this model and fund other campus-related initiatives that rely on increased scholarship. In addition to the type of course like the Peel Commission game, there are other, broader campus initiatives that should be promoted.

First, as noted in chapter 3, many campuses are helping students avoid intellectual stress, rather than cultivating an environment in which they relish being unsettled by ideas. Colleges and universities need to do more to equip students to handle difficult and disturbing issues. They should emphasize – maybe even with banners and other reminders – that students are in college to have their thinking shaken up, their minds stirred. Students should learn to think clearly about what happens to their reasoning powers when someone expresses an opinion that feels like a gut punch. *Why* does it feel this way? *How* does my thinking change when my identity is connected to an issue of perceived social justice, and someone just expressed an idea that undercuts my group, my sense of right and wrong, or both? *What* are my presumptions, my values? *When* do I (ever) question my thinking, and test it, rather than set up walls and rationales to defend it? Workshops, seminars, classes, and programs can help students enjoy learning how to create UNSAFE intellectual spaces, safely.

There are good reasons to be skeptical of the value of core curricula, but given that students from Right and Left, and pro-Palestinian and pro-Israel, seem eager to censor perspectives with which they disagree, there should be courses (or at least dense first-year units) on the history and importance of free speech and academic freedom. The need for such courses goes beyond the Israel/Palestine conflict. If too many of today's college students think that they have a right to be sheltered from disturbing ideas, I worry both about the academic world and our democratic politics. If the academy erects higher and higher intellectual walls so that people will refrain from saying what they think for the fear of offending, our pursuit of knowledge will suffer. Faculty – and especially students – need the intellectual space to think "outside the box," to try out ideas, *and to be wrong*. Without a culture that allows for, in fact encourages, intellectual error, progress will be difficult, if not impossible.

I worry about our politics too, because of the inversion among too many young people about the ideas of power and state; they look to the state to prevent speech they view as hateful, not to protect everyone's ability to express opinions. Some students justify shouting down a Milo or a Bannon or a Murray or a Coulter or a Netanyahu or an Oren, earnestly believing that they have a moral responsibility to suppress hateful speech, and that the law either allows them to do so or should allow them to do so. Rather than consider the long history of the state suppressing speech *the state* sees as dangerous (opposition to war, promotion of civil rights, etc.), many students seem comfortable with the idea that the state should regulate expression.

I'm troubled as I write this – in early fall of 2019 – how students who are insisting on "no platforming" for ideas they find reprehensible are not seeing the especial danger to free speech in an environment in which the president of the United States refers to the free press as "the enemy of the people," bans reporters from covering the news, and talks about withdrawing licenses for television networks and regulating search engines that don't prioritize articles that are favorable to him.

Finally, faculty have a responsibility too. Yes, the environment is so charged that professors – even those with tenure – will be condemned for putting scholarship above partisanship. But, as historian and Israel studies professor Derek Penslar says, scholars researching Palestine and Israel have more in common than what divides them. They may have starkly different views of historical events, yet they frequently attend the same conferences, use the same sources, and read what the other writes. "A [joint] field of Israel/Palestine Studies is ... a necessity," Penslar states. "It is a necessity because scholars of Israel and Palestine scrutinize the same small bit of land, the same events, and often the same people. They have much to learn from each other."[19]

Penslar also sees the difficulty: "[T]he joint field will remain an impossibility so long as its would-be practitioners remain wedded to conceptual frameworks that are Procrustean beds – which, as the legend has it, destroy those who lie on them."[20] Studying Israel and Palestine separately makes little sense. It is, as Penslar notes, the same place, and the same peoples. As scholar Seth Anziska points out, there "is no Jewish history, or history of Zionism without the context of Jewish-Muslim and wider Jewish-Arab relations, and there is no history of the Middle-East without navigating the history of Jews and their aspirations."[21] Where else in the world would scholars divide one subject into two distinct sections? A scholar might be more interested in the Catholic or Protestant experience in Northern Ireland, or the black or white experience in the American South, or the Hindu or Muslim experience in Kashmir, but they don't put up walls as if they are examining entirely unrelated questions and history.

Penslar is right that the ghettoization of Israel studies and Palestine studies hurts both. His plea that "academic conversation about Israel/Palestine can and should refract, rather than reflect, the conflict"[22] is compelling. Other faculty – as well as university leaders – should add their voices to his. Otherwise, we risk the further segregation of the academy into "Palestine only" and "Israel only" fountains of knowledge.

I began this book with a vignette of Spokane, Washington, and how its Jewish community and peace and justice activists were refusing to work together, or even meet, because of their different positions on Israel. There's more to that story. In 1987 Bill Wassmuth – the Idaho parish priest who had his house firebombed after he spoke out against the Aryan Nations – founded the Northwest Coalition against Malicious Harassment, a regional organization fighting hate. Police, religious leaders, labor movement officials, activists, and others looked to Bill and the Coalition not only to fight the white supremacists in the region but also other manifestations of bigotry and hatred (like anti-gay ballot initiatives).

In the early 1990s, working at AJC and by then a veteran of the Northwest Coalition's annual meetings, Bill asked me to give a keynote. "What do you want me to do?" I asked. "Challenge us to do something we're not already doing," he said. This was no easy task. The Northwest Coalition was the best regional organization fighting hate, and when I spoke around the country I referred to it as a model. What advice could I possibly offer? But then I thought about the people who came to the Coalition's annual conferences (which rotated around the region). Law enforcement, people from ethnic and religious organizations, politicians, labor officials, and others all came to the meetings because of their day jobs, and the importance of tackling hate in the community for their employer's mission. The academics who attended, conversely, were there mostly because of personal interest.

Many of these academics worked in fields (sociology, political science, and others) that had something to say about human hate, but no one was harnessing that knowledge, pulling it together in an interdisciplinary manner, and applying it to the work on the ground. The Coalition, AJC, ADL, and every other group that had a mission of countering one or more forms of bigotry or hatred were defining their programs and making budgetary choices based on presumptions, not testable theories that came out of the academy. Wouldn't it be useful to have a better understanding of how hate could be impacted, what additional theories could prove helpful, what tools the groups could use to measure success, and so forth?

My challenge to the group was to find an academic, intellectual home for the study of hate, someplace that could pull the different fields that touched hate into an interdisciplinary whole. Bill liked the idea, so he and I looked for a university that would take on this task. The schools we approached in the Pacific Northwest loved the project, but would ask "where's the funding?" and we said, well, we don't have any.

The 1996 Northwest Coalition annual conference was to be held in Spokane, Washington. Morris Dees, the co-founder of the Southern Poverty Law Center,[23] was the main keynote speaker and draw. Then, shortly before the meeting, Gonzaga University – which is in Spokane, and was the site of the conference – was in turmoil. Two black law students received threatening letters, the second year in a row the school's few black law students had been targeted.

"The only good nigger is a dead nigger," the 1996 letter said. "But we won't kill you ... How loud do you think niggers can scream? How fast do you think [one of the black students] can run? We want to find out."[24] The school was looking for ideas of what to do and turned to Bill, who immediately invited Morris Dees and me to meet with him and key people at the university. We told them about the idea of a hate studies institute.

That's how the Gonzaga Institute for Hate Studies was born. It has had fits and starts, but because of the commitment of Gonzaga faculty and administrators, it has continued for two decades now, holding an international conference every two years and publishing the *Journal of Hate Studies*.

George Critchlow attended the initial meeting with me and Bill and Morris. George was a law professor and later dean of the law school. He is now retired, but we remain friends, and one day he called me, perplexed. George is active in the Peace and Justice Action League of Spokane (PJALS), and was struggling to understand why the Jewish community was calling the group antisemitic. He had never heard any antisemitism expressed. What was going on? What could be done? The issue, of course, was Israel – PJALS had a static page on its website endorsing BDS, and there were other flare-ups over Israel in recent years that had led to the divide and recriminations.

Perhaps because people on both sides knew me (I remain on the advisory board of the Institute, and have spoken at the synagogue on antisemitism), perhaps because Spokane is a small enough community that everyone active in progressive politics probably knows everyone else, perhaps because of the memory of organized white supremacists in the area, I was asked to help the warring communities get over this divide.

About forty key people were invited to a full-day workshop. Each had to promise to read eighty pages of material about Jews, about Israel, about the history of antisemitism, and, most importantly, how we think about hate. There were ground rules – there would be no vilification, no demonization. People committed to listen. And they promised to say what they thought (otherwise, the day would be wasted).

I led the morning's discussions about Jewish history and anti-semitism, and midday took them through some of the material discussed in chapter 1 of this book, about hatred and how we think about issues that threaten our identity and values of perceived social justice. With this background, they were ready to discuss Israel and Zionism. For example, we had read Derek Penslar's essay "What If a Christian State Had Been Established in Modern Palestine?"[25] In his thought experiment, instead of Jews, Palestine was settled by Swabian Templers, a German "Protestant sect that established several colonies in pre-1914 Palestine." Would antipathy to a state made up of ingathered Christians with ties to the land differ from that towards the Jewish state of Israel?

We discussed the tension between Israel as a democracy and as a Jewish state. As long as Israel has a Jewish majority, the potential contradiction might be managed. But what happens if, decades down the road, there's a Jewish minority inside the "green line"? At the magical movement when there's one more non-Jew than Jew, or perhaps one more Israeli of Arab origin than Jew, does Israel at that point cease to be a democracy, if it still considers itself a Jewish state? We wrestled with such questions, and with others about antisemitism, Jewish history, Palestinian aspirations, the BDS movement, and so forth.

There were people in the room who were fervent Israel supporters, and those who were active pro-Palestinian organizers. But they listened. One of the pro-Palestinian participants said that he had been unaware of the history of Jews being boycotted, and why BDS resonates so negatively with many Jews who are aware of this history. Conversely, pro-Israel activists listened when I said I had been on an academic panel with a Palestinian pro-BDS professor who, despite whatever one thinks about BDS, had a point: during the Second Intifada, people were saying Palestinians should find a non-violent way to make their case, and BDS is non-violent. Jewish pro-Israel activists also got a better sense of what it was like to be a Palestinian, going through checkpoints, having your history – and even your contemporary existence – diminished and marginalized. And of course pro-Palestinian participants left the workshop understanding why many Jews worry about threats to the existence of Israel.

The day was a success, partly because people came prepared to find a way forward, to listen and learn, and when appropriate to apologize for acts and omissions. There was a willingness to find ways to work together in the community, and to continue learning. The sense of connection to the Israel/Palestine conflict wasn't reduced. But this small community understood the necessity of prioritizing their relationships with each other, to improve the lives of the people in the city they shared.

I suspect that this model cannot be so easily replicated in too many other communities. Spokane's activists knew each other, many knew me (and looked to me as an honest broker), and they understood that if they didn't find a way to work together, it wouldn't really matter for Middle East peace, but would benefit local white supremacists.

If partisans on conflicting sides of the Israel/Palestine debate can find a way to open their minds, imagine, learn, and see the value of doing so for the community in which they live, why can't college students do this too?[26] Just as the mayor of Spokane supported the initiative, why can't college presidents do more to cultivate the environment where students and faculty engage the full range of issues around Israel and Palestine, in an environment that appreciates academic freedom and free speech, and understands how human beings not only hate but also how hatreds impact their thinking?

Hatred over Israel and Palestine has killed many people over the last century and more. But hatred more generally may have killed more people than any other human malady. It continues to affect our politics, and ruins lives around the world, including those of children. The economic cost in hate – wars, workplace discrimination, and so forth – has not (yet) been computed, but it must be staggering.[27] We still know way too little about hate despite the good work of the Institute for Hate Studies, and the newly created Bard Center for the Study of Hate, which I am honored to direct.[28]

I don't expect that partisans on either side of the Israel/Palestine campus debate will stop trying to arm students to be proxy warriors in this battle, and stoking hatred while they do so. I hope some, who profess to care about these young people and value our colleges and universities, see the wisdom in another approach: innovating ways to increase knowledge, while protecting and promoting academic freedom and free speech.

Acknowledgments

This book could not have appeared without the faith, support, and help of many people.

First, my agent Eric Myers, who believed in this project, and worked tirelessly to make sure it found the right home. Eric is more than an agent. He is a friend, sounding board, and co-conspirator.

Also first, my friend Derek Penslar. Derek read an early draft and also made it his mission that the book find the right publisher. His careful reading of that draft, and many parts of redrafts, improved the book immeasurably.

Thanks to the following friends and colleagues who read parts or the entire manuscript, and/or offered corrections, additions, and other valuable support. Of course, their help doesn't mean they agree with everything I wrote, and any mistakes are my own. Seth Anziska, Shula Bahat, Kenneth Bob, Lee Bollinger, Greg Britton, George Critchlow, Lois Frank, Natasha Gill (who, as always, forced me to think of things in a new way), David Greenberg, Jonathan Haidt, Evan Harrington, Harry Hellenbrand, Suzannah Heschel, David Hirsh, Frederic Hof, Elizabeth Jackson, Steven Jacobs, Kristin Lane, Joe Levin, Jonathan Levine, Richard Levitt, Sharon Musher, Cary Nelson, Floyd Norris, Geri Palast, Hank Reichman, Ross Rudolph, Paul Scham, Arden Shenker, Etaiy Shisgal, David M. Stone, Alan Sussman, Steve Trachtenberg, Avi Weinryb (a diligent and thoughtful reader and researcher, about whom it is impossible to say enough), Mike Whine, Allen Zerkin, and Steven Zipperstein. Thanks also to Lisa Eisen and Alicia Meeks Hunter, who helped when I needed some critical information. And thanks to Bard student Artun Ak, who provided early research help, Tom Keenan and Danielle Riou of the Bard Human Rights Project, and to my fellow Bard alums, Eric Warren Goldman and Barbara Grossman, who were beyond supportive and encouraging.

Thanks to Evan Harrington for permission to print generous segments of his article from the *Journal of Hate Studies*, Kenneth Bob for permission to quote from The Third Narrative website, Phillip Weiss for allowing me to reproduce a large part of his Mondoweiss blog post about Vassar, and Daniel Holtzman for permission to use a student's article from *New Voices*.

Although not directly involved in the production of *The Conflict over the Conflict*, conversations and collaboration over many years with friends and colleagues helped me think about many aspects of this book – free speech, hate, antisemitism, Israel, Palestinian advocacy, the campus, and others. From my AJC days I especially appreciate Michele Anish, Shula Bahat, Andy Baker, Yehudit Barsky, Harvey Belkin, Roslyn Bell, Deidre Berger, David Bernstein, Marc Dworkin, David Elcott, Richard Foltin, Anita Fricklas, Felice Gaer, E. Robert Goodkind, Cyma Horowitz, Linda Krieg, Wendy Lecker, Irving Levine, Jonathan Levine, Noam Marans, Rebecca Neuwirth, the late Sam Rabinove, Bruce Ramer, Ed Rettig, Simone Rodan-Benzaquen, David Rosen, Geri Rozanski, the late Gary Rubin, Danielle Samuelon, Ann Schaffer, Michael Schmidt, Linda Senat, Harold Shapiro, Emily Soloff, Diane Steinman, Marc Stern, and Jeff Weintraub.

From my days directing the Justus and Karin Rosenberg Foundation, in addition to the board members, I thank the two advisory boards, all of whom had important insights about the campus and the Israel/Palestine debate: Barry Alperin, Mimi Alperin, Dottie Bennett, Marty Bresler, Michael Brooks, Dianne Cohen, Richard Cohen, Lois Frank, Norman Gelman, Susannah Heschel, Steven Jacobs, Marty Kaplan, Frederick Lawrence, Deborah Lipstadt, Joe Mendels, Ora Mendels, Carol Nelkin, Lee Pelton, Derek Penslar, Jehuda Reinharz, Arleen Rifkind, Robert Rifkind, Stephen J. Trachtenberg, and Steven Zipperstein.

From my twenty years on the board of advisors of the Gonzaga Institute for Hate Studies, I want to thank everyone involved with the Institute and those supporting it in the Spokane community, in particular: Bob Bartlett, James Beebe, Joan Braune, Melissa Click, George Critchlow, Carmen de la Cruz, Joanie Eppinga, Kem Gambrell, Melissa Hart, Kristine Hoover, the late Eva Lassman, Bobbi League, Adrieane Leithauser, Brian Levin, Marshall Mend, James Mohr, Molly Pepper, Barbara Perry, the late Jan Polek, Mary Lou Reed, Raymond Reyes, Jerri Shepard, Pavel Shlossberg, John Shuford, Lisa Silvestri, Joanne Smieja, Tony Stewart, Sima Thorpe, James Waller, the late Bill Wassmuth, and Larry Weiser.

Discussions with others over the decades helped me shape my thinking on the issues addressed in this book, and I'm thankful to all of them. Some are listed above. Others are Floyd Abrams, Eric Alterman, Jane Ashworth, Aliza Becker, Ernst Benjamin, Michael Berenbaum, Roger Berkowitz, Chip Berlet, Esta Bigler, Leon Botstein, Suzette Bronkhorst, Stacy Burdette, Gillian Butler, Margaret Butler, Candace Carponter, Neil Cogan, Joe Cohn, Will Creeley, the late Leonard Dinnerstein, Matt Duss, Ronald Eissens, Ethan Felson, Jamie Fishman, Ira Forman, Pat Foster, Sam Freedman, Steven Gardiner, Todd Gitlin, Andrew Goldberg, Paul Goldenberg, Samantha Hill, Jeremy Jones, Anthony Julius, Greg Kaster, Ahmad Khalidi, Simon Klarfeld, Michael Lerner, Rachel Lerner, Larry Levine, Danny Levitas, James Libson, Michael Lieberman, Greg Lukianoff, Marilyn Mayo, Shahanna McKinney-Baldon, David Myers, Mary Nathan, Jeremy Newmark, Rafal Pankowski, Pamela Paresky, Debra Pemstein, Dina Porat, Steve Queener, Martin Raffel, Dave Rich, Gregg Rickman, Hannah Rosenthal, Rachel Sandalow-Ash, Ronnie Stauber, Rachel Timoner, Eric Ward, Esti Webman, Kate Wittenstein, Tamar Wynschogrod, Lenny Zeskind, Erin Ziegler, and Simone Zimmermann. And I can't say thank you enough to the many Bard administrators and faculty (too many to name) who have, over the many years, given me the benefit of their wisdom as I pondered the vexing question of hate. I'm particularly in the debt of the group of faculty who are meeting every three weeks to read texts about hate; I've learned so much from you.

A special thanks to Nadine Strossen. I've known and admired Nadine for many years, which is why I went to her when I was looking for someone else to write a report on the campus and the Israel/Palestine debate. Despite her incredibly busy schedule, she graciously agreed to write the foreword for this book. One of the best by-products of this book has been the opportunity to get to know Nadine even better. She is one of my heroes.

Many thanks to Natalie Fingerhut at the University of Toronto Press, who immediately and enthusiastically saw the value of this book. Working with her and her many talented colleagues made the production and promotion of *The Conflict over the Conflict* a pleasure. Thank you to Anna Del Col, Ani Deyirmenjian, David Drummond, Janice Evans, Sebastian Frye, Matthew Gatien, Jane Kelly, Beth McAuley, Breanna Muir, Chris Reed, and Tanya Rohrmoser.

Thanks also to my cousin Eloise Malek and my sister Alice Stern. Alice, a librarian, read the entire manuscript and offered valuable advice. I think I can also count on her to buy a book for her institution.

To my children Daniel Stern and Emily Stern. This is my fifth book, and the first one written with my children as adults. It was wonderful to share the manuscript (and the book proposal before that), and to discuss ideas with them.

And finally to my wife, Margie Slome. She not only read the manuscript (multiple times as it evolved), she was my rock. She also didn't kill me when I commandeered our dining-room table as a huge desk for many months. I love her always.

Notes

Prologue

1 Simpson, Blevins, and Auge, "The Murder of Alan Berg."
2 Keneally, "Ruby Ridge Siege."
3 Weinstein, "Furrow Gets 5."
4 Prager, "Racism Drives Off."
5 Carter, "FBI Dissecting Bomb."
6 Woo, "Bill Wassmuth."
7 Hosack, "Victoria Keenan and Jason Keenan vs. Aryan Nations Judgment."
8 It was first slated to become a "peace park" but is being sold to support human rights education in the region. Sokol, "North Idaho College."
9 Richey, "Failed Martin Luther King Day Parade."
10 Glover, "Racist Flyers Posted."
11 Students Supporting Israel, *What Really Happened at UCLA.*
12 Sekar, "Photo."
13 JTA and TOI Staff, "Stanford Undergraduate."
14 Rachel Sandalow-Ash, interview with author, Brooklyn, NY, 22 January 2016.
15 Now called the Celebrate Israel Parade.
16 Stavis, Memorandum, "Re: National Lawyers Guild Convention."

1. Thinking about Thinking

1 Dr. Robert Leahy quoted in Lukianoff and Haidt, *Coddling of the American Mind*, 242.
2 Kahneman, *Thinking Fast and Slow*, 12, 14.
3 Lukianoff and Haidt, *Coddling of the American Mind*, 58.

4 If the Holocaust didn't happen, then World War II historians from the United States, Britain, Germany, Israel, and elsewhere would all have to be either incompetent or in on a huge conspiracy, or both.

5 Weiss, *Israel Supporter Refuses to Share Bard Stage.*

6 Ghayrat and Adams, "Anti-Zionist Activists."

7 Ghayrat and Adams, "Anti-Zionist Activists."

8 Jewish Telegraphic Agency, "Stony Brook."

9 Jewish Telegraphic Agency, "Stony Brook."

10 Waller, "Our Ancestral Shadow," 126–7.

11 This phenomenon occurs inside what appear to outsiders as homogenous groups too. Jews might seem as one community to their non-Jewish neighbors, but inside the community, groups defined by differences in religious observance or political positions sometimes are at loggerheads, or worse.

12 Waller, "Our Ancestral Shadow," 128.

13 There is some evidence, however, that our definitions of who is part of our "ingroup" and who is part of the "outgroup" has some flexibility. See, especially regarding race, Kurzban, Tooby, and Cosmides, "Can Race Be Erased?"

14 Waller, "Our Ancestral Shadow," 129.

15 Waller, "Our Ancestral Shadow," 129–30.

16 Waller, "Our Ancestral Shadow," 129.

17 See Greenwald and Pettigrew, "With Malice toward None"; Weisel and Böhm, "'Ingroup Love' and 'Outgroup Hate'"; and Brewer, "The Psychology of Prejudice."

18 Harrington, "The Social Psychology of Hatred."

19 McLeod, "Robbers Cave."

20 Recent scholarship suggests ethical problems with the experiment, and also allegations that Sherif and his team manipulated some of the boys' behavior. See Shariatmadari, "A Real-Life Lord of the Flies"; Haslem, "The Lost Boys." Yet Sherif's observations about realistic conflict theory and superordinate goals have been supported by other research. See, for example, Brief et al., "Community Matters," and Gaertner et al., "Reducing Intergroup Conflict."

21 Hohman and Hogg, "Fearing the Uncertain," 32.

22 Grant and Hogg, "Self-Uncertainty," 539.

23 Grant and Hogg, "Self-Uncertainty," 539.

24 Hogg, Meehan, and Farquharson, "The Solace of Radicalism," 1061.

25 Hogg, Adelman, and Blagg, "Religion in the Face," 73.

26 Hogg, Adelman, and Blagg, "Religion in the Face," 75.

27 There is also research starting to explore more deeply why and how humans dehumanize others. See, for example, Haslam and Lougham, "Dehumanization and Infrahumanization," and Haslam and Stratemeyer, "Recent Research on Dehumanization."

28 Hogg, Adelman, and Blagg, "Religion in the Face," 74.

29 Cikara, Botvinick, and Fiske, "Us versus Them." See also Change, Krosch, and Ciraka, "Effects of Intergroup."

30 Of course, as noted before, we each have multiple identities. We may be men, women, parent, child, sports fan, and so on. But for many, religious or ethnic affiliations are central to how we view ourselves, especially when we see those identities challenged by others.

31 AMCHA Initiative, "Disruptions." This page allows the following: "Search incidents involving the suppression of speech/movement/ assembly of Jewish and Zionist students on US college and university campuses from 2015 to present day."

32 While there is some dispute about whether the term was linked to the taking of American Indian scalps, there is little debate it is a pejorative term similar to these other slurs. See Democracy Now!, "Meet the Navajo Activist," and Goddard, "'I Am a Red-Skin.'"

33 Pyrillis, "Perspectives."

34 While beyond the scope of this chapter, women in positions of leadership experience greater difficulty than men in having their authority respected. See, for example, Vial, Napier, and Brescoll, "A Bed of Thorns."

35 Harrington, "Social Psychology," 55.

36 Harrington, "Social Psychology," 55.

37 Perry, *Behind the Shock Machine*.

38 Beardsley, "Fake TV Game Show."

39 Harrington, "Social Psychology," 53.

40 For example, the level of atrocity in Southern lynchings increased when the lynch mob was larger. See Mullen, "Atrocity as a Function."

41 Haidt, *Righteous Mind*, 1.

42 Haidt, *Righteous Mind*, 53.

43 Haidt, *Righteous Mind*, 59.

44 Haidt, *Righteous Mind*, xxiii.

45 Haidt, *Righteous Mind*, 34.

46 Haidt, *Righteous Mind*, 103.

47 Haidt, *Righteous Mind*, 164.

48 Haidt, *Righteous Mind*, 174.

49 Haidt, *Righteous Mind*, 312.

50 Kahneman, *Thinking Fast*, 21.

51 Kahneman, *Thinking Fast*, 20, 22, 23.
52 Kahneman, *Thinking Fast*, 45.
53 Kahneman, *Thinking Fast*, 51.
54 Kahneman, *Thinking Fast*, 86–7.
55 Kahneman, *Thinking Fast*, 416.
56 Kahneman, *Thinking Fast*, 103.
57 Kahneman, *Thinking Fast*, 225.
58 Kahneman, *Thinking Fast*, 225.
59 Kahneman, *Thinking Fast*, 329–30.
60 Kahneman, *Thinking Fast*, 330.
61 Nathan-Kazis, "Campus 'Apartheid Week.'"
62 National Centre for Education Statistics, "Fast Facts." The denominator is 4,583 for two- and four-year colleges. Jews aren't evenly distributed across them all, of course, and it is probable that IAW is more likely to occur at the colleges where Jews are enrolled than, say, rural community colleges, but the percentage is still miniscule.
63 Kahneman, *Thinking Fast*, 354.
64 Kahneman, *Thinking Fast*, 367.
65 Kahneman, *Thinking Fast*, 381.
66 Vallone, Ross, and Lepper, "Hostile Media."
67 Vallone, Ross, and Lepper, "Hostile Media," 582.
68 Vallone, Ross, and Lepper, "Hostile Media," 582.
69 See, for example, Hollancer, "CAMERA Op-Ed."
70 See, for example, Johnson, "NYT's BDS," and Norton, "Journalists Blast NY Times."
71 "Myside bias," as social psychologists refer to the phenomenon, shows how partisans with strong views and identities, who see their side as just and its opposite as either unjust or dangerous, frequently ignore evidence that could undermine their beliefs.
72 Ginges et al., "Sacred Bounds."
73 National Centre for Education Statistics, "Fast Facts."
74 College students also organized against South African Apartheid, which was a distant battle. The difference was that almost everyone wanted an end to Apartheid, whereas the campus has fervent supporters of each side of the Israeli/Palestinian conflict.

2. Zionism and 1948

1 Regular, "Terrorize the Enemy."
2 Eban, "Zionism and the U.N."

3 This was the same week that Marlon Brando's motorhome was stopped in Oregon with leaders of the American Indian Movement in it.

4 United Nations General Assembly, "Resolution 3379."

5 Jewish Virtual Library, "Zionism."

6 During the Inquisitions, Jews who "confessed" and converted to Christianity were generally not killed.

7 Penslar, *Theodor Herzl*, 68.

8 Herzl, "Theodor Herzl."

9 Balfour, "The Balfour Declaration."

10 Indeed, Jews in Mandatory Palestine referred to themselves as Palestinian Jews.

11 Scham, "Modern Jewish History."

12 Peoples Press Palestine Book Project, *Our Roots*, 11–12.

13 Some will dismiss Sari Nusseibeh because he is part of an older Palestinian generation, or because he is one of the Palestinians whom Jews tend to quote. Regardless of what you may think about him, engage his observation about the implications of the focus on "justice" alone.

14 Nusseibeh and David, *Once upon a Country*, 508. Israeli writer Yossi Klein Halevi, in his *Letters to My Palestinian Neighbor*, makes a similar point, calling out "the sin of not seeing, of becoming so enraptured with one's own story, the justice and poetry of one's national epic, that you cannot acknowledge the consequences to another people of fulfilling the whole of your own people's dreams," 106.

15 Herzl, *Complete Diaries*, 88–9, cited in Penslar, "Herzl and the Palestinian Arabs," 67.

16 Athnet, "Historical Facts about Lacrosse."

17 The Onondaga, part of that confederacy, had had a part in my American Indian Movement case, giving sanctuary to Dennis Banks.

18 Palestinian Campaign for the Academic and Cultural Boycott of Israel (PACBI), "Palestinians Urge."

19 Pearl, "BDS and Zionophobic Racism," 229.

20 Grant and Hogg, "Self-Uncertainty."

21 Seth Anziska, "MS," e-mail message to author, 3 July 2019.

22 Of course, some people bent on killing Jews like the idea of Jews moving to Israel. Hezbollah leader Sheikh Hassan Nasrallah reportedly said, "If they all gather in Israel, it will save us the trouble of going after them worldwide." Editorial Board, "Nasrallah's Nonsense."

23 Pileggi, "New Deputy Defense Minister."

24 Beaumont, "Anger at Netanyahu."

25 Bedein, "Abba Eban."

26 Ravid, "Deputy Foreign Minister."
27 That an issue becomes a movement isn't necessarily a reflection that it is the most important one at any political moment. Whether it founders or inspires is also related to who raises it, how, its historical time, its ability to energize questions of identity and morality, and so forth. These political issues, however, are usually seen as matters of us vs. them.
28 Morris, ed., *Making Israel*.
29 Estrin and Bashir, "Hamas Leader Implies," and Toameh, "Hamas Vows Gaza."

3. Free Speech and Academic Freedom

1 Stone, "Statement on Principles of Free Expression."
2 *Terminiello v. Chicago*.
3 Mill, "On Liberty," 10.
4 Stern, *Bigotry on Campus*, 1.
5 Freitag, "3 Jewish Students."
6 Stern, *Bigotry on Campus*, foreword.
7 "Headers and Text of Email Machado Sent."
8 Bollinger, "Cardozo Lecture."
9 Bollinger, "Cardozo Lecture."
10 Bollinger, "Cardozo Lecture."
11 "Current Topics and Notes," 912.
12 "Text of Conant's Speech."
13 *Sweezy v. New Hampshire*, 354 US, 234.
14 *Sweezy*, 354 US, 242.
15 *Sweezy*, 354 US, 243.
16 *Sweezy*, 354 US, 244.
17 *Sweezy*, 354 US, 250.
18 *Sweezy*, 354 US, 261–3.
19 Chemerinsky and Gillman, "What Students Think."
20 In *HATE: Why We Should Resist It with Free Speech, Not Censorship*, Nadine Strossen notes that today, "[a] prime target for suppression would include expressions by the Black Lives Matter movement, which has been attacked as 'hate speech' and even blamed for spurring murder of police officers" (16, 17). She also recalls the attempts to suppress pro-abolitionist speech before the Civil War, even in the North, because of fear it might lead to slave rebellions.
21 Contreras, "Controversial Cardinal."
22 For a further explanation of why the term "hate speech" is problematic, see Nossel, "To Fight."

23 See, for example, Neuman, "Boston Right."
24 Bollinger, "President Bollinger's Statement."
25 Global Research, "Full Transcript."
26 Egan, "Outrage Turns."
27 For the 8 October 2007 cover of the *New Yorker*, see https://www
    .newyorker.com/magazine/2007/10/08; for the *Saturday Night Live* skit
    of 29 September 2007, see "Iran So Far," NBC, https://www.nbc.com
    /saturday-night-live/video/iran-so-far/n12159. Note: The video may
    not be available in some areas.
28 The Southern Poverty Law Center filed a suit against Anglin on behalf of
    one of the targeted Jews. See Southern Poverty Law Center, "Complaint."
    A federal judge ruled, in summer 2019, that Anglin had to pay millions of
    dollars in damages. https://www.splcenter.org/presscenter/federal
    -judge-adopts-magistrate-judges-recommendation-neo-nazi-must-pay
    -more-14m-jewish.
29 Stern, "How to Honor MLK."
30 Bannon did not speak. See Grieve, "Prof Who Would've Talked."
31 Rose, "Safe Spaces."
32 Merriam-Webster, "Microaggression."
33 University of New Hampshire, "Bias-Free Language Guide."
34 FIRE, "Best of 'The Torch.'"
35 Committee on Freedom of Expression at the University of Chicago,
    "Report of the Committee on Freedom of Expression."
36 The Investigative Project on Terrorism, "Students for Justice."
37 Cohen, "Psychology Association."

4. Durban and Its Aftermath

 1 "Boycotting Israel: New Pariah on the Block."
 2 Some of the material in this chapter first appeared in my 2006 book
    Antisemitism Today.
 3 COBASE (Cooperative Tecnico Scientifica de Base), "Are the NGO's Forum and
    WCAR Racist?" (Rome: COBASE, 2001). Cited in Stern, *Antisemitism Today*, 24.
 4 Puddington, "The Wages of Durban."
 5 Melchior, "Briefing to the Foreign Press."
 6 Arab Lawyers Union, "That Is the Fact ... Racism of Zionism & 'Israel,'"
    cited in Stern, *Antisemitism Today*, 28.
 7 "Statement of the Jewish Caucus on the NGO Process," cited in Stern,
    Antisemitism Today, 29.

8 Coslov and Davidson, "The Durban Experience," 11, cited in Stern, *Antisemitism Today*, 31.

9 Jones, "Durban Daze."

10 "Statement of the Jewish Caucus on the NGO Process," cited in Stern, *Antisemitism Today*, 31.

11 Shehori and Sheleg, "Israel, US Leave Durban."

12 Krauthammer, "Disgrace in Durban," 15.

13 Koplin, "Grid of Campus Divestment Activity."

14 Arenson, "Harvard President."

15 Greenberg, "Columbia President."

16 Schevitz, "UC Berkeley's Conflicts."

17 Zoloth, "Where Is the Outrage?"

18 BBC News, "Canada Protests."

19 Berzon, "Anti-Israeli Activity."

20 Sideman and Stern, "Minutes."

21 Zoloth, "Where Is the Outrage?"

22 Maggio, "Intimidation-Free Campuses."

23 American Jewish Committee, "College Presidents."

24 Katznelson et al., "Ad Hoc Grievance Committee Report."

25 Sherman, "The Mideast."

26 Popper, "Students."

5. The Academic Boycott of Israel

1 Gideon Toury quoted in Goldenberg and Woodward, "Israeli Boycott Divides Academics."

2 Bateson et al., "More Pressure."

3 Goldenberg and Woodward, "Israeli Boycott Divides Academics."

4 Quoted in Goldenberg and Woodward, "Israeli Boycott Divides Academics."

5 Gerstenfeld, "The Academic Boycott."

6 Wilkie was disciplined. See Cassidy, "Oxford Professor."

7 Palestinian Campaign for the Academic and Cultural Boycott of Israel, "The PACBI Call for Academic Boycott Revised."

8 Hirsh, "The Myth of Institutional Boycotts."

9 Magidor and Nusseibeh, "Counter Boycott."

10 See Levi, "Letter to Sally Hunt."

11 BDS Cookbook, "National Association of Teachers."

12 Bollinger, "Statement by President."

13 Alvarez, "Professors in Britain."
14 Redden, "A First for the Israel Boycott."
15 Antler et al., "To the Members."
16 Antler et al., "To the Members."
17 "Re: ASA Update," e-mail message to author, 25 November 2013.
18 "ASA Update," e-mail message to author, 24 November 2013.
19 "Re: ASA Update," e-mail message.
20 Musher, "The Closing," 114.
21 Musher, "The Closing," 116.
22 Association of American Universities, "AAU Statement."
23 American Association of University Professors, "AAUP Statement."
24 Schmidt, "Backlash."
25 In December 2013 another small group – the Native American Studies Association – also announced a boycott of Israeli academic institutions. See Redden, "Native American Studies."
26 Kotzin, "Politics," 457.
27 And some individuals inside AJC (unbeknownst to me at the time) wanted to do so too.
28 Jaschik, "MLA Vote."
29 The Third Narrative, "Alliance for Academic Freedom."
30 At the AHA, historian Jeffrey Herf and the Academic Engagement Network (led by former University of California president Mark Yudof and Kenneth Waltzer) also had a role defeating the resolutions.
31 One was introduced and defeated in the summer of 2019. See https://www.algemeiner.com/2019/08/12/major-academic-association-votes-down-bds-resolution/.
32 Nelson, "Micro-Boycotts," 4.
33 Nelson, *Israel Denial*, 32–3.
34 Palestinian Campaign for the Academic and Cultural Boycott of Israel, "PACBI Guidelines." Note that the paragraph says Israelis should be treated "like all other offenders in the same category, not better or worse," but of course no other group of academics is so targeted.
35 Palestinian Campaign for the Academic and Cultural Boycott of Israel, "PACBI Guidelines."
36 Zakim and Mohamed, "Best of Intentions." See also Nelson, *Israel Denial*, 36.
37 Nelson, *Israel Denial*, 37.
38 Moshe, "University of Michigan."
39 Schlissel and Philbert, "Letter: Important Questions."

40 Nelson, "How the Israel Boycott."
41 Jewish Telegraphic Agency, "U of Michigan."
42 Beaumont, "Israel Brands."
43 Ravid, "Netanyahu Tells."
44 Goodstein, "New Israel."
45 Goodstein, "New Israel."
46 How different is this from NATFHE's resolution in the UK, attempting to reject Israeli academics unless they spoke out against their government?
47 Howe, "US Denial." In 1966, the Lyndon B. Johnson administration, under pressure, ultimately allowed Neruda and others to attend an International PEN congress under a "group waiver."
48 Landau, "Israel Publishes."
49 Israel has apparently said it would only refuse entry to "leaders" involved in the BDS groups, but that's hardly reassuring. Is a leader the head of the organization, someone on the board, someone on its speakers' bureau list, a significant financial supporter?
50 CBS News, "US Student Appeals," and Associated Press, Reuters, and Gilad Morag, "Court Hears."
51 Halbfinger, "Israel Can't Deport."
52 Other academics, less friendly to Israel, have used Israel's anti-BDS law to underpin efforts to end their school's study abroad programs. This happened with a faculty vote at Pitzer College, but the call to cut the program was rejected by the president (see Redden, "Pitzer President"), and at a program at New York University, which was boycotting its own NYU campus in Israel (see Sales, "NYU Department").

6. Stopping and Chilling Speech; Heckler's Veto, Legal Threats

1 Muslim Student Union at University of California, Irvine, "Ambassador Michael Oren Visits UCI."
2 Tammi Rossman-Benjamin, "Serious Concerns about a UC Hastings Event," e-mail to author, 24 March 2011.
3 Nelson, *Israel Denial*, 262.
4 Muslim Student Union at University of California, Irvine, "Ambassador Michael Oren Visits UCI."
5 LaHood et al., "Amici Curiae Brief."
6 Majeed, "Irvine 11 Case," 372.
7 Majeed, "Irvine 11 Case," 372.
8 Abdulrahim, "11 Students Arrested."
9 Weiner, "Threat to Freedom."

10 Weiner, "Threat to Freedom."
11 Huffpost, "'Irvine 11.'"
12 One had already completed community service, so only ten were tried. See Cruz, Williams, and Anton, "'Irvine 11.'"
13 The term "heckler's veto" is also used when speech is silenced not because, as here, of an actual heckler but for fear of what those opposing the speaker might do if an event is allowed to proceed.
14 Cruz, "11 Muslim."
15 LaHood et al., "Amici Curiae Brief."
16 Williams, Cruz, and Anton, "Students Guilty," and LaHood et al., "Amici Curiae Brief." Part of the pro-Palestinian argument went beyond the assertion that disrupting speech is an exercise of free speech. They also claimed there was selective prosecution – that others who had disrupted other speeches were not prosecuted, while pro-Palestinian activists were. Regardless of the merit of the claim of unequal protection of the law, materially interfering with the ability of a speaker to talk is a violation of free speech and academic freedom.
17 Etaiy Shisgal, "Re: Thanks Again," e-mail message to author, 29 July 2019. The email contained a spreadsheet entitled "Event Disruptions 2010–2019."
18 ICC's list mentions the following sixteen episodes on a total of twelve campuses where programs or events could not be held or completed between 2010 and the end of spring semester 2019: 2010–11 University of California, Irvine (Michael Oren disruption, but as noted in the text, he was able to complete his speech); 2014–15 Loyola University Chicago (disruption of a Birthright tabling); 2015–16 University of California, Irvine (Aharon Barak disruption), Tufts University (Taste of Israel disrupted), University of Minnesota (Moshe Halbertal disruption), University of Texas at Austin (Professor Ami Pazhazur disruption), University of Chicago (Bassam Eid disruption), Northwestern University (Bassam Eid event cancelled), Brown University (Janet Mock event cancelled), San Francisco State University (Nir Barkat disruption), University of California, Irvine (Beneath the Helm disruption); 2016–17 University of Texas at Austin (Save a Child's Heart fundraiser disrupted), University of California, Santa Cruz (Israeli Independence Day Celebration disrupted), University of California, Irvine (Reservists on Duty disruption); 2017–18 University of Virginia (Reservists on Duty disruption), University of California, Santa Barbara (student senate meeting disrupted).
19 But there is history for using this tactic by some Jewish groups in other contexts, most particularly the disruption of the Bolshoi Ballet during

the battle for Soviet Jewry in August 1974. See Anti-Defamation League, "About the Jewish Defense League."

20 Rossman-Benjamin, "Serious Concerns."
21 Rossman-Benjamin, "Serious Concerns."
22 Kenneth S. Stern, "RE: Serious Concerns about a UC Hastings Event," e-mail to David Harris, 25 March 2011.
23 David Harris, "RE: Serious Concerns about a UC Hastings Event," e-mail response to Kenneth S. Stern, 25 March 2011.
24 Palestine Legal and Center for Constitutional Rights, *The Palestinian Exception*, 88–9.
25 The letter was dated 25 March 2011 from Marc D. Stern to Frank H. Wu, noted to be sent by email as "RE: Litigating Palestine: Can Courses Secure Palestine Rights?" Copy in author's possession.
26 Israel on Campus Coalition, "2016–2017 Year End Report." The 2017–18 numbers are consistent: 3,336 pro-Israel events and 1,213 anti-Israel events, although as an official of the ICC noted, the numbers tell a limited story because of the "visceral nature of certain events." Etaiy Shisgal, "Re: Thanks," e-mail message to author, 29 July 2019. The email contained a spreadsheet entitled "2011–2019 BDS Campaigns."
27 JTA, "College Campuses."
28 Shisgal, "Re: Thanks" – "2011–2019 BDS Campaigns."
29 Shisgal, "Re: Thanks" – "Event Disruptions 2010–2019."
30 Frommer, "For Second Time," and May, "Students Supporting Israel."
31 Widge, "Poster REMIX D'affiches."
32 AMCHA Initiative, "Incidents."
33 Boycott Roger Waters, Facebook post.
34 Jewish News Syndicate, "Jewish Students."
35 JTA, "College Campuses."
36 CONN Students in Solidarity with Palestine, "Not a Real Eviction."
37 JTA and Chandler, "UPDATE."
38 The Jewish Voice, "CUNY Report."
39 Saxe et al., "Antisemitism."
40 Kosmin and Keysar, "National Demographic."
41 Wright et al., "The Limits."
42 During the writing of this book, Jews were gunned down at the Tree of Life Synagogue in Pittsburgh, Pennsylvania, and at the Chabad synagogue in Poway, California. See https://www.peacejusticestudies.org/chronicle/antisemitism-through-a-hate-studies-lens/.
43 Shukman, "Meet the Neo-Nazi."
44 Jewish Telegraphic Agency, "Fliers Found."
45 Solomon, "'End Jewish Privilege.'"

46 Movement for Black Lives, "Invest-Divest."
47 Waltzer, "From 'Intersectionality.'"
48 Canary Mission, "Home Page," and Jasper, "Dear Canary Mission." The website probably dropped the "if you're racist" line – it did not appear on the homepage when I visited it on 27 May 2019, but it did appear on previous visits, as this New Voices piece also documents. See http://newvoices.org/2019/01/17/dear-canary-mission-if-youre-reading-this-im-not-afraid-of-you/.
49 Greenberg et al., "The Blacklist in the Coal Mine."
50 I serve on its executive committee and co-authored its statement about Canary Mission.
51 Greenberg et al., "The Blacklist in the Coal Mine."
52 Nossel, "Statement of Suzanne Nossel ... on 'Examining Anti-Semitism on College Campuses.'"
53 Nathan-Kazis, "Campus 'Apartheid Week'"; Israel on Campus Coalition, "2016–2017 Year End Report"; and Nathan-Kazis, "REVEALED." See also Nathan-Kazis, "Second Major."
54 Canary Mission, "About Us."
55 Telephone interview with author, 31 March 2005.
56 Shisgal, "Re: Thanks Again" – "2011–2019 BDS Campaigns."
57 Likewise, the Jewish Virtual Library notes that there were 130 such resolutions between 2005 and 2019, two-thirds of which were defeated. These resolutions appeared at sixty-eight schools, which is at less than 3 per cent of four-year colleges. (The Jewish Virtual Library reports that the resolutions appeared at less than 2 per cent of four-year colleges, but it says there are a total of 4,298 four-year colleges, a higher number of such colleges than the National Center for Educational studies lists [3,004] from US Department of Education data.) Resolutions were passed at thirty-eight schools, meaning about 1 per cent of four-year institutions. See Jewish Virtual Library, "Anti-Semitism." The Israel on Campus Coalition (ICC) data from 2011 to 2019 are similar. The ICC's criteria are likely somewhat different, but they show sixty-six BDS initiatives passing out of 178 proposed (many are repeat efforts in succeeding years at the same campus). The 2018–19 ICC data show eight BDS initiatives passing out of twenty proposed on fifteen campuses (and also nine out of ten non-BDS resolutions passing that were supportive of anti-Israel or pro-Palestinian advocacy, such as resolutions condemning Canary Mission or proclaiming that SJP is not antisemitic). Shisgal, "Re: Thanks," e-mail message to author.
58 Roth and Goldberg, "Jewish Students."
59 Anti-Defamation League, "Background Information," 5.
60 Schneiderman, "A Field Geologist," 316, 322.

61 Schneiderman, "A Field Geologist," 322.

62 Weiss, "Ululating at Vassar."

63 Of course, professors and administrators should apprise students of risks associated with fieldwork, including discriminatory policies of the countries they will be visiting.

64 McEvoy, "NYU SJP Demands."

65 Palestine Legal, "Year-in-Review."

66 Palestine Legal and Center for Constitutional Rights, *The Palestinian Exception*, 72.

67 Palestine Legal and Center for Constitutional Rights, *The Palestinian Exception*, 93.

68 AMCHA Initiative, "20 Groups Write."

69 AMCHA Initiative, "20 Groups Write."

70 Palestine Legal and Center for Constitutional Rights, *The Palestinian Exception*, 56.

71 Gaither, "Berkeley Course."

72 AMCHA Initiative, "Serious Concerns." In full disclosure, one of the recipients of this letter, Harry Hellenbrand of CSU, Northridge, is a friend and high school classmate.

73 Klein and Tuchman, "Letter from Zionist Organization of America to Professor Abu-Lughod."

74 US Department of Education, "About OPE."

75 Klein and Tuchman, "Letter from Zionist Organization of America to Professor Abu-Lughod."

76 Schmidt, "Supporters of Israel."

77 In late summer 2019, the Department of Education sent a letter to the Duke-UNC Consortium on Middle East Studies, essentially threatening the funding of the program, noting, inter alia, a possible lack of "balance," evidenced by "a considerable emphasis placed on ... understanding the positive aspects of Islam, while there is an absolute absence of any similar focus on the positive aspects of Christianity, Judaism, or any other religion" (see https://www.federalregister.gov /documents/2019/09/17/2019-20067/notice-of-a-letter-regarding-the -duke-unc-consortium-for-middle-east-studies).

   Apparently, the investigation into the Duke-UNC consortium was precipitated when Congressman George Holding (Republican of North Carolina) complained to the Department of Education about a Duke-UNC program entitled "Conflict over Gaza: People, Politics and Possibilities." Holding alleged the event included "distorted facts," had a "radical anti-Israel bias," and included a "brazenly anti-Semitic

song" (see https://www.nytimes.com/2019/09/19/us/politics
/anti-israel-bias-higher-education.html?action=click&module=Top
%20Stories&pgtype=Homepage).

There was apparently no full video of the performance, and there were differences of opinion about whether it was antisemitic or bad parody. The Foundation for Individual Rights in Education issued a statement noting the differences between Title VI regulatory requirements, such as the adequacy of a school's library collection, and academic matters. FIRE decried the department's "sharp deviation from past practice" by involving itself in the "'sifting and winnowing' of ideas best facilitated by the academy," and called the Department of Education's action "a threat to academic freedom" (see https://www.thefire.org/fire-statement-on-department-of-education -letter-to-duke-unc-consortium-for-middle-east-studies/).

78 Klein and Tuchman, "Letter from Zionist Organization of America to Professor Abu-Lughod."
79 Gershman, "Professor Khalidi."
80 Purnick, "Some Limits."
81 Lipstadt, Freedman, and Seidler-Feller, "American Jewry," 29–30.
82 Fidler et al., "Letter to Brooklyn College."
83 Hikind, "Hikind Calls."
84 Butler, "Judith Butler's Remarks."
85 LaHood and Sainath, "Letter from Palestine Legal."
86 LaHood and Sainath, "Letter from Palestine Legal."
87 LaHood and Sainath, "Letter from Palestine Legal."
88 LaHood and Sainath, "Letter from Palestine Legal."
89 Ryan, "Memorandum of Law."
90 In fact, some pro-Israel advocates continue to try and silence SJP, through law. As I was finishing the copy edits of this book, *The Guardian* wrote an exposé about efforts to pass state-based legislation adopting and applying the antisemitism definition to campuses (see chapter 7). The story included a link to uncovered emails, including one by "Randy Fine, a Republican from Florida who was instrumental in passing in May the first state law outlawing antisemitism in public education" (see https://www .theguardian.com/us-news/2019/oct/16/conservative-activists-want -to-outlaw-antisemitism-in-public-education-why-is-that-a-bad-thing). An email from Fine to various elected officials said the legislation would limit "racist speech," and declared that "Students for Justice in Palestine is now treated the same way as the Ku Klux Klan – as they should be" (see https://assets.documentcloud.org/documents/6455535/Anti -Semitism-Bill-Discussed-at-ALEC-Emails.pdf).

91 *Ahmad Awad v. Fordham University.*
92 Newton, "CC Rejects Williams Initiative for Israel."
93 Moore and Payan, "Why."
94 Williams College Office of the President, "College Council."
95 This perspective is also much like Kenneth Marcus's refusal to debate Dima Khalidi. Anti-normalizers, one presumes, believe Zionists are "anti-Palestinian deniers," who deny Palestinians what is rightfully theirs and diminish their suffering, inflicted by Zionists. But as with Marcus's take on pro-Palestinian activists, this point of view is troubling, especially on a campus, where stark differences about Israel and Palestine need to be heard and debated, and are – or should be – seen as a different category from whether one debates a Holocaust denier or, for that matter, a flat-earther.
96 Mael, "On Many."
97 PACBI, "Israel's Exceptionalism."
98 For further reading about the rationale behind anti-normalization, see *+972 Magazine*, "What Is Normalization?": "It is helpful to think of normalization as a 'colonization of the mind,' whereby the oppressed subject comes to believe that the oppressor's reality is the only 'normal' reality that must be subscribed to, and that the oppression is a fact of life that must be coped with. Those who engage in normalization either ignore this oppression, or accept it as the status quo that can be lived with. In an attempt to whitewash its violations of international law and human rights, Israel attempts to re-brand itself, or present itself as normal – even enlightened – through an intricate array of relations and activities encompassing hi-tech, cultural, legal, LGBT and other realms."
99 Salaita, "A Moral Case."
100 Pessah, "Why Palestinian."
101 Salaita, "Zionists Should Be Excluded."
102 Salaita, "Zionists Should Be Excluded."
103 Former colleagues in mainstream Jewish organizations tell me that children and grandchildren of many of their lay leaders belong to IfNotNow.
104 Hillel International, "Hillel Israel Guidelines."
105 Derek J. Penslar, e-mail message to author, 4 October 2018.
106 Open Hillel, "Mission and Vision."
107 Kelman et al., "Safe and on the Sidelines."
108 Pink, "Camp Ramah."
109 Wikiquote, "Abba Eban," accessed 14 July 2019, https://en.wikiquote .org/wiki/Abba_Eban.

7. The Antisemitism Awareness Act

1 Creely, "State Department's Anti-Semitism."
2 Bergman and Wetzel, "Manifestations of Anti-Semitism."
3 European Monitoring Centre on Racism and Xenophobia, *Manifestations of Antisemitism in the EU 2002–2003.*
4 Associated Press and Haaretz Service, "Montreal Attack."
5 See European Forum on Antisemitism, "Working Definition of Antisemitism."
6 Bulgarian Chairmanship of OSCE, "Berlin Declaration."
7 European Forum on Antisemitism, "Working Definition."
8 Special Envoy to Monitor and Combat Anti-Semitism, "Defining Anti-Semitism."
9 Stern, "The Working Definition of Antisemitism – A Reappraisal." In my remarks I also said: "The challenge is that inside the Jewish community, those who use the working definition incorrectly may be perceived as strong defenders against antisemitism, while those who seek to protect its integrity and utility for major institutions – if they speak out about this problem – may be seen as weak and ineffectual. In this particular case, I spoke privately with the director of the lead Jewish group involved and tried to educate him about why his misuse of the definition was a problem. And I also communicated with the university president, sharing with him the intent of the definition and underscoring that it is a useful tool for identifying and analyzing antisemitism, and understanding when and how leaders should speak out against it, but was never meant to provide a framework for eviscerating free speech or academic freedom, let alone labeling anyone an antisemite."
10 Ali, "Dear Colleague Letter."
11 Blanchard, "Letter to Superintendent Roach."
12 *Jessica Felber v. Mark G. Yudof.*
13 Rossman-Benjamin, "Complaint to San Francisco," 1.
14 Rossman-Benjamin, "Complaint to San Francisco," 3.
15 Rossman-Benjamin, "Complaint to San Francisco," 7.
16 Rossman-Benjamin, "Complaint to San Francisco," 10.
17 Rossman-Benjamin, "Complaint to San Francisco," 13.
18 Klein and Tuchman, "Zionist Organization," 4.
19 Klein and Tuchman, "Letter from Zionist Organization of America." This allegation was not included in the ZOA's 20 July 2011 complaint letter to the Office of Civil Rights of the US Department of Education.
20 Klein and Tuchman, "Letter from Zionist Organization of America." ZOA's 20 July 2011 complaint letter to the Office of Civil Rights of the

US Department of Education said the film "inflames hatred of Jews and Israel by promoting the incendiary falsehood that the Palestinian Arabs are innocent victims and Israelis their brutal occupiers and oppressors."

21 Klein and Tuchman, "Zionist Organization."
22 Klein and Tuchman, "Zionist Organization."
23 Klein and Tuchman, "Letter from Zionist Organization of America." The ZOA's 20 July 2011 complaint letter to the Office of Civil Rights of the US Department of Education does not allege that the event was intended to coincide with Holocaust Remembrance Day (which was two days earlier, something that was alleged in its earlier letter to the president of Rutgers University, see https://www.amchainitiative.org/wp-content /uploads/2013/08/ZOA-letter-to-Rutgers-4_6_11.pdf), but said the program "falsely and outrageously analogized the Nazis' treatment of the Jews to Israel's policies and practices toward Palestinian Arabs." (There was also an allegation of discrimination, but the ZOA's objection was also to expression.) See also Rossman-Benjamin, "Why I Filed Title VI Complaint," in which she defends having included in her complaint a conference entitled "Alternative Histories Within and Beyond Zionism," and a class taught by a professor whom had chosen readings which "contain language that clearly meets the working definition of anti-Semitism adopted by the US Department of State ... As a result of their experiences with such university-sponsored, anti-Semitic expression, Jewish students ... have expressed feeling emotionally and intellectually harassed and intimidated by their professors, isolated from their fellow students and unfairly treated by administrators."
24 Rossman-Benjamin, "Retaliation," 306.
25 Nelson and Stern, "Cary Nelson and Kenneth Stern Pen."
26 Marcus, "Standing up for Jewish Students."
27 AMCHA Initiative, "Letter to UC President Napolitano."
28 AMCHA Initiative, "Letter to UC President Napolitano."
29 Sherman, "UC President Napolitano."
30 Stern, "Should a Major University?"
31 Guttman, "Could California Ban?"
32 Stern, "Letter to Janet Napolitano."
33 Rosenberg and Stern, "How UC Can Respond."
34 Committee on Educational Policy, "Adoption of the Report."
35 Stern, "Letter to Members of Congress."
36 Stern, "Will Campus Criticism of Israel Violate Federal Law?"
37 Case, "Genocide Begins with Words."
38 Marcus, "This Is Very Important."

39 Stern and Benjamin, "How Legislative Efforts."
40 Anti-Semitism Awareness Act of 2016, pamphlet circulated to support legislation.
41 See Simon Wiesenthal Center, "Other Universities."
42 JNS.org, "20 Organizations Say."
43 Simon Wiesenthal Center, "Other Universities."
44 Woodell, "Anti-Semitism Bill."
45 Stern, "Statement of Kenneth S. Stern … on 'Examining Anti-Semitism on College Campuses.'"
46 The politicization of the definition became even clearer in the summer of 2019. On 16 July 2019 Representative Ilhan Omar (Democrat from Minnesota), who had previously made statements about Israel that invoked antisemitic tropes, introduced a resolution in the House supporting the right to boycott, associating it with free speech. While not mentioning Israel, this resolution was seen as responding to an anti-BDS resolution that had been introduced in the House (https://schneider.house.gov/media/press-releases/schneider-zeldin-nadler-wagner-introduce-bipartisan-resolution-supporting-two) as well as to anti-BDS legislation in a number of states, requiring contractors doing business with the state government to pledge that they were not boycotting Israel. According to the ACLU and others, demanding such a pledge before a teacher or disaster relief official could contract with the state seemed like an unconstitutional loyalty oath. Omar's resolution spoke of the long history of boycotts, including the Boston Tea Party, those of the civil rights era, and against Japan, the Soviet Union, Apartheid South Africa and Nazi Germany (see https://www.congress.gov/bill/116th-congress/house-resolution/496/text). Fox News reported that following Omar's resolution, a pro-Israel philanthropist praised the Department of State for adding this example from the definition to its website: "Drawing comparisons of contemporary Israeli policy to that of the Nazis" (see https://www.foxnews.com/politics/state-dept-updates-definition-of-anti-semitism-following-omars-anti-israel-resolution.print). The reference to Nazi analogies had been in the 2010 version of the State Department definition, but it was not included in the version it had online in May 2019 (see http://web.archive.org/web/20190516145928/https://www.state.gov/defining-anti-semitism/).
47 Stern, "Statement of Kenneth S. Stern … on 'Examining Anti-Semitism on College Campuses.'"
48 You don't have to be a Jewish activist for Palestinians to be called a "kapo" or antisemite; a Jew who simply disagrees with a charge of antisemitism can be labeled such things too. Bard's Hannah Arendt

Center held a conference on antisemitism and racism in October 2019. About twenty student SJP members protested one of the speakers – Ruth Wisse – who was a staunch Israel supporter and had also said disturbing things in the past about Arabs. Unlike the protest of Oren at University of California, Irvine, Bard's SJP protestors were mostly silent, standing with handmade signs. The few students who spoke were immediately ushered out, and later the group left quickly, with a chant. The delay totaled about two minutes; the program was completed, including the discussion between Wisse and the moderators and the question and answer period.

Batya Ungar-Sargon, the opinion editor of *The Forward*, was one of the moderators, and was to be part of a panel the following day too. But, at that session the next day, she read a statement and walked out, asserting that the demonstration the day before was antisemitic, claiming that other members of the conference had encouraged the demonstration, and that no one had spoken out.

Ungar-Sargon then wrote an opinion piece with the title "I was protested at Bard for being a Jew" (https://forward.com/opinion/433082/i-was-protested-at-bard-college-for-being-a-jew/). Her view of the events was challenged by me (I was there and moderated another session on antisemitism), by Roger Berkowitz (the event organizer), by Shahanna McKinney-Baldon (the person Ungar-Sargon falsely accused of "egging on" the protestors), and others, including *Times of Israel* blogger Tamar Wyschogrod, who had written early on that Ungar-Sargon's description of events seemed a "weak, self-serving piece." The video of the conference, quickly shared, also refuted Ungar-Sargon's claims (https://totalwebcasting.com/view/?func=VOFF&id=bard&date=2019-10-10&seq=1). Berkowitz, McKinney-Baldon, and Wyschogrod are all well-respected professionals, each working in their own fields, with long records opposing antisemitism. They shared some of the comments they received via emails and tweets with me: "kapo," "Jews are being killed on college campuses in America, and … you are creating that environment," "I demand you apologize for impersonating a Jew," "You are a Jew hater," "unabashed Jew basher," "you are an antisemite," "you've outed yourself as an antisemite," "you're clearly an antisemite," and "you are an affirmative action Jew [to McKinney-Baldon, who is both Jewish and African American]."

49 TOI Staff, "Citing Anti-Semitism."
50 Stern, "Statement of Kenneth S. Stern … on 'Examining Anti-Semitism on College Campuses.'"

51 Trump, "Executive Order on Combating Anti-Semitism."
52 Marcus, "Letter to Susan B. Tuchman."
53 Kushner, "Jared Kushner."
54 Stern, "I Drafted the Definition of Antisemitism."
55 Oster, "After Israel Visit." See also Adley, "NJ Anti-Semitism Bill." For South Carolina, see Cohn, "Problematic Anti-Semitism Bill Passes in South Carolina." For Florida, see National Coalition against Censorship, "Florida Anti-Semitism Bill Threatens Free Speech."

8. Blueprint for Rational Campus Discussion on Israel and Palestine

 1 Botstein, "Bard President Responds."
 2 Kahneman, *Thinking Fast*, 361.
 3 "Seattle – Anti-Israel Ad."
 4 *Seattle Mideast Awareness Campaign v. King County.*
 5 8 Members of the Alliance for Academic Freedom, "Everyone Lost at Dartmouth."
 6 8 Members of the Alliance for Academic Freedom, "Everyone Lost at Dartmouth."
 7 8 Members of the Alliance for Academic Freedom, "Everyone Lost at Dartmouth."
 8 Jewish Telegraphic Agency, "J Street U."
 9 Barnard College, "Reacting to the Past."
10 Natasha Gill, "Book!" e-mail message to author, 19 June 2019.
11 Natasha Gill, "Revisions," e-mail message to author, 30 July 2019.
12 As we have seen, some in the Jewish community say BDS is by definition antisemitic. It is not. A college student who supports BDS isn't necessarily a Jew-hater. Those who claim BDS is antisemitic likely view anti-Zionism always as antisemitism, denying Jews the right to self-determination. Would it be fair to put that label on a Palestinian whose concerns are not Jews because they are Jews, but Jews because they happen to be the ones that took over what he/she sees as his/her homeland? The people promoting BDS (as opposed to many of its supporters) do tend to be anti-Zionist. Because opposition to the existence of a Jewish state alongside a Palestinian one is a formula for perpetual conflict, apparently without concern about how many Jews and Palestinians die in this fight, one can argue that BDS is both antisemitic and anti-Palestinian in effect.
13 Jewish Voice for Peace, "URGENT Support."
14 Foreman, "Daoud's Facebook Post."
15 Stanford College Republicans, "Facebook Post."

16 Jewish Voice for Peace, "URGENT Support."
17 Foreman, "Daoud's Facebook Post."
18 American Jewish Committee, "AJC Welcomes."
19 Penslar, "Toward a Joint Field."
20 Penslar, "Toward a Joint Field."
21 Seth Anziska, "MS," e-mail message to author, 3 July 2019.
22 Penslar, "Toward a Joint Field."
23 In 2019 Morris Dees was fired from the SPLC. See Hassan, Zraick, and Blinder, "Morris Dees, a Co-Founder of the Southern Poverty Law Center, Is Ousted."
24 Hansen, Jordan, and Pra, "Hate Mail."
25 Penslar, "What If a Christian State."
26 At Bard I helped the Hannah Arendt Center convene a two-day "off the record" workshop with students, faculty, and outside experts, including a leader of a mainstream Jewish organization, a former president of a progressive Jewish group focused on Israel, and BDS leaders (Jewish and non-Jewish). The discussion was intense, but productive.
27 Helping scholars create such an annual index is one of the goals of the Bard Center for the Study of Hate.
28 See bcsh.bard.edu. As of this writing, in addition to Bard and Gonzaga, there are three other hate studies entities: the International Network for Hate Studies – http://www.internationalhatestudies.com/; the California State University, San Bernardino's Center for the Study of Hate and Extremism – https://csbs.csusb.edu/hate-and-extremism-center; and the Centre on Hate, Bias and Extremism at the University of Ontario Institute of Technology – http://socialscienceandhumanities.uoit.ca /centre-on-hate-bias-and-extremism/.

Bibliography

Abdulrahim, Raja. "11 Students Arrested after Disrupting Israeli Ambassador's Speech at UC Irvine." *Los Angeles Times*, 9 February 2010. https://latimesblogs.latimes.com/lanow/2010/02/11-students-arrested-for-disrupting-israeli-ambassadors-speech-at-uc-irvine-.html.

Adley, Hannan. "NJ Anti-Semitism Bill Would Stifle Free Speech, Advocates Say." *New Jersey Record*, 9 July 2019. https://www.northjersey.com/story/news/2019/07/09/nj-antisemitism-bill-would-bar-certain-criticisms-israel-schools-raising-free-speech-concerns/1673997001/?fbclid=IwAR26aiktmh9_LzfmHC2zueugGhmzoXzi7wDcuW_Cy6nzEjVCKrXaKldSQRo.

Ahmad Awad v. Fordham University, No. 153826/2017, slip op. (Supreme Court of the State of New York, 29 July 2019). https://ccrjustice.org/sites/default/files/attach/2019/04/107_3-4-19_Fordham%20opposition%20to%20motion%20to%20amend%20petition%20web.pdf.

Ali, Russlynn. "Dear Colleague Letter." US Department of Education. 26 October 2010. https://www2.ed.gov/about/offices/list/ocr/letters/colleague-201010.pdf.

Almog, Schmuel. "What's in a Hyphen?" *SICSA Report: Newsletter of the Vidal Sassoon International Center for the Study of Antisemitism* (Summer 1989). https://web.archive.org/web/20120114044903/https://sicsa.huji.ac.il/hyphen.htm.

Alvarez, Lizette. "Professors in Britain Vote to Boycott 2 Israeli Schools." *New York Times*, 8 May 2005. https://www.nytimes.com/2005/05/08/world/europe/professors-in-britain-vote-to-boycott-2-israeli-schools.html?searchResultPosition=1.

AMCHA Initiative. "Disruptions." AMCHA Initiative. Accessed 24 May 2019. https://amchainitiative.org/sjp-disruption-of-jewish-events/#disruption-of-jewish-events/display-by-date3/.

– "Letter to UC President Napolitano regarding Adopting US State Department Definition of Antisemitism to Protect Jewish Students." AMCHA Initiative. 19 March 2015. https://amchainitiative.org/letter -to-uc-president-napolitano-regarding-adopting-u-s-state-department -definition-of-antisemitism-to-protect-jewish-students.

– "Serious Concerns about Abuse of CSU Resources and Name." AMCHA Initiative. 13 February 2012. https://amchainitiative.org/pappe_at _csu/.

– "20 Groups Write to Chancellor Wilcox regarding Serious Concerns about Political Indoctrination in UCR Course." AMCHA Initiative. 16 April 2015. https://amchainitiative.org/serious-concerns-about-political -indoctrination-in-ucr-course.

American Association of University Professors. "AAUP Statement on ASA Vote to Endorse Academic Boycott of Israel." News release. AAUP. 16 December 2013. https://www.aaup.org/sites/default/files/files /AAUPStatementASAVote.pdf.

American Jewish Committee. "AJC Welcomes Stanford University Developments Repudiating Student's Threats against Zionists." News release. American Jewish Committee. 3 August 2018. https://www .marketwatch.com/press-release/ajc-welcomes-stanford-university -developments-repudiating-students-threats-against-zionists-2018-08-03.

– "College Presidents Decry Intimidation on Campuses." Scholars for Peace in the Middle East. 15 October 2002. http://spme.org/campus-news -climate/college-presidents-decry-intimidation-on-campuses/639.

Anti-Defamation League (ADL). "About the Jewish Defense League." Accessed 27 May 2019. https://www.adl.org/education/resources/profiles/jewish -defense-league.

– "Background Information on Students for Justice in Palestine (SJP)." November 2018. ADL. https://www.adl.org/media/12176/download.

Anti-Semitism Awareness Act of 2016. Pamphlet Circulated to Support Legislation. N.p., 2016.

Antler, Joyce et al. "To the Members of the National Council of the American Studies Association." 15 November 2013. https://www.telospress.com /opposing-the-israel-boycott-by-the-american-studies-association/.

Arenson, Karen W. "Harvard President Sees Rise in Anti-Semitism on Campus." New York Times, 21 September 2002. https://www.nytimes.com/2002/09/21 /us/harvard-president-sees-rise-in-anti-semitism-on-campus.html.

Associated Press and Haaretz Service. "Montreal Attack on Jewish School Was to Avenge Yassin Death." Haaretz, 5 April 2004. https://www.haaretz .com/1.4773961.

Associated Press, Reuters, and Gilad Morag. "Court Hears US Student's Appeal against Detention." *Ynetnews*. 11 October 2018. https://www.ynetnews.com/articles/0,7340,L-5368698,00.html.

Association of American Universities. "AAU Statement on Boycott of Israeli Academic Institutions." News release. Association of American Universities. 20 December 2013. https://www.aau.edu/sites/default/files/AAU-Files/News/aau-executive-committee-statement-on-israel-boycott-12-20-13.pdf.

Athnet. "Historical Facts about Lacrosse." Accessed 5 June 2019. https://www.athleticscholarships.net/history-of-lacrosse.htm.

Balfour, Arthur James. "The Balfour Declaration." Israeli Ministry of Foreign Affairs. 2 November 1917. https://mfa.gov.il/mfa/foreignpolicy/peace/guide/pages/the%20balfour%20declaration.asp.

Barnard College. "Reacting to the Past." Barnard College. Accessed 28 May 2019. https://web.archive.org/web/20190402200616/https://reacting.barnard.edu/reacting-home.

Bateson, Patrick, et al. "More Pressure for Mid-East Peace." *The Guardian*, 6 April 2002. https://www.theguardian.com/world/2002/apr/06/israel.guardianletters.

BBC News. "Canada Protests Stop Netanyahu Speech." BBC News. 10 September 2002. http://news.bbc.co.uk/2/hi/americas/2248555.stm.

BDS Cookbook. "National Association of Teachers in Further and Higher Education Case Study." Stop BDS. May 2006. http://www.stopbds.com/?page_id=1839.

Beardsley, Eleanor. "Fake TV Game Show 'Tortures' Man, Shocks France." NPR. 18 March 2010. https://www.npr.org/templates/story/story.php?storyId=124838091.

Beaumont, Peter. "Anger at Netanyahu Claim Palestinian Grand Mufti Inspired Holocaust." *The Guardian*, 21 October 2015. https://www.theguardian.com/world/2015/oct/21/netanyahu-under-fire-for-palestinian-grand-mufti-holocaust-claim.

– "Israel Brands Palestinian-led Boycott Movement a 'Strategic Threat.'" *The Guardian*, 3 June 2015. https://www.theguardian.com/world/2015/jun/03/israel-brands-palestinian-boycott-strategic-threat-netanyahu.

Bedein, David. "Abba Eban: The June 1967 Map Represented Israel's 'Auschwitz' Borders." Israel Behind the News. 17 November 2002. https://israelbehindthenews.com/abba-eban-the-june-1967-map-represented-israels-auschwitz-borders/3838/.

Bergman, Werner, and Juliane Wetzel. "Manifestations of Anti-Semitism in the European Union: First Semester 2002 Synthesis Report." European

Monitoring Centre on Racism and Xenophobia. Accessed 14 July 2019.
https://web.archive.org/web/20060113170036/UK-ORG-BOD
.SUPPLEHOST.ORG/EUMC/EUMC.PDF.

Berzon, Corinne. "Anti-Israeli Activity at Concordia University 2000–2003."
Jerusalem Center for Public Affairs. 25 September 2008. http://jcpa.org
/article/anti-israeli-activity-at-concordia-university-2000-2003/.

Blanchard, Timothy C.J. "Letter to Superintendent Roach Re Case No. 02-11-
1270 Vestal Central School District." US Department of Education. 21 May
2012. https://www2.ed.gov/about/offices/list/ocr/docs/investigations
/more/02111270-a.pdf.

Bollinger, Lee. "Cardozo Lecture on Academic Freedom." Columbia
University Office of the President. 23 March 2005. http://www.columbia
.edu/cu/president/printable/docs/communications/2004-2005/050323
-cardozo-lecture.html.

– "President Bollinger's Statement about President Ahmadinejad's Scheduled
Appearance." Columbia University Office of the President. 19 September
2017. http://www.columbia.edu/cu/news/07/09/ahmadinejad2.html.

– "Statement by President Lee C. Bollinger on British University and
College Union Boycott." Columbia University Office of the President. 12
June 2007. http://www.columbia.edu/cu/news/07/06/boycott.html.

Botstein, Leon. "Bard President Responds to Critics of Far-Right Figure's
Talk." *The Chronicle of Higher Education*, 24 October 2017. https://www
.chronicle.com/article/Bard-President-Responds-to/241538.

"Boycotting Israel: New Pariah on the Block." *The Economist*, 13 September
2007. https://www.economist.com/international/2007/09/13/new
-pariah-on-the-block.

Boycott Water Rogers. "Facebook post." Facebook. 10 May 2019. https://www
.facebook.com/BoycottRogerWaters/photos/a.1142043365926921
/1555108497953737/?type=3&theater.

Brewer, Marilynn B. "The Psychology of Prejudice: Ingroup Love or
Outgroup Hate?" *Journal of Social Issues* 55, no. 3 (1999): 429–44.

Brief, Arthur P., Elizabeth E. Umphress, Joerg Dietz, John W. Burrows, Rebecca
M. Butz, and Lotte Scholten. "Community Matters: Realistic Group Conflict
Theory and the Impact of Diversity." *Academy of Management Journal* 48, no. 5
(October 2005): 830–44.

Bulgarian Chairmanship of OSCE. "Berlin Declaration." Organization for
Security and Cooperation in Europe. 29 April 2004. https://www.osce
.org/cio/31432?download=true.

Butler, Judith. "Judith Butler's Remarks to Brooklyn College on BDS." *The
Nation*, 7 February 2013. https://www.thenation.com/article/judith
-butlers-remarks-brooklyn-college-bds/.

Canary Mission. "About Us." Accessed 27 May 2019. https://canarymission
.org.
– "Home Page." Accessed 13 July 2019. https://canarymission.org.
Caplan, Neil. *The Israel-Palestine Conflict: Contested Histories.* 2nd ed. New
York: Wiley-Blackwell, 2019.
Carter, Mike. "FBI Dissecting Bomb to Crack Spokane Case." *The Seattle Times*
(Seattle, WA), 8 February 2011. https://www.seattletimes.com/seattle
-news/fbi-dissecting-bomb-to-crack-spokane-case/.
Case, Jonathan. "Genocide Begins with Words." *The State* (Columbia, SC),
[1 May 2017?]. https://www.thestate.com/opinion/letters-to-the-editor
/article146719154.html.
Cassidy, Sarah. "Oxford Professor Is Suspended for Rejecting Israeli Student."
Independent, 28 October 2003. https://www.independent.co.uk/news
/education/education-news/oxford-professor-is-suspended-for-rejecting
-israeli-student-93405.html.
CBS News. "US Student Appeals Detention in Israel over Alleged Boycott
Link." CBS News. 11 October 2018. https://www.cbsnews.com/news
/lara-alqasem-american-student-held-israel-bds-boycott-movement-appeal
-detention/.
Change, Linda W., Amy R. Krosch, and Mina Ciraka. "Effects of Intergroup
Threat on Mind, Brain and Behavior." *Current Opinion in Psychology* 11
(2016): 69–73.
Chemerinsky, Erwin, and Howard Gillman. "What Students Think about
Free Speech." *Chronicle of Higher Education*, 3 April 2016. https://www
.chronicle.com/article/What-Students-Think-About-Free/235897.
Cikara, Mina, Matthew M. Botvinick, and Susan T. Fiske. "Us versus Them:
Social Identity Shares Neural Responses to Intergroup Competition and
Harm." *Psychological Science* 22, no. 3 (2011): 306–13.
Cohen, Debra Nussbaum. "Psychology Association Faces Pressure to Boycott
Israel." Jewish Telegraph Agency. 19 June 2018. https://www.jta
.org/2018/06/19/united-states/psychology-association-faces-pressure
-boycott-israel?utm_source=JTA%20Maropost&utm_campaign=JTA&utm
_medium=email&mpweb=1161-4838-32500.
Cohn, Joe. "Problematic Anti-Semitism Bill Passes in South Carolina." FIRE.
17 April 2018.
Committee on Educational Policy. "Adoption of the Report of the Regents
Working Group on Principles against Intolerance." Regents of the University
of California. 24 March 2016. https://web.archive.org/web/20170311080737
/https://regents.universityofcalifornia.edu/aar/mare.pdf.
Committee on Freedom of Expression at the University of Chicago. "Report
of the Committee on Freedom of Expression." University of Chicago.

Accessed 26 May 2019. https://provost.uchicago.edu/sites/default/files/documents/reports/FOECommitteeReport.pdf.

CONN Students in Solidarity with Palestine. "Not a Real Eviction: Eviction Notice." Accessed 27 May 2019. http://49yzp92imhtx8radn224z7y1-wpengine.netdna-ssl.com/wp-content/uploads/2016/05/CSSP-Conn-college-eviction-notices-2016.jpg.

Contreras, Brian. "Controversial Cardinal Conversations Speaker Murray Sparks Peaceful Anti-Racist Rally." *Stanford Daily*, 23 February 2018. https://www.stanforddaily.com/2018/02/23/controversial-cardinal-conversation-speaker-murray-sparks-peaceful-anti-racist-rally/.

Coslov, Max, and H. Ron Davidson. "The Durban Experience." *AJC Journal*, November 2001, 11.

Creely, Will. "State Department's Anti-Semitism Definition Would Likely Violate First Amendment on Public Campuses." FIRE. 22 May 2015. https://www.thefire.org/state-departments-anti-semitism-definition-would-likely-violate-first-amendment-on-public-campuses/.

Cruz, Nicole Santa. "11 Muslim Student Union Members Charged with Disrupting Israeli Ambassador's Speech at UC Irvine." *Los Angeles Times*, 5 February 2011. https://www.latimes.com/local/la-xpm-2011-feb-05-la-me-0205-uci-protesters-20110205-story.html.

Cruz, Nicole Santa, Lauren Williams, and Mike Anton. "'Irvine 11': 10 Students Sentenced to Probation, no Jail Time." *Los Angeles Times*, 23 September 2011. https://latimesblogs.latimes.com/lanow/2011/09/irvine-11-sentenced-probation-no-jail-time.html.

"Current Topics and Notes." *American Law Review*, Volume 51. New York: Little, Brown and Company, 1917.

Democracy Now! "Meet the Navajo Activist Who Got the Washington Redskins' Trademark Revoked: Amanda Blackhorse." Democracy Now! 19 June 2014. https://www.democracynow.org/2014/6/19/meet_the_navajo_activist_who_got.

Eban, Abba. "Zionism and the U.N." *New York Times*, 3 November 1975. https://www.nytimes.com/1975/11/03/archives/zionism-and-the-un.html.

Editorial Board. "Nasrallah's Nonsense." *New York Sun*, 11 March 2005. https://www.nysun.com/editorials/nasrallahs-nonsense/10439/.

Egan, Mark. "Outrage Turns to Laughter at Ahmadinejad NY Speech." Reuters. 25 September 2007. https://www.reuters.com/article/us-iran-ahmadinejad-scene/outrage-turns-to-laughter-at-ahmadinejad-ny-speech-idUSN2428553420070925.

8 Members of the Alliance for Academic Freedom. "Everyone Lost at Dartmouth." Inside Higher Education. 19 June 2017. https://www

.insidehighered.com/views/2017/06/19/why-n-bruce-duthus-withdrawal
-dean-faculty-dartmouth-defeat-all-sides-essay?utm_source=Inside+Higher
+Ed&utm_campaign=e146624ade-DNU20170619&utm_medium=email&utm
_term=0_1fcbc04421-e146624ade-197369437&mc_cid=e146624ade&mc
_eid=009055881d.

Estrin, Daniel, and Abu Bakar Bashir. "Hamas Leader Implies 'Hundreds of
Thousands' of Palestinians May Breach Israel Border." NPR. 10 May 2018.
https://www.npr.org/sections/parallels/2018/05/10/610062464/hamas
-leader-implies-hundreds-of-thousands-of-palestinians-may-breach-israel
-bor.

European Forum on Antisemitism. "Working Definition of Antisemitism."
Accessed 27 May 2018. https://web.archive.org/web/20151207170121
/https://european-forum-on-antisemitism.org/definition-of-antisemitism
/english-english.

European Monitoring Centre on Racism and Xenophobia. Manifestations of
Antisemitism in the EU 2002–2003. Vienna: EUMC, 2004. https://fra
.europa.eu/sites/default/files/fra_uploads/184-as-main-report.pdf.

Fidler, Lewis A., et al. "Letter to Brooklyn College President Karen L. Gould."
29 January 2013. https://coreyrobin.files.wordpress.com/2013/02/letter
-from-lew-fidler.pdf.

FIRE. "Best of 'The Torch': 'Can We Take a Joke?' New FIRE-Supported Film
Examines Collision between Comedy and Outrage." FIRE. 7 August 2015.
https://www.thefire.org/best-of-the-torch-can-we-take-a-joke-new-fire
-supported-film-examines-collision-between-comedy-and-outrage/.

Foreman, Holden. "Daoud's Facebook Post, Originally Threatening to
'Physically Fight' Zionists, Sparks Debate." Stanford Daily, 22 July 2018.
https://www.stanforddaily.com/2018/07/22/norcliffe-ra-threatens-to
-physically-fight-zionists-in-facebook-post.

Freitag, Michael. "3 Jewish Students Beaten by Men Yelling Ethnic Slurs in
Brooklyn." New York Times, 9 October 1989. https://www.nytimes
.com/1989/10/09/nyregion/3-jewish-students-beaten-by-men-yelling
-ethnic-slurs-in-brooklyn.html?searchResultPosition=1.

Frommer, Rachel. "For Second Time in a Year, University of California
-Irvine Students Require Police Escort from IDF-Related Event Due to
Intense Protests." The Algemeiner, 12 May 2017. https://www.algemeiner
.com/2017/05/12/for-second-time-in-a-year-university-of-california
-irvine-students-require-police-escort-from-idf-related-event-due-to
-intense-protests/.

Gaertner, L., John F. Dovidio, B.S. Banker, M. Houlette, K.M. Johnson, and
E.A. McGlynn. "Reducing Intergroup Conflict: From Superordinate Goals

to Decategorization, Recategorization, and Mutual Differentiation." *Group Dynamics: Theory, Research, and Practice* 4, no. 1 (2000): 98–114.

Gaither, Chris. "Berkeley Course on Mideast Raises Concerns." *New York Times*, 16 May 2002. https://www.nytimes.com/2002/05/16/us/berkeley -course-on-mideast-raises-concerns.html.

Gershman, Jacob. "Professor Khalidi Might Be Bound for Princeton." *New York Sun*, 3 March 2005. https://www.nysun.com/new-york/professor-khalidi -might-be-bound-for-princeton/9996/.

Gerstenfeld, Manfred. "The Academic Boycott against Israel and How to Fight It." 1 September 2003. Jerusalem Center for Public Affairs. http://www .jcpa.org/phas/phas-12.htm.

Ghayrat, Gary, and Mike Adams. "Anti-Zionist Activists Protest Israeli Independence Day Celebration." *The Statesman* (Stony Brook, NY), 22 April 2018. https://www.sbstatesman.com/2018/04/22/anti-zionist-activists -protest-israeli-independence-day-celebration/.

Ginges, Jeremy, Scott Atran, Douglas Medin, and Khalil Shikaki. "Sacred Bounds on Rational Resolution of Violent Political Conflict." *Proceedings of the National Academy of Sciences of the United States of America* 104, no. 18 (1 May 2007): 7357–60. https://www.pnas.org/content/pnas/104/18/7357 .full.pdf.

Global Research. "Full Transcript of Ahmadinejad Speech at Columbia University." Global Research. 25 September 2007. https://www .globalresearch.ca/full-transcript-of-ahmadinejad-speech-at-columbia -university/6889.

Glover, Jonathan. "Racist Flyers Posted in Downtown Spokane." *Spokesman-Review* (Spokane, WA), 19 March 2018. http://www.spokesman.com /stories/2018/mar/19/racist-flyers-posted-in-downtown-spokane/.

Goddard, Ives. "'I Am a Red-Skin': The Adoption of a Native American Expression (1769–1826)." *European Review of Native American Studies* 19, no. 2 (2005): 1–20. http://esq.h-cdn.co/assets/cm/15/06/54d44abb4e540 _-_redskin.pdf.

Goldenberg, Suzanne, and Will Woodward. "Israeli Boycott Divides Academics: Sackings on Two Obscure Journals Fuel Debate on Cooperation with Universities." *The Guardian*, 8 July 2002. https://www.theguardian .com/uk/2002/jul/08/highereducation.israel.

Goodstein, Laurie. "New Israel Law Bars Foreign Critics from Entering the Country." *New York Times*, 7 March 2017. https://www.nytimes.com/2017/03/07/world /middleeast/israel-knesset-vote-boycott-bds-reform-judaism.html.

Grant, Fiona, and Michael A. Hogg. "Self-Uncertainty, Social Identity Prominence and Group Identification." *Journal of Experimental Social Psychology* 48 (2012): 538–42.

Greenberg, David, Rebecca Lesses, Jeffry V. Mallow, Deborah Dash Moore, Sharon Ann Musher, Cary Nelson, Kenneth S. Stern, and Irene Tucker. "The Blacklist in the Coal Mine." Tablet. 26 October 2016. https://www .tabletmag.com/scroll/216271/the-blacklist-in-the-coal-mine-canary -missions-fear-mongering-agenda-college-campuses.

Greenberg, Eric J. "Columbia President Blasts Divestment Petition." *New York Jewish Week*, 8 November 2002. http://jewishweek.timesofisrael .com/columbia-president-blasts-divestment-petition/.

Greenwald, Anthony G., and Thomas F. Pettigrew. "With Malice toward None and Charity for Some: Ingroup Favoritism Enables Discrimination." *American Psychologist* 69, no. 7 (2014): 669–84.

Grieve, Pete. "Prof Who Would've Talked to Bannon, 'Early Hitler' Speaking at Convocation." *Chicago Maroon*, 9 December 2018. https://www .chicagomaroon.com/article/2018/12/10/professor-invited-bannon -uchicago-give-conv/.

Griffin, Robert J. "Ideology and Misrepresentation: A Response to Edward Said." *Critical Inquiry* 15, no. 3 (1989): 611–25.

Guttman, Nathan. "Could California Ban Anti-Israel Campus Protests as 'Anti-Semitic' Hate?" *Forward*, 10 June 2015. https://forward.com/news /national/309450/what-is-anti-semitism/.

Haidt, Jonathan. *The Righteous Mind: Why Good People Are Divided by Politics and Religion*. New York: Vintage Books, 2013.

Halbfinger, David M. "Israel Can't Deport US Student over Past Support for Boycott." *New York Times*, 18 October 2018. https://www.nytimes .com/2018/10/18/world/middleeast/israel-student-deport-boycott.html.

Halevi, Yossi Klein. *Letters to My Palestinian Neighbor*. New York: Harper, 2018.

Hansen, Dan, S. Isamu Jordan, and Mike Pra. "Hate Mail Revisits Gonzaga Campus One Year Later, Two Black Law Students Receive Threatening Letters." *Spokesman-Review* (Spokane, WA), 23 March 1996. http://www .spokesman.com/stories/1996/mar/23/hate-mail-revisits-gonzaga-cus -one-year-later/.

Harrington, Evan. "The Social Psychology of Hatred." *Journal of Hate Studies* 3, no. 1 (2004): 49–82. https://jhs.press.gonzaga.edu/articles/abstract/10.33972/jhs.20.

Haslam, Nick, and Steve Lougham. "Dehumanization and Infrahumanization." *Annual Review of Psychology* 65 (2014): 399–423.

Haslam, Nick, and Michelle Stratemeyer. "Recent Research on Dehumanization." *Current Opinion in Psychology* 11 (2016): 25–9.

Haslem, Alex. "The Lost Boys: Inside Muzafer Sherif's Robbers Cave Experiments (Gina Perry Scribe [2018])." *Nature*, 17 April 2018. https://www.nature.com /articles/d41586-018-04582-7.

Hassan, Adeel, Karen Zraick, and Alan Blinder. "Morris Dees, a Co-Founder of the Southern Poverty Law Center, Is Ousted." *New York Times*, 14 March 2019. https://www.nytimes.com/2019/03/14/us/morris-dees-southern -poverty-law-center-fired.html.

"Headers and Text of Email Machado Sent." computingcases.org. Accessed 26 May 2019. https://web.archive.org/web/20150711122234/https:// computingcases.org/case_materials/machado/support_docs/machado _case_narr/Email.html.

Herzl, Theodor. *Complete Diaries*. Edited by Patai Raphael and translated by Harry Zohn. New York: Herzl Press, 1960.

– "Theodor Herzl: The Jewish State." History Muse Net. Accessed 9 July 2019. http://historymuse.net/readings/HerzlTHEJEWISHSTATE.htm.

Hikind, Dov. "Hikind Calls for Brooklyn College President's Resignation." News release. Assemblyman Dov Hikind. 30 January 2013. http:// dovhikind.blogspot.com/2013/01/hikind-calls-for-brooklyn-college .html.

Hillel International. "Hillel Israel Guidelines." Accessed 27 May 2019. https://www.hillel.org/jewish/hillel-israel/hillel-israel-guidelines.

Hirsh, David. "The Myth of Institutional Boycotts." Inside Higher Ed. 4 January 2014. https://www.insidehighered.com/views/2014/01/07 /essay-real-meaning-institutional-boycotts.

– "Say No to an Eye for an Eye." *The Guardian*, 2 June 2006. https://www .theguardian.com/commentisfree/2006/jun/02/dontboycotttheboycotters.

Hogg, Michael A., Janice R. Adelman, and Robert D. Blagg. "Religion in the Face of Uncertainty: An Uncertainty-Identity Theory Account of Religiousness." *Personality and Social Psychology Review* 14, no. 1 (2010): 72–83.

Hogg, Michael A., Christie Meehan, and Jayne Farquharson, "The Solace of Radicalism: Self-Uncertainty and Group Identification in the Face of Threat." *Journal of Experimental Social Psychology* 46 (2010): 1061–66.

Hohman, Zackary P., and Michael A. Hogg. "Fearing the Uncertain: Self-Uncertainty Plays a Role in Mortality Salience." *Journal of Experimental Social Psychology* 57 (2015): 31–42.

Hollancer, Ricki. "CAMERA Op-Ed: The New York Times Continues Its Anti-Israel Smear Campaign." CAMERA. 16 April 2018. https://www.camera .org/article/camera-op-ed-the-new-york-times-continues-its-anti-israel -smear-campaign/.

Hosack, Charles W. "Victoria Keenan and Jason Keenan vs. Aryan Nations Judgment," 8 September 2000, Southern Poverty Law Center. https://www.splcenter.org/sites/default/files/d6_legacy_files /keenanvaryannations_judgment.pdf.

Howe, Marvine. "US Denial of Visa over Politics of Foreigners: The Battle Is Heating Up." *New York Times*, 28 July 1985. https://www.nytimes .com/1985/07/28/world/us-denial-of-visas-over-politics-of-foreigners-the -battle-is-heating-up.html.

Huffpost. "'Irvine 11' Charged for Disturbing Michael Oren's Speech." Huffpost. 7 February 2011. https://www.huffpost.com/entry/irvine-11 -charged-for-dis_n_819596.

Hurvitz, Karen D. "Verified Complaint for Declaratory and Injunctive Relief; John Doe et al v. Robert Manning et al, Commonwealth of Massachusetts Superior Court Department." FIRE. 26 April 2019. https://d28htnjz2elwuj .cloudfront.net/wp-content/uploads/2019/04/26162834/Complaint -Against-UMass-Amherst.pdf.

Investigative Project on Terrorism, The. "Students for Justice in Palestine Is a Terrorist Organization." Stop the Jew Hatred on Campus. 15 July 2017. https://stopthejewhatredoncampus.org/news/students-justice-palestine -terrorist-organization.

Israel on Campus Coalition. "2016–2017 Year End Report." Accessed 27 May 2019. https://web.archive.org/web/20190104054938/https:// israelcc.org/wp-content/uploads/2017/09/2016-2017-Year-End-Report .pdf.

Jaschik, Scott. "MLA Vote to Criticize Israel Falls Short." Inside Higher Ed. 5 June 2014. https://www.insidehighered.com/news/2014/06/05/mla -members-back-resolution-israel-not-margin-make-statement-official -policy.

Jasper, Zoe. "Dear Canary Mission, If You're Reading This, I'm Not Afraid of You." *New Voices Magazine*. 17 January 2019. http://newvoices.org /2019/01/17/dear-canary-mission-if-youre-reading-this-im-not-afraid -of-you/.

Jessica Felber v. Mark G. Yudof (United States District Court for the Northern District of California). Civil Rights Complaint for Damages Re Endangerment of Health and Safety of Jewish University of California Student Jessica Felber; Request for Jury Trial, March 3, 2011, allegation number 55. https://www.berkeleyside.com/wp-content /uploads/2011/03/felber-v.-yudof-et-al-complaint-11.pdf.

Jewish News Syndicate. "Jewish Students Berate BDS Planned Vote at University of Maryland during Passover." Jewish News Syndicate, 18 April 2019. https://www.jns.org/jewish-students-slam-bds-vote-at-university -of-maryland-during-passover/.

Jewish Telegraphic Agency. "Fliers Found at Cornell Read 'Just Say No to Jewish Lies.'" Jewish Telegraphic Agency. 23 October 2017. https://www

.jta.org/2017/10/23/united-states/fliers-found-at-cornell-read-just-say-no
-to-jewish-lies.

–   "J Street U Elects Muslim Student as President." Jewish Telegraphic Agency.
19 August 2015. https://www.jta.org/2015/08/19/united-states/j-street
-u-elects-muslim-student-as-president.

–   "Stony Brook University's Muslim Chaplain under Fire from Pro-
Palestinian Students for Defending Campus Hillel." Jewish Telegraphic
Agency. 8 May 2018. https://www.jta.org/2018/05/08/united-states
/stony-brook-universitys-muslim-chaplain-fire-pro-palestinian-students
-defending-campus-hillel.

–   "U of Michigan Punishes Professor for Refusing to Recommend Student
for Study in Israel." Jewish Telegraphic Agency. 10 October 2018. https://
www.jta.org/2018/10/10/united-states/u-michigan-sanctions
-professor-refusing-recommend-student-study-israel.

Jewish Virtual Library. "Anti-Semitism: Campus Divestment Resolutions
in the USA (2005–2019)." Jewish Virtual Library. Accessed 27 May 2019.
https://www.jewishvirtuallibrary.org/campus-divestment-resolutions.

–   "Zionism: A Definition of Zionism." Accessed 25 May 2019. jewishvirtuallibrary
.org.

Jewish Voice, The. "CUNY Report Faults Bklyn College for Ejection of
Jewish Students at BDS Event." The Jewish Voice. 17 April 2013. http://
thejewishvoice.com/2013/04/17/cuny-report-faults-bklyn-college-for
-ejection-of-jewish-students-at-bds-event/.

Jewish Voice for Peace. "URGENT Support Hamzeh Daoud, a Palestinian
Muslim Student Targeted by the Right, Who Now Risks Expulsion from
Stanford University." Accessed 28 May 2019. https://docs.google.com
/document/u/1/d/1nYK1dsjiDI1AS8UkJp2Hz3PukQ5YAhgmCQ1AAcAl9QI
/mobilebasic.

JNS.org. "Judge Dismisses Lawsuit to Stop Anti-Israel Event at U Mass
Amherst." The Algemeiner, 5 May 2019. https://www.algemeiner
.com/2019/05/05/judge-dismisses-lawsuit-to-stop-anti-israel-event-at
-umass-amherst/.

–   "20 Organizations Say UC Riverside Offering Anti-Semitic Class." Jewish
News Syndicate. 10 April 2015. https://www.jns.org/20-organizations
-say-uc-riverside-offering-anti-semitic-class/.

Johnson, Adam. "NYT's BDS Debate Excludes BDS Proponents." FAIR. 6 April
2017. https://fair.org/home/nyts-bds-debate-excludes-bds-proponents/.

Jones, Jeremy. "Durban Daze: When Antisemitism Becomes 'Anti-Racism.'"
Zionism and Israel Information Center. October 2001. http://www
.zionism-israel.com/issues/Durban_anti_semitism2.html.

JTA. "College Campuses Are Actually Becoming More Pro-Israel, Study Says." *Forward*, 18 September 2017. https://forward.com/fast-forward /383102/college-campuses-are-actually-becoming-more-pro-israel-study -says.

JTA and Doug Chandler. "UPDATE: Brooklyn College Probing Removal of Students from Anti-Israel Event." *New York Jewish Week*, 10 February 2013. https://jewishweek.timesofisrael.com/update-brooklyn-college-probing -removal-of-students-from-anti-israel-event/.

JTA and TOI Staff. "Stanford Undergraduate Threatens to 'Physically Fight' the 'Zionist Students.'" *The Times of Israel*, 24 July 2018. https://www .timesofisrael.com/stanford-undergraduate-threatens-to-physically-fight -the-zionist-students/.

Kahneman, Daniel. *Thinking Fast and Slow*. New York: Farrar, Straus and Giroux, 2011.

Katznelson, Ira, et al. "Ad Hoc Grievance Committee Report." University of Columbia. 28 March 2005. https://web.archive.org/web/20050405201959 /http://www.columbia.edu/cu/news/05/03/ad_hoc_grievance_committee _report.html.

Kelman, Ari Y., Abiya Ahmed, Ilana Horwitz, Jeremiah Lockwood, Marva Shalev Marom, and Maja Zuckerman. "Safe and on the Sidelines: Jewish Students and the Israel-Palestine Conflict on Campus." Stanford Graduate School of Education, 2017. https://stanford.app.box.com/v /SafeandontheSidelinesReport.

Keneally, Meghan. "Ruby Ridge Siege, 25 Years Later, a 'Rallying Cry' for Today's White Nationalists." abcNEWS. 18 April 2017. https://abcnews.go.com /Politics/ruby-ridge-siege-25-years-called-rallying-cry/story?id=49296439.

Klein, Morton A., and Susan B. Tuchman. "Letter from Zionist Organization of America to Professor Abu-Lughod." Center for Constitutional Rights. 27 May 2015. https://ccrjustice.org/sites/default/files/attach/2015/06 /letter%20to%20Middle%20East%20Institute%20at%20Columbia%20U .%205-27-15_1.pdf.

– "Letter from Zionist Organization of America to Richard L. McCormick, President, Rutgers." 6 April 2011. https://web.archive.org/web /20111008012924/https://zoa.org/media/user/images/letter%20to %20Rutgers%20President%20McCormick%204-6-11.pdf.

– "Zionist Organization of America Complaint to Office of Civil Rights, New York Office, US Department of Education, regarding Rutgers University." AMCHA Initiative. 20 July 2011. https://www.amchainitiative.org/wp -content/uploads/2012/10/ZOAs-Title-VI-complaint-agst-Rutgers-7-20-11 .pdf.

Koplin, Steven. "Grid of Campus Divestment Activity." Unpublished raw data, American Jewish Committee, New York, 2002.

Kosmin, Barry A., and Ariela Keysar. "National Demographic Survey of American Jewish College Students 2014 ANTI-SEMITISM REPORT." Louise D. Brandeis Center and Trinity College. February 2015. https://www.trincoll.edu/NewsEvents/NewsArticles/Documents/Anti-SemitismReportFinal.pdf.

Kotzin, Michael C. "Politics and the Modern Language Association: Reflections before and after the MLA Vote." In *The Case against Academic Boycotts of Israel*, edited by Cary Nelson and Gabriel Noah Brahm, 452–60. Detroit: MLA Members for Scholars' Rights, 2014.

Krauthammer, Charles. "Disgrace in Durban: The U.N. Conference on Racism Was Worse than Just Hot Air." *The Weekly Standard*, 17 September 2001. http://www.resisttyranny.com/pnac/web.archive.org/web/20040205130034/www.newamericancentury.org/Krauthammer-Sept17.pdf.

Kurzban, Robert, John Tooby, and Leda Cosmides. "Can Race Be Erased? Coalitional Computation and Social Categorization." *Proceedings of the National Academy of Sciences of the United States of America* 98, no. 26 (December 18, 2001): 15387–92.

Kushner, Jared. "Jared Kushner: President Trump Is Defending Jewish Students." *New York Times*, 11 December 2019. https://www.nytimes.com/2019/12/11/opinion/jared-kushner-trump-anti-semitism.html.

LaHood, Maria C., et al. "Amici Curiae Brief of the Center for Constitutional Rights and Jewish Voice for Peace in Support of Defendants and Appellants in People of the State of California v. Ali Sayeed et al., Superior Court for the State of California County of Orange Appellate Division." Center for Constitutional Rights. 9 October 2013. https://ccrjustice.org/sites/default/files/assets/files/Irvine%2011%20Brief%2010%2009%20FINAL%20COMPLETE.pdf.

LaHood, Maria C., and Radhika Sainath. "Letter from Palestine Legal and Center for Constitutional Rights to Fordham President McShane Re Ban on Students for Justice in Palestine at Fordham University." 17 January 2017. https://static1.squarespace.com/static/548748b1e4b083fc03ebf70e/t/587e4768ebbd1a5151d66011/1484670829707/Letter+to+Fordham-Civil+Rights+Orgs+1-17-17+Public+BLOG.pdf.

Landau, Noa. "Israel Publishes BDS Blacklist: These Are the 20 Groups Whose Members Will Be Denied Entry." *Haaretz*, 7 January 2018. https://www.haaretz.com/israel-news/israel-publishes-bds-blacklist-these-20-groups-will-be-denied-entry-1.5729880.

Levi, Margaret. "Letter to Sally Hunt." American Political Science Association. 13 May 2015. https://www.biu.ac.il/academic_freedom/files/aut1.pdf?ArticleID=153162.

Lipstadt, Deborah E., Samuel G. Freedman, and Chaim Seidler-Feller. *American Jewry and the College Campus: Best of Times or Worst of Times?* New York: American Jewish Committee, 2005. http://ajcarchives.org/ajcarchive/DigitalArchive.aspx. [To access document, enter the title in the search window.]

Lukianoff, Greg, and Jonathan Haidt. *Coddling of the American Mind: How Good Intentions and Bad Ideas Are Setting up a Generation for Failure.* New York: Penguin, 2018.

Mael, Daniel. "On Many Campuses, Hate Is Spelled SJP." *The Tower*, October 2014. http://www.thetower.org/article/on-many-campuses-hate-is-spelled-sjp/.

Maggio, Paula. "Intimidation-Free Campuses: College Presidents Speak out about AJC Statement." Campus Watch. 15 November 2002. https://www.meforum.org/campus-watch/8133/intimidation-free-campuses-college-presidents.

Magidor, Menachem, and Sari Nusseibeh. "Counter Boycott by British Association of University Teachers: Joint Hebrew University–Al-Quds University Statement on Academic Cooperation Signed in London." Israel-Academic-Monitor.com. 19 May 2005. http://www.israel-academia-monitor.com/index.php?type=large_advic&advice_id=1297&page_data[id]=178&userid=&cookie_lang=en%20&BLUEWEBSESSIONSID=7824ae974fb4fa29a9195df22345122c.

Majeed, Faiza. "The Irvine 11 Case: Does Nonviolent Student Protest Warrant Criminal Prosecution." *Law and Inequality: A Journal of Theory and Practice* 30, no. 2 (2012): 371–99. https://scholarship.law.umn.edu/cgi/viewcontent.cgi?referer=https://www.google.com/&httpsredir=1&article=1185&context=lawineq.lahood.

Marcus, Kenneth L. "Letter to Susan B. Tuchman, Zionist Organization of America, Re: Rutgers University – OCR Case No. 02-11-2157." Inside Higher Education. 27 August 2018. https://www.insidehighered.com/sites/default/server_files/media/Rutgers%20Appeal.pdf.

– "Standing up for Jewish Students." *Jerusalem Post*, 9 September 2013. https://www.jpost.com/Opinion/Op-Ed-Contributors/Standing-up-for-Jewish-students-325648.

– "This Is Very Important." Twitter. 1 May 2017. https://twitter.com/Klmarcus.

May, Jacob. "Students Supporting Israel Vindicated at Irvine." Students Supporting Israel. 22 February 2018. https://brandeiscenter.com/students-supporting-israel-vindicated-irvine/.

McEvoy, Jemima. "NYU SJP Demands Further Action from NYU after Death Threats." *Washington Square News* (New York, NY), 1 May 2017. https://nyunews.com/2017/05/01/nyu-sjp-demands-further-action-from-nyu-after-death-threats.

McLeod, Sam. "Robbers Cave." Simple Psychology. 2008. Accessed 27 May 2019. https://www.simplypsychology.org/robbers-cave.html.

Mearsheimer, John, and Stephen Walt. *The Israel Lobby and US Foreign Policy*. New York: Farrar, Straus and Giroux, 2008.

Melchior, Michael. "Briefing to the Foreign Press by Deputy Foreign Minister Rabbi Michael Melchior." Israel Ministry of Foreign Affairs. 9 August 2001. https://mfa.gov.il/mfa/pressroom/2001/pages/briefing%20to%20the%20foreign%20press%20by%20dep%20fm%20melchior%20-.aspx.

Merriam-Webster. "Microaggression." Accessed 10 June 2019. https://www.merriam-webster.com/dictionary.

Mill, John Stuart. "On Liberty." 1859. Reprint, Kitchener, ON: Bartouche Books, 2001. https://socialsciences.mcmaster.ca/econ/ugcm/3ll3/mill/liberty.pdf.

Moore, Joseph, and Jesus Payan. "Why We Opposed WIFI: Challenging WIFI's Complicity in State Violence." *The Williams Record* (Williamstown, MA), 1 May 2019. https://williamsrecord.com/2019/05/why-we-opposed-wifi-challenging-wifis-complicity-in-state-violence.

Morris, Benny, ed. *Making Israel*. Ann Arbor, MI: University of Michigan Press, 2007. https://is.muni.cz/el/1423/podzim2015/SAN277/um/59355238/Morris_2007_-_Making_Israel.pdf?lang=en.

– *1948: A History of the First Arab-Israeli War*. New Haven, CT: Yale University Press, 2009.

Moshe, Shiri. "University of Michigan 'Disappointed' after Professor Refuses to Write Recommendation Letter for Student Studying Abroad in Israel." *The Algemeiner*, 17 September 2018. https://www.algemeiner.com/2018/09/17/university-of-michigan-professor-refuses-to-write-recommendation-letter-for-student-studying-abroad-in-israel/.

Movement for Black Lives. "Invest-Divest." Accessed 27 May 2019. https://policy.m4bl.org/invest-divest.

Mullen, Brian. "Atrocity as a Function of Lynch Mob Composition: A Self-Attention Perspective." *Personality and Social Psychology Bulletin* 12, no. 2 (1986): 187–97. https://journals.sagepub.com/doi/10.1177/0146167286122005.

Musher, Sharon Ann. "The Closing of the American Studies Association's Mind." In *The Case against Academic Boycotts of Israel*, edited by Cary Nelson and Gabriel Noah Brahn, 105–18. Detroit: MLA Members for Scholars' Rights, 2014.

Muslim Student Union at University of California, Irvine. "Ambassador Michael Oren Visits UCI." News release. Archive Today. 8 February 2010. http://archive.li/VYejw.

Nathan-Kazis, Josh. "Campus 'Apartheid Week' Drew Little, Varied Response." *Forward*, 3 March 2010. https://forward.com/news/126455/campus-apartheid-week-drew-little-varied-res.

– "REVEALED: Canary Mission Blacklist Is Secretly Bankrolled by Major Jewish Federation." *Forward*, 3 October 2018. https://forward.com/news/national/411355/revealed-canary-mission-blacklist-is-secretly-bankrolled-by-major-jewish.

– "Second Major Jewish Charity Admits Funding Group Tied to Canary Mission Blacklist." *Forward*, 11 October 2018. https://forward.com/news/national/411895/second-major-jewish-charity-admits-funding-canary-mission-blacklist/.

– "Shadowy Blacklist of Student Activists Wins Endorsement of Mainstream Pro-Israel Group." *Forward*, October 3, 2017.

National Centre for Education Statistics. "Fast Facts: Educational Institutions." Accessed 12 November 2019. https://nces.ed.gov/fastfacts/display.asp?id=84.

National Coalition Against Censorship. "Florida Anti-Semitism Bill Threatens Free Speech Update: Bill Signed." 30 May 2019. https://ncac.org/news/florida-anti-semitism-bill-threatens-free-speech.

Nelson, Cary. "How the Israel Boycott Can Compromise Faculty and Harm Students." *The Chronicle of Higher Education*, 25 September 2018. https://www.chronicle.com/article/How-the-Israel-Boycott-Can/244626.

– *Israel Denial: Anti-Zionism, Anti-Semitism, and the Faculty Campaign against the Jewish State.* Bloomington: Academic Engagement Network and Indiana University Press, 2019.

– "Micro-Boycotts, Anti-Zionism and Anti-Semitism in the Personal Boycott Movement." Unpublished manuscript [2018?].

Nelson, Cary, and Kenneth S. Stern. "Cary Nelson and Kenneth Stern Pen Open Letter on Campus Antisemitism." American Association of University Professors. 20 April 2011. https://www.aaup.org/news/cary-nelson-and-kenneth-stern-pen-open-letter-campus-antisemitism#.XOyPjNNKiRs.

Neuman, Scott. "Boston Right-Wing 'Free Speech' Rally Dwarfed by Counterprotesters." NPR. 19 August 2017. https://www.npr.org/sections/thetwo-way/2017/08/19/544684355/bostons-free-speech-rally-organizers-deny-links-to-white-nationalists.

Newton, William. "CC Rejects Williams Initiative for Israel." 1 May 2019. *The William Record.* https://williamsrecord.com/2019/05/cc-rejects-williams-initiative-for-israel/.

+972 *Magazine.* "What Is Normalization?" +972 *Magazine*, 27 December 2011. https://972mag.com/what-is-normalization/31368/.

Norton, Ben. "Journalists Blast NY Times for Pro-Israel Bias and 'Grotesque' Distortion of Illegal Occupation of Palestine." Salon. 27 May 2016. https://www.salon.com/2016/05/26/journalists_blast_ny_times_for_grotesque_pro_israel_bias_and_distortion_of_illegal_occupation_of_palestine/.

Nossel, Suzanne. "Statement of Suzanne Nossel, Executive Director PEN America, before the House Committee on the Judiciary Hearing on 'Examining Anti-Semitism on College Campuses.'" 7 November 2017. https://docs.house.gov/meetings/JU/JU00/20171107/106610/HHRG-115-JU00-Wstate-NosselS-20171107.pdf.

– "To Fight 'Hate Speech,' Stop Talking about It." PEN America. 3 June 2016. https://pen.org/press-clip/to-fight-hate-speech-stop-talking-about-it/.

Nusseibeh, Sari, and Anthony David. *Once upon a Country: A Palestinian Life.* New York: Farrar, Straus and Giroux, 2007.

Open Hillel. "Mission and Vision." Accessed 27 May 2019. http://www.openhillel.org/about.

Oster, Marcy. "After Israel Visit, Florida Governor Signs Bill against Anti-Semitism into Law." *The Times of Israel*, 3 June 2019. https://www.timesofisrael.com/after-israel-visit-florida-governor-signs-bill-against-anti-semitism-into-law.

Palestine Legal. "Year-in-Review: Palestine Legal Responded to 308 Suppression Incidents in 2017, Nearly 1000 in Last 4 Years." Accessed 27 May 2019. https://palestinelegal.org/2017-report.

Palestine Legal, and Center for Constitutional Rights. *The Palestinian Exception to Free Speech: A Movement under Attack in the US.* Center for Constitutional Rights. September 2015. https://ccrjustice.org/sites/default/files/attach/2015/09/Palestine%20Exception%20Report%20Final.pdf.

Palestinian Campaign for the Academic and Cultural Boycott of Israel (PACBI). "Israel's Exceptionalism: Normalizing the Abnormal." PACBI. 31 October 2011. http://www.pacbi.org/etemplate.php?id=1749.

– "The PACBI Call for Academic Boycott Revised: Adjusting the Parameters of the Debate." PACBI. 28 January 2006. http://www.pacbi.org/etemplate.php?id=1051.

– "PACBI Guidelines for the International Academic Boycott of Israel (Revised July 2014)." PACBI. 31 July 2014. http://www.pacbi.org/etemplate.php?id=1108.

– "Palestinians Urge Iroquois Nationals to Withdraw from Lacrosse Championships in Israel." PACBI. 4 July 2018. https://bdsmovement.net/news/palestinians-urge-iroquois-nationals-withdraw-lacrosse-championships-israel.

Pearl, Judea. "BDS and Zionophobic Racism." In *Anti-Zionism on Campus: The University, Free Speech, and BDS*, edited by Andrew Pessin and Doron S. Ben-Atar, 224–35. Bloomington: Indiana University Press, 2018.

Penslar, Derek J. "Herzl and the Palestinian Arabs: Myth and Counter-Myth." *Journal of Israeli History* 24, no. 1 (2005): 55–77.

– *Theodor Herzl: The Charismatic Leader*. New Haven, CT: Yale University Press, 2020.

– "Toward a Joint Field of Israel/Palestine Studies." Unpublished manuscript, 2018.

– "What If a Christian State Had Been Established in Modern Palestine." In *What Ifs of Jewish History from Abraham to Zionism*, edited by Gavriel D. Rosenfeld, 142–64. Cambridge: Cambridge University Press, 2016.

Peoples Press Palestine Book Project. *Our Roots Are Still Alive: The Story of the Palestinian People*. New York: Institute for Independent Social Journalism, 1981.

Perry, Gina. *Behind the Shock Machine: The Untold Story of the Notorious Milgram Psychology Experiments*. New York: New Press, 2013.

Pessah, Tom. "Why Palestinian Advocacy Groups Don't Partner with Hillel." New Voices. 2 July 2014. http://newvoices.org/2014/07/02/sjphillel.

Pessin, Andrew, and Doron S. Ben-Atar, eds. *Anti-Zionism on Campus: The University, Free Speech, and BDS*. Bloomington: Indiana University Press, 2018.

Pileggi, Tamar. "New Deputy Defense Minister Called Palestinians 'Animals.'" *Times of Israel*, 11 May 2015. https://www.timesofisrael.com /new-deputy-defense-minister-called-palestinians-animals/.

Pink, Aiden. "Camp Ramah Says No Way to IfNotNow's Harsh Criticism of Israel." *Forward*, 13 June 2018. https://forward.com/news/national /403027/camp-ramah-says-no-way-to-ifnotnows-harsh-criticism-of-israel /?utm_content=daily_Newsletter_MainList_Title_Position-1&utm_source =Sailthru&utm_medium=email&utm_campaign=Daily%20-%20M-Th %202018-06-14&utm_term=The%20Forward%20Today%20Monday-Friday.

Popper, Nathanial. "Students, Outsiders Spar at Columbia Conference." *Forward*, 11 March 2005. https://forward.com/news/3067/students -outsiders-spar-at-columbia-conference/.

Prager, Mike. "Racism Drives Off Black Law Students." *Spokesman-Review* (Spokane, WA), 25 June 1995. http://www.spokesman.com/stories/1995 /jun/25/racism-drives-off-black-law-students/.

Puddington, Arch. "The Wages of Durban: A Carnival of Hate, the World Conference against Racism Was Also a Prelude to the Events of September 11." Commentary. November 2001. https://www.commentarymagazine .com/articles/the-wages-of-durban/.

Purnick, Joyce. "Some Limits on Speech in Classrooms." *New York Times*, 28
February 2005. https://www.nytimes.com/2005/02/28/nyregion/some
-limits-on-speech-in-classrooms.html.

Pyrillis, Rita. "Perspectives: University of Illinois Misses a Teachable
Moment on the Mascot." Diverse Issues in Higher Education. 22 February
2007. Retrieved from https://diverseeducation.com/article/7053/.

Ravid, Barak. "Deputy Foreign Minister: 1967 Borders Are Auschwitz
Borders." *Haaretz*, 2 January 2014. https://www.haaretz.com/1967
-borders-are-auschwitz-borders-1.5307464.

– "Netanyahu Tells Knesset Panel: We Have Defeated the BDS Movement."
Haaretz, 25 July 2016. https://www.haaretz.com/israel-news/netanyahu
-tells-knesset-panel-we-have-defeated-the-bds-movement-1.5415364.

Redden, Elizabeth. "A First for the Israel Boycott." Inside Higher Ed. 23
April 2013. https://www.insidehighered.com/news/2013/04/24/asian
-american-studies-association-endorses-boycott-israeli-universities.

– "Native American Studies Group Joins Israel Boycott." Inside Higher Ed.
18 December 2013.

– "Pitzer President Rejects College Council Vote to Suspend Israel Study
Abroad." Inside Higher Ed. 15 March 2019. https://www.insidehighered
.com/quicktakes/2019/03/15/pitzer-president-rejects-college-council-vote
-suspend-israel-study-abroad.

Regular, Arnon. "Terrorize the Enemy, Arafat Says on Nakba." *Haaretz*, 16
May 2004. https://www.haaretz.com/1.4833521.

Richey, Warren. "Failed Martin Luther King Day Parade Bomber Gets 32-Year
Sentence." *Christian Science Monitor*, 20 December 2011. https://www
.csmonitor.com/USA/Justice/2011/1220/Failed-Martin-Luther-King-Day
-parade-bomber-gets-32-year-sentence.

Rose, Flemming. "Safe Spaces on College Campuses Are Creating Intolerant
Students." Huffpost. 12 June 2017. https://www.huffpost.com/entry/safe
-spaces-college-intolerant_b_58d957a6e4b02a2eaab66ccf.

Rosenberg, Justus, and Kenneth S. Stern. "How UC Can Respond to Bigoted
Speech without Censorship." *San Francisco Chronicle*, 21 August 2015.
https://www.sfchronicle.com/opinion/article/How-UC-can-respond-to
-bigoted-speech-without-6456502.php.

Rossman-Benjamin, Tammi. "Complaint to San Francisco Office of Office
of Civil Rights, Department of Education, about Title VI Violations at
University of California, Santa Cruz." 25 June 2009. https://spme.org
/spme-research/analysis/title-vi-complaint-6-25-09/9581/.

– "Retaliation: The High Price of Speaking Out about Campus Antisemitism
and What It Means for Jewish Students." In *Anti-Zionism on Campus: The*

University, Free Speech, and BDS, edited by Andrew Pressin and Doron
    S. Ben-Atar, 298–316. Bloomington: Indiana University Press, 2018.
– "Why I Filed Title VI Complaint." *Forward*, 8 February 2012. https://
    forward.com/opinion/150968/why-i-filed-title-vi-complaint/.
Roth, Gabrielle, and Joseph Goldberg. "Jewish Students: A Blacklist of BDS
    Supporters Is Hurting Our Efforts to Defend Israel on Campus." *Jewish
    Telegraphic Agency*. 23 April 2018. https://www.jta.org/2018/04/23/opinion
    /jewish-students-blacklist-bds-supporters-hurting-efforts-defend-israel-campus.
Ryan, James G. "Memorandum of Law in Support of Respondent's Motion
    to Dismiss Petitioner's Verified Petition in Matter of Ahmad Awad et al. v.
    Fordham University, in Supreme Court of the State of New York, County
    of New York." IAPPS Courts. 5 June 2017. https://iapps.courts.state
    .ny.us/fbem/DocumentDisplayServlet?documentId=s1kq/rY6nO
    /9gqiouGRoCQ==&system=prod.
Said, Edward. *The Question of Palestine*. New York: Vintage Books, 1992.
Salaita, Steven. "A Moral Case against Normalisation with Israel." The
    New Arab. 31 August 2017. https://www.alaraby.co.uk/english
    /comment/2017/8/31/a-moral-case-against-normalisation-with-israel.
– "Zionists Should Be Excluded from Left-Oriented Protests." Mondoweiss.
    30 January 2018. https://mondoweiss.net/2018/01/zionists-excluded
    -oriented/.
Sales, Ben. "NYU Department Votes to Boycott School's Campus in Israel."
    Jewish Telegraph Agency. 3 May 2019. https://www.jta.org/2019/05/03
    /united-states/nyu-department-votes-to-boycott-schools-campus-in
    -israel?utm_source=JTA%20Maropost&utm_campaign=JTA&utm_medium
    =email&mpweb=1161-10645-32500.
Saxe, Leonard, Theodore Sasson, Graham Wright, and Shahar Hecht.
    "Antisemitism and the College Campus: Perceptions and Realities."
    Maurice and Marilyn Cohen Center for Modern Jewish Studies of
    Brandeis University. July 2015. https://www.brandeis.edu/cmjs/pdfs
    /birthright/AntisemitismCampus072715.pdf.
Scham, Paul. "Israeli Historical Narratives." In *Routledge Handbook on the
    Israeli-Palestinian Conflict*, edited by Joel Peters and David Newman,
    33–44. New York: Routledge, 2013.
– "Modern Jewish History: Traditional Narratives of Israeli and Palestinian
    History." Jewish Virtual Library. Accessed 24 May 2019. http://www
    .jewishvirtuallibrary.org/traditional-narratives-of-israeli-and-palestinian
    -history.
Scham, Paul, Walid Salem, and Benjamin Pogrund, eds. *Shared Histories: A
    Palestinian-Israeli Dialogue*. New York: Routledge, 2005.

Schevitz, Tanya. "UC Berkeley's Conflicts Mirror Mideast's Pain/Tension Growing between Jewish, Palestinian Students." *San Francisco Chronicle*, 5 April 2002. https://www.sfgate.com/education/article/UC-Berkeley-s -conflicts-mirror-Mideast-s-pain-2855314.php.

Schlissel, Mark, and Martin A. Philbert. "Letter: Important Questions around Issues of Personal Beliefs, Our Responsibilities as Educators, and Anti-Semitism." Public Affairs University of Michigan. 9 October 2018. https:// publicaffairs.vpcomm.umich.edu/statement-regarding-boycott-of-israel -universities/.

Schmidt, Peter. "Backlash against Israel Boycott Throws Academic Association on Defensive." *New York Times*, 5 January 2014. https://www.nytimes .com/2014/01/06/us/backlash-against-israel-boycott-throws-academic -association-on-defensive.html%20accessed%20June%2016.

– "Supporters of Israel Say Programs in Middle East Studies Misuse US Funds." *The Chronicle of Higher Education*, 17 September 2014. https:// www.chronicle.com/blogs/ticker/supporters-of-israel-say-programs-in -middle-east-studies-misuse-u-s-funds/86245.

Schneiderman, Jill S. "A Field Geologist in Politicized Terrain." In *Anti-Zionism on Campus: The University, Free Speech, and BDS*, edited by Andrew Pessin and Doron S. Ben-Atar, 317–32. Bloomington: Indiana University Press, 2018.

"Seattle – Anti-Israel Ad Can Be Barred from Seattle Buses, Appeals Court Rules." Vos Iz Neias? 18 March 2015. https://vosizneias.com/2015/03/18 /seattle-anti-israel-ad-can-be-barred-from-seattle-buses-appeals-court-rules/.

Seattle Mideast Awareness Campaign v. King County (9th Cir. Mar. 18, 2015). http:// cdn.ca9.uscourts.gov/datastore/opinions/2015/03/18/11-35914.pdf.

Sekar, Megana. "Photo: Students Protest Lack of Representation at Indigenous Peoples Unite Event." *Daily Bruin* (Los Angeles, CA), 17 March 2018. https://dailybruin.com/2018/05/17/photo-students-protest-lack-of -representation-at-indigenous-peoples-unite-event/.

Shariatmadari, David. "A Real-Life Lord of the Flies: The Troubling Legacy of the Robbers Cave Experiment." *The Guardian*, 16 April 2018. https://www .theguardian.com/science/2018/apr/16/a-real-life-lord-of-the-flies-the -troubling-legacy-of-the-robbers-cave-experiment.

Shavit, Ari. *My Promised Land: The Triumph and Tragedy of Israel*. New York: Spiegel and Grau, 2013.

Shehori, Dalia, and Yair Sheleg. "Israel, US Leave Durban; Peres Dubs Meet a Farce." *Haaretz*, 4 September 2001. https://www.haaretz.com /1.5427327.

Sherman, Eliezer. "UC President Napolitano Supports Adopting State Department Definition of Antisemitism." *The Algemeiner*, 21 May 2015. http://www.algemeiner.com/2015/05/21/uc-president-napolitano -supports-adopting-state-department-definition-of-antisemitism.

Sherman, Scott. "The Mideast Comes to Columbia." *The Nation*, 4 April 2005. https://www.thenation.com/article/mideast-comes-columbia/.

Shukman, Harry. "Meet the Neo-Nazi Coming to Put Up White Pride Posters on Your Campus." The Tab. 15 February 2017. https://thetab .com/us/2017/02/15/nathan-damigo-identity-evropa-60697.

Sideman, Richard, and Kenneth S. Stern. Memorandum, "Minutes of June 6, 2002 Conference Call." American Jewish Committee. 6 June 2002.

Simon Wiesenthal Center. "Other Universities Should Follow British University's Cancellation of 'Israel Apartheid Week.'" News release. 21 February 2017. http://www.wiesenthal.com/about/news/wiesenthal -center-other.html.

Simpson, Kevin, Jason Blevins, and Karen Auge. "The Murder of Alan Berg in Denver: 25 Years Later." *Denver Post*, 17 June 17 2009. https://www .denverpost.com/2009/06/17/the-murder-of-alan-berg-in-denver-25-years -later/.

Smithsonian National Museum of the American Indian. "Did You Know?" Accessed 19 November 2019. https://americanindian.si.edu/nk360 /didyouknow#topq2.

Sokol, Chad. "North Idaho College Foundation Plans to Sell Former Site of Aryan Nations Compound." *Spokesman-Review* (Spokane, WA), 18 April 2019. http://www.spokesman.com/stories/2019/apr/18/north-idaho -college-foundation-plans-to-sell-forme/.

Solomon, Daniel J. "'End Jewish Privilege' Poster Circulates on Chicago College Campus." *Forward*, 16 March 2017. https://forward.com/fast -forward/366240/end-jewish-privilege-poster-circulates-on-chicago -college-campus.

Southern Poverty Law Center. "Complaint: Tonya Gersh v. Andrew Anglin." Southern Poverty Law Center. 18 April 2017. https://www.splcenter.org /sites/default/files/documents/whitefish_complaint_finalstamped.pdf.

Special Envoy to Monitor and Combat Anti-Semitism. "Defining Anti- Semitism." 8 June 2010. US Department of State Archived Content. https://2009-2017.state.gov/j/drl/rls/fs/2010/122352.htm.

Stanford College Republicans. "Facebook Post." Facebook. 21 July 2018. https:// www.facebook.com/StanfordGOP/posts/scr-is-disgusted-by-a-threat-of -violence-issued-by-hamzeh-daoud-a-rising-junior-/1789635307785617/.

Stavis, Morton. Memorandum, "Re: National Lawyers Guild Convention, Seattle, Washington, August 1977." 15 September 1977.

Stern, Kenneth S. *Antisemitism Today: How It Is the Same, How It Is Different, and How to Fight It.* New York: American Jewish Committee, 2006.

– *Bigotry on Campus: A Planned Response.* New York: American Jewish Committee, 1990.

– "How to Honor MLK Legacy in Whitefish, Montana." CNN. 13 January 2017. https://www.cnn.com/2017/01/13/opinions/kkk-plans-march-on -mlk-day-stern/index.html.

– "I Drafted the Definition of Antisemitism. Rightwing Jews Are Weaponizing It." *The Guardian*, 13 December 2019. https://www.theguardian.com /commentisfree/2019/dec/13/antisemitism-executive-order-trump -chilling-effect.

– "Letter to Janet Napolitano." Justus & Karin Rosenberg Foundation. 21 March 2016. https://web.archive.org/web/20160804140228/http:// jkrfoundation.org/wp-content/uploads/2016/03/Napolitano-letter -032116b21032016-1.pdf.

– "Letter to Members of Congress: RE: Oppose H.R. 6421/S. 10 'The Anti-Semitism Awareness Act of 2016.'" Justus & Karin Rosenberg Foundation. 6 December 2016. https://web.archive.org/web/20181008124315/http:// jkrfoundation.org/wp-content/uploads/2016/12/Stern-Letter-links -corrected.pdf.

– "The Need for an Interdisciplinary Field of Hate Studies." *Journal of Hate Studies* 3, no. 1 (2004): 7–35. https://jhs.press.gonzaga.edu/articles /abstract/10.33972/jhs.18.

– "Should a Major University System Have a Particular Definition of Anti-Semitism?" *Jewish Journal* (Los Angeles, CA), 22 June 2015. https:// jewishjournal.com/opinion/175207/.

– "Statement of Kenneth S. Stern, Executive Director Justus & Karin Rosenberg Foundation, before the House Committee on the Judiciary Hearing on 'Examining Anti-Semitism on College Campuses.'" 7 November 2017. https://docs.house.gov/meetings/JU/JU00 /20171107/106610/HHRG-115-JU00-Wstate-SternK-20171107.pdf.

– "Will Campus Criticism of Israel Violate Federal Law?" *New York Times*, 12 December 2016. https://www.nytimes.com/2016/12/12/opinion/will -campus-criticism-of-israel-violate-federal-law.html?_r=0.

– "The Working Definition of Antisemitism – A Reappraisal." In *10th Biannual Seminar on Antisemitism: Proceedings.* Tel Aviv: Kantor Center for the Study of Contemporary European Jewry, 2010. http://www.kantorcenter.tau .ac.il/working-definition-antisemitism-six-years-after. Also available at

https://web.archive.org/web/20170228140344/http://kantorcenter.tau
.ac.il/sites/default/files/proceeding-all_3.pdf.

Stern, Kenneth S., and Ernst Benjamin. "How Legislative Efforts to Define
Antisemitism Threaten Academic Freedom." *Academe Blog*. 5 May 2017.
https://academeblog.org/2017/05/05/how-legislative-efforts-to-define
-antisemitism-threaten-academic-freedom/.

Stone, Geoffrey. "Statement on Principles of Free Expression." UChicago
News. July 2012. https://web.archive.org/web/20180309043741/https://
freeexpression.uchicago.edu/page/statement-principles-free-expression.

Strossen, Nadine. *HATE: Why We Should Resist It with Free Speech, Not
Censorship*. New York: Oxford University Press, 2018.

Students Supporting Israel (SSI). "What Really Happened at UCLA." *SSI Blog*.
The Jerusalem Post, 22 May 2018. https://www.jpost.com/Blogs/Students
-Supporting-Israel-SSI-blog/What-really-happened-at-UCLA-558086.

Sweezy v. New Hampshire, 354 US 234 (June 17, 1957). https://scholar.google
.com/scholar_case?case=10026374859124601238.

Terminiello v. Chicago, 337 US 1 (May 16, 1949). JUSTIA, US Supreme Court.
Accessed 26 May 2019. https://supreme.justia.com/cases/federal/us/337/1/.

"Text of Conant's Speech." *Harvard Crimson*, 23 June 1949. https://www
.thecrimson.com/article/1949/6/23/text-of-conants-speech-pbthe-full/.

Third Narrative, The. "Alliance for Academic Freedom." The Third Narrative.
22 December 2014. https://thirdnarrative.org/get-involved/alliance-for
-academic-freedom/.

Toameh, Khaled Abu. "Hamas Vows Gaza Protests to Last until Palestinians
'Return to All of Palestine.'" *Times of Israel*, 9 April 2018. https://www
.timesofisrael.com/hamas-vows-gaza-protests-to-continue-until-they
-return-to-all-of-palestine.

TOI Staff. "Citing Anti-Semitism, UK University Nixes Israel Apartheid
Week." *Times of Israel*, 21 February 2017. https://www.timesofisrael.com
/citing-anti-semitism-uk-university-nixes-israel-apartheid-week/.

Trump, Donald J. "Executive Order on Combating Anti-Semitism." The
White House. 11 December 2019. https://www.whitehouse.gov
/presidential-actions/executive-order-combating-anti-semitism/.

United Nations General Assembly. "Resolution 3379: Elimination of All
Forms of Racial Discrimination." 10 November 1975. https://unispal
.un.org/UNISPAL.NSF/0/761C1063530766A7052566A2005B74D1.

University of New Hampshire. "Bias-Free Language Guide." Accessed 26
May 2019. http://d3n8a8pro7vhmx.cloudfront.net/therebel/pages/2166
/attachments/original/1438599745/UNH_Bias-Free_Language_Guide_PDF
.pdf?1438599745.

US Department of Education. "About OPE – International and Foreign Language Education." Accessed 27 May 2019. https://www2.ed.gov/about/offices/list/ope/iegps/index.html.

Vallone, Robert P., Lee Ross, and Mark R. Lepper. "The Hostile Media Phenomenon: Biased Perception and Perceptions of Media Bias in Coverage of Beirut Massacre." *Journal of Personality and Social Psychology* 49, no. 3 (1985): 577–85. https://www.ssc.wisc.edu/~jpiliavi/965/hwang.pdf.

Vial, Andrea C., Jaime L. Napier, and Victoria L. Brescoll. "A Bed of Thorns: Female Leaders and the Self-Reinforcing Cycle of Illegitimacy." *The Leadership Quarterly* 27 (2016): 400–14.

Waller, James. "Our Ancestral Shadow: Hate and Human Nature in Evolutionary Psychology." *Journal of Hate Studies* 3, no. 1 (2004): 121–32. https://jhs.press.gonzaga.edu/articles/abstract/10.33972/jhs.25.

Waltzer, Kenneth. "From 'Intersectionality' to the Exclusion of Jewish Students: BDS Makes a Worrying Turn on US Campuses." Fathom. July 2018. http://fathomjournal.org/from-intersectionality-to-the-exclusion-of-jewish-students-bds-makes-a-worrying-turn-on-us-campuses.

Weiner, Justus Reid. "The Threat to Freedom of Speech about Israel: Campus Shout-Downs and the Spirit of the First Amendment." *Jewish Political Studies Review* 25, nos. 1–2 (2013). http://jcpa.org/article/the-threat-to-freedom-of-speech-about-israel/.

Weinstein, Henry. "Furrow Gets 5 Life Terms for Racist Rampage." *Los Angeles Times*, 27 March 2001. https://www.latimes.com/archives/la-xpm-2001-mar-27-me-43302-story.html.

Weisel, Ori, and Robert Böhm. "'Ingroup Love' and 'Outgroup Hate' in Intergroup Conflict between Natural Groups." *Journal of Experimental Social Psychology* 60 (2015): 110–20.

Weiss, Philip. "Israel Supporter Refuses to Share Bard Stage with Dima Khalidi and Cites Stereotypes about Jews Smelling Bad." Mondoweiss. 23 October 2016. https://mondoweiss.net/2016/10/supporter-stereotypes-smelling/.

– "Ululating at Vassar: The Israel/Palestine Conflict Comes to America." Mondoweiss. 20 March 2014. https://mondoweiss.net/2014/03/ululating-israelpalestine-conflict/.

Widge. "Poster REMIX D'affiches: Israeli Apartheid Week, BDS Movement." Burning Billboard. 25 February 2016. http://burningbillboard.org/2016/02/25/poster-remix-daffiches-israeli-apartheid-week-bds-movement/.

Williams, Lauren, Nicole Santa Cruz, and Mike Anton. "Students Guilty of Disrupting Speech in 'Irvine 11' Case." *Los Angeles Times*, 24 September 2011. https://www.latimes.com/local/la-xpm-2011-sep-24-la-me-irvine-eleven-20110924-story.html.

Williams College Office of the President. "College Council Vote on Williams Initiative for Israel." 3 May 2019. https://president.williams.edu/letters-from-the-president/college-council-vote-on-williams-initiative-for-israel.

Woo, Elaine. "Bill Wassmuth, 61; Ex-Priest Led Anti-Hate Group, Helped to Bankrupt Aryan Nations." *Los Angeles Times*, 31 August 2002. https://www.latimes.com/archives/la-xpm-2002-aug-31-me-wassmuth31-story.html.

Woodell, Mike. "Anti-Semitism Bill Met with Mixed Reaction on Campus as Statehouse Session Winds Down." *Daily Gamecock* (Columbia, SC), 20 April 2017. https://www.dailygamecock.com/article/2017/04/anti-semitism-bill-on-agenda.

Wright, Graham, Michelle Shain, Shahar Hecht, and Leonard Saxe. "The Limits of Hostility: Students Report on Antisemitism and Anti-Israel Sentiment at Four US Universities." Brandeis University. December 2017. https://www.brandeis.edu/ssri/pdfs/campusstudies/LimitsofHostility.pdf.

Zakim, Michael, and Feisal G. Mohamed. "The Best of Intentions: Debating the ASA Boycott." *Dissent*, 5 November 2014. https://www.dissentmagazine.org/online_articles/best-of-intentions-asa-boycott-bds-debate.

Zoloth, Laurie. "Where Is the Outrage? Pogrom at SFSU." San Francisco Bay Area Independent Media Center (Indybay). 20 May 2002. https://www.indybay.org/newsitems/2002/05/20/1285821.php.

Index

Milton Keynes UK
Ingram Content Group UK Ltd.
UKHW030703021124
450385UK00003B/68/J